All the World and Her Husband

All the World and Her Husband

Women in Twentieth-Century Consumer Culture

Edited by

MAGGIE ANDREWS and MARY M. TALBOT

CASSELL
London and New York

Cassell
Wellington House, 125 Strand, London WC2R 0BB
370 Lexington Avenue, New York, NY 10017–6550

First published 2000

British Library Cataloguing-in-Publication Data
A catalogue record for this book is available from the British Library.

ISBN   0–304–70151–3 (hardback)
        0–304–70152–1 (paperback)

Designed and typeset by Ben Cracknell Studios
Printed and bound in Great Britain by Biddles Ltd, Guildford and King's Lynn

Contents

The Contributors

Alia Al-Khalidi is a lecturer in advertising and design communication at Southampton Institute. Her PhD, 'Menstruation in visual and material culture: a critical analysis of the mediation of female sanitary products 1880–1958', is near completion.

Maggie Andrews is Head of Media and Film Studies at King Alfred College, Winchester. She is the author of *The Acceptable Face of Feminism: A History of the Women's Institute* (Lawrence & Wishart, 1997) and a variety of articles. She is now working on the relationship between popular culture and feminism in the 1980s and 1990s.

Jen Browne has recently completed an MPhil at Southampton Institute on the subject of consumption linked to do-it-yourself in 1950s Britain. After graduating from the Open University, she completed an MA in the history of design at Middlesex University in 1990. Since 1989 she has lectured part-time in design history and cultural studies at several British art colleges.

Mary Bucholtz is assistant professor of linguistics and discourse studies in the Department of English at Texas A&M University. In addition to work on language in the media, she has worked on issues of language and racial identity. She is the editor of *Gender Articulated: Language and the Socially Constructed Self* (Routledge, 1995, with Kira Hall) and *Reinventing Identities: From Category to Practice in Language and Gender Studies* (with A.C. Liang and Laurel A. Sutton; Oxford University Press, forthcoming).

Deborah Cameron is Professor of English Language at Strathclyde University. She is the author of *Feminism and Linguistic Theory* (Macmillan, 2nd edition, 1992), *The Feminist Critique of Language: A Reader* (Routledge; 2nd edition, 1998) and *Verbal Hygiene* (Routledge, 1995) and co-authored *Researching Language* (1992).

Alison J. Clarke is a lecturer in design history and material culture at the University of Southampton/Winchester School of Art and Visiting Professor at the University of Applied Arts, Vienna. Her recent publications include 'Tupperware: suburbia, sociality and mass consumption', in Roger Silverstone (ed.), *Visions of Suburbia* (Routledge, 1997) and 'Window shopping at home: classifieds, catalogues and new consumer skills', in Daniel Miller (ed.), *Material Cultures* (UCl/Chicago University Press, 1998).

Anne M. Cronin is a sociology lecturer at Lancaster University. She is currently writing a book on advertising, cultural belonging and visual culture.

Joanne Entwistle is a senior lecturer in communications and cultural studies at the University of North London. She is the author of *The Fashioned Body* (Polity Press, forthcoming). Her research interests include the sociology of the body, fashion and feminist cultural theory.

Jane Hobson teaches in language and discourse studies and in cultural studies at the University of Western Sydney (Nepean). Her current research interests coalesce around technologies of intimacy, in particular the mass-produced communication texts, greeting cards, and the mass communication texts of radio. She is the author of 'Cannibalism and community: the commodification and consumption of "gay" and "lesbian" identity', in *QueerZone, Working Papers in Feminist Cultural Studies*, 4, 1997.

Sallie McNamara is a lecturer in media studies at Chichester Institute. She is currently researching women, leisure, pleasure and consumption in the inter-war years.

Mica Nava is a professor in the Department of Cultural Studies at the University of East London. She is author of *Changing Cultures: Feminism, Youth and Consumerism* (1992) and co-editor (with Alan O'Shea) of *Modern Times: Reflections on a Century of English Modernity* (1996) and (with Andrew Blake, Iain MacRury and Barry Richards) of *Buy This Book: Studies in Advertising and Consumption* (1997).

Deborah S. Ryan is an associate lecturer with the Open University on the MA in Popular Culture. Following the completion of her PhD, 'The Daily Mail Ideal Home Exhibition and suburban modernity, 1908–1951' (University of East London, 1995), she wrote *The Ideal Home Through the Twentieth Century* (Hazar, 1997). Her recent publications include 'Staging the imperial city: pageant of empire, 1911', in F. Driver and D. Gilbert (eds), *Imperial Cities: Landscape, Space and Identity* (Manchester University Press, 1998) and 'The man who staged the empire and lived in Sibford Gower: remembering Frank Lascelles, 1875–1934', in C. Breward and M. Kwint (eds), *Material Memories* (Berg, forthcoming).

Mary M. Talbot is a senior lecturer in linguistics at the University of Sunderland. Recent publications include *Fictions at Work: Language and Social Practice in Fiction* (Longman, 1995), *Studies in Valency 1* (with Lene Schøsler, Odense University Press, 1995), *Language and Gender: An Introduction* (Polity, 1998) and contributions to numerous collections on language in social life, particularly print media.

Penny Tinkler is a lecturer in the Department of Sociology and Deputy Director of Women's Studies at the University of Manchester. She has written articles on adolescent girlhood, leisure and popular culture between 1900 and 1950 and is currently researching young women and smoking, 1920–1970. She is the author of *Constructing Girlhood: Popular Magazines for Girls Growing up in England, 1920–1950* (Taylor & Francis, 1995).

Barbara Usherwood teaches historical and theoretical aspects of graphic design at the University of Teesside. Previous publications include 'The Design Museum: form follows funding', in Victor Margolin and Ruchard Buchanan (eds), *The Idea of Design* (MIT Press, 1996) and 'Transnational publishing: the case of *Elle Decoration*', in M. Nava *et al.* (eds), *Buy This Book: Studies in Advertising and Consumption* (Routledge, 1997).

Rosie Whorlow is a part-time tutor and student at Chichester Institute, studying girls and motorbike culture. She is particularly interested in oral history, narratives and interview techniques.

Janice Winship is a lecturer in media studies in the School of Cultural and Community Studies, University of Sussex.

Acknowledgements

The original impetus for this collection was a one-day conference on 'Consumer Culture and Women's Power' organized by Maggie Andrews at Southampton Institute in January 1996. The conference was a joint endeavour by what was then the Consumer Culture Research Centre at Southampton Institute and the Southern Women's History Network. Five of the chapters in this volume have been developed from the papers presented there and other chapters come from the work of post-graduate students working in the Consumer Culture Research Centre.

Thanks are therefore due to those in the Southern Women's History Network such as Jacqui Melbourne, who helped with the conference organization, and to those working in the centre at that time – Professor Mike Richards and Ron Cowdrey – whose stimulating contributions in discussions helped to bring about this collection. A special thank-you also goes out to Sarah Ward, who worked in the centre during 1996 and helped with this book in many practical ways through typing and making phone calls and coffee.

1. *Introduction: women in consumer culture*

Maggie Andrews and Mary M. Talbot

'I'd rather have my credit card than my vote.'

'As a single parent I'd rather have my dishwasher now
than some dream of a socialist revolution in the future.'

(Open University students)

Women's relationship with consumption may be contradictory, troubling and
at times traumatic, but one thing is certain: it is unavoidable. Whether it is
buying the weekly shopping or a suit for work, looking at adverts in
magazines or on the shopping channel, enjoying the Ideal Home Exhibition
or a Boyzone concert, consumption in a variety of forms is part of many
women's everyday life. In westernized capitalist societies it is an inevitable
experience that is part of being female. Indeed, it is a sphere where femininity
is performed, where versions of femininity are legitimated and negotiated,
or contested and rejected. The significant part that consumption plays in so
many women's lives justifies its study by feminists. We need to understand
what it means and to explore how changes – such as the introduction of self-
service food shopping or the commercialization of female sanitary products –
affect our lives.

There has been a significant emphasis in women's studies on bringing
female experience into the academic world, on the rejection of condescension
towards the study of female experience and the challenge to dominant value
systems that accompanies this rejection. One feature of this has been the need
to pull together the lived experiences of women with the concerns of feminist
study, without which academic feminism becomes more a case of career

positioning and advancement than political engagement. Many of the
contributors to this book write from a position of engagement based on
personal experience: they write about DIY because they do it (Jen Browne,
Chapter 9), about romantic novels because they read them (Sallie McNamara,
Chapter 6), about Boyzone concerts and young girls' experience of fandom
as they watch their daughters go through this (Maggie Andrews and Rosie
Whorlow, Chapter 17). For many writers of this book, and we hope for its
readers, the personal is also a space for political enquiry. Such enquiries bridge
gaps between the academic and non-academic parts of our lives. They attempt
to understand struggles and experiences in the lives of women around us,
not in an uncritically celebratory way but, at least, with some engaged
empathy.

While not all the contributors to this book write from personal experience,
they all share the aim of understanding women's experiences and struggles
in relation to consumer culture in the twentieth century. Consumption is taken
in a broad sense. It involves not just the purchasing and using up of items
produced by the commercial world, but also bringing meaning to items,
appropriating them, making them, indeed taking them, as one's own. In
arguing for this perception of consumption we perceive it not in isolation but
as intimately tied up with production as an area of creativity and constraint.
Indeed, as Hugh Mackay (1997) has argued, the very constraints imposed
may produce creativity. This point is well illustrated in Jen Browne's chapter
on DIY ('do-it-yourself' home improvements), in which we see individuals
forced, by financial constraint and post-war shortages, to be creative in their
use of bought materials. They have to be creative in using materials they have
bought, or consumed, in order to produce something.

Consumption is but one point on what Richard Johnson (1986) calls the
cultural circuit, consisting of representation, identity, consumption, production
and regulation. Strictly speaking, it cannot be explored on its own; other points
in the cultural circuit inevitably come into play. This volume, because of its
focus on gender, addresses the inter-relationships of identity and consumption
and also the complexity of issues surrounding representation in the
articulation of consumer culture, particularly through advertising.

We refer to consumer *culture* not just to be fashionable (as a symptom of
the recent turn towards culture) but because in very many ways the act of
consumption for women brings them into participation in a culture: a
community of other consumers. This may be an imagined community of
teleshoppers (Bucholtz, Chapter 13 and 1999) or young readers of magazines
(Talbot, 1992, 1995). There is, of course, considerable debate about how 'real'
or imagined a cultural community based on consumption is. In contrast with
communities based on kinship or workplace relations, not very real at all,

perhaps, but, at times, a consumption community has a perceivable spatial dimension – when women or girls are found together in one place, such as the Ideal Home Exhibition (Deborah Ryan, Chapter 2). Whether this is more or less real than, say, the cultural community of soap opera fans, who sit in their homes regularly reading magazine and tabloid newspaper stories about soap stars (Moores, 1996), is one of the questions which we want this book to raise.

Consumption is multi-faceted and conditional, given different meanings by different groups at different times. Consider, for example, the articulation of gender. Not so long ago a man pushing a supermarket trolley would probably have felt his masculinity put into question by this activity as much as by pushing a pram. Such differentiation is not, however, something that has just emerged in the twentieth century. In his diaries in the seventeenth century, Samuel Pepys describes how he and his wife have been shopping but are put in turmoil by the need to acquire provisions (Latham and Matthews, 1978). This is *marketing*, involving barter, and is seen as an activity fit for a member of the lower orders: a job for their household servant. This careful distinction between shopping and marketing in relation to class is one that two or three centuries later articulated a discourse of gender.

The middle-class woman's relationship with consumption emerged in a somewhat contradictory way as the notion of middle-class life itself emerged in the nineteenth century. Leonora Davidoff and Catherine Hall (1987) have explored how the Industrial Revolution relied upon an increase in sales for the domestic market, in pottery, fabrics and chocolate to name but a few. This purchasing was tied up with the emergence of the new domestic ideology of middle-classness, which was pivoted upon a notion of women in the home but, as time progressed, on the necessity for women to go *outside* the home to purchase *for* the home. As Rachel Bowlby has observed (1985), the department stores at the end of the nineteenth century provided a space for women to go outside the home, under the auspices of shopping for the home. The department stores were in the public sphere, but in their very construction, architecture and aura they presented themselves as part of the private sphere. Bowlby argues that they are a new public space for women which can provide a new source of freedom and independence (see both Janice Winship, Chapter 3, and Mica Nava, Chapter 4, for discussion).

Whether or not one agrees with Bowlby's speculations, the significance of the new public spheres provided through consumerism should not be underestimated or undermined. Jürgen Habermas (1989), in his work on the role of the eighteenth-century coffee house, sees such spaces as an important spatial location for discussion and debate crucial for democracy. This view must be treated with extreme caution, of course, in so far as it leads to a celebration of consumption and the public sphere. As in Habermas's original work, the class-specific nature of the new public spheres provided through consumerism is a severe limitation.

This limitation does not, however, prevent us from acknowledging the part consumerism can play in political arenas. Diane Atkinson (1992) has examined the central place of consumer culture in the campaign for women's suffrage. The department stores in London were the object of a certain amount of suffrage activity in the form of window smashing, on the one hand. On the other, the women's suffrage organization in Britain (the Women's Social and Political Union) had its own department store, which played a key role in their publicity campaigns. This store sold all manner of items, from playing cards to tea caddies: all in the suffragette colours of purple, white and green. Such merchandising took the public suffrage campaigns back into the domestic sphere.

This merging and fluidity in the relation between the public and the private in consumer culture remain throughout the twentieth century. We do not mean to suggest here that there is a steady shift – from women being positioned in the private sphere to them being positioned in the public sphere – which consumption is facilitating. Some cultural critics have put forward this view. Erica Carter (1984) sees consumer culture as empowering in the visibility it gives women, especially younger women at, for example, pop concerts and the shopping mall. What some case studies in this book *do* suggest is increased fluidity in twentieth-century consumption between the home and the public sphere (see, in particular, Mary Bucholtz's chapter on an American shopping channel and Alison Clarke's on television advertising and 'armchair shopping').

Another valuable way of viewing women's identities and positions in consumer culture is in terms of their subjection in discourses. Tensions and concerns about consumerism are articulated and played out in discourses in which women are the subject. In the twentieth century, the need to understand consumers has led to the development of discourse technologies (in Norman Fairclough's sense (1989)) for scrutinizing them. Market research brought science to the art of second-guessing the needs and whims of that group of shoppers often assumed to be most important, namely, women. Such attempts by manufacturers and department stores to manage, predict and control were attempts to rationalize the irrational consumer, the irrational impulses of consumption being perceived as feminine (see Nava, this volume). These attempts were (and continue to be) driven by a concern to establish predictability and stability in the market-place; for this, control of the capricious consumer was essential. Knowledge of the consumer facilitated power over her.

However, it is important to note that the contributors to this book do not share with the Frankfurt School a dismissive view of consumers as passive victims of manufacturers' manipulations (Negus, 1997). This negative perception of the consumer led to consumption being seen as a despised field of study. This dismissive attitude towards consumption is reinforced when the consumers are women (see Radway, 1987; also Browne, Chapter 9; Andrews and Whorlow, Chapter 17). We reject such a position here, not in favour of an uncritical reclamation of consumption, but rather to argue that consumption should be seen as contradictory and problematic when applied to women. In doing so, we acknowledge a debt to the work of Daniel Miller, for example, his study of women shoppers in London, whose behaviour he analyses in terms of the contradictory pulls of duty and pleasure (1997).

This is a post-disciplinary collection, in which research into the history of consumption rubs shoulders with case studies based on participant observation or close investigation of verbal interaction. The ordering of its chapters is roughly chronological with loose groupings. The collection begins with the study from which it borrowed its title: 'All the world and her husband'. We have co-opted this phrase for the volume as a whole because we think it conveys succinctly the book's focus on the feminized world of domesticity and shopping, in which men are, for once, in the margins. The phrase – taken from the *Daily Mail* newspaper's report on its first Ideal Home Exhibition in London in 1908 – heads Deborah Ryan's opening chapter, in which she explores the consumer aspirations of women, as reflected in the newspaper and its exhibition before World War II. Janice Winship's chapter examines the rise of the chain store in 1930s Britain, while exploring three complementary theoretical positions on consumption and the consumer: shopping as *empowerment*, as *flânerie* and as *(self-)discipline*. Mica Nava also explores early twentieth-century consumer culture, examining in particular attempts to rationalize the consumer in order to control her. Nava's chapter also reminds us that, in looking at the twentieth century, we need to be aware of the problems with selective, popular perceptions of the past. Nava's chapter blurs the notion of any easy association between the acceptance of consumption and post-modernism. She points to a post-modern approach to Oxford Street in Virginia Woolf's magazine writing: perhaps surprising, given that Woolf is seen by some as the archetypal modernist.

The chapters that follow also serve as reminders that popular narratives of historical progress are problematic. In a study of the commercialization of female hygiene products – and the discourses of femininity and of menstruation which are articulated through their advertising – Alia Al-Khalidi emphasizes continuity rather than change or progress. The invention referred to in her title, 'the greatest invention of the century', is the sanitary towel, but the century in which it was invented was the nineteenth. There has been little change in the discourses in which menstruation is represented. There is a similar challenge to the popular perception of historical progress and liberalization in Sallie McNamara's chapter on the historical romances of Georgette Heyer. She emphasizes that, in their consumption of popular novels in the inter-war period, women were involved in a culture in which gender was represented in a somewhat fluid way, with elements recognizable to students of queer theory. Gender-bending, at least in the realms of fantasy, suggests possibilities for liberation of a sort, or some alternatives to dominant discourses of gender. In the chapter on magazines that follows, Penny Tinkler debunks another myth of progress, showing that adolescent girls were active participants in consumer culture long before the 'birth' of the teenage consumer in the 1950s.

The 1950s has popularly become the period of 'Never had it so good', of the consumer boom. The chapters looking at this period, however, contain a different story. They tell of the negotiated relationship women maintained with a rhetoric of consumerism which they could rarely afford: a story of making-do, and also of control and resistance. While the chapters looking at this period deal with British consumerism, the American cultural influence is very clear. Barbara Usherwood's chapter on the introduction of American retailing methods to Britain examines the control over consumers – predominantly women – in a new kind of shopping environment. In foisting self-service shopping onto an unwilling public, grocers were balancing control of the shopping process with appeal to their customers. The subject of the next chapter is the way financial constraints and shortages in post-war Britain stimulated creativity, with the help of the burgeoning home-improvements industry. In it Jen Browne explores DIY in the home, in which, as her case studies show, women tended to be key decision-makers. In looking at both DIY and the consumption of 'As Seen on TV' gadgets, which Alison Clarke explores in the next chapter, the American influence on patterns of consumption is emphasized. Furthermore, this area of consumption emphasizes the fluidity between public and private spheres in relation to consumption and how such apparently labour-saving devices served as gifts of modernity to women. The role of consumer goods in the maintenance of relationships is a significant aspect of women's relationship with consumption (also explored later in Hobson's chapter on 'non-occasion cards'). Mica Nava has suggested that women's enthusiasm for consumerism may have stemmed from the positions of authority it gave them and have thus paved the way for the modern women's movement:

Consumption has offered women new areas of authority and expertise; new sources of income, a new sense of consumer rights and one of the consequences of these developments has been a heightened entitlement outside the sphere of consumerism which may well have contributed to the emergence of feminism. (Nava, 1989)

The next two chapters, however, provide a necessary note of caution. Anne Cronin's concentrates on advertising in the 1990s and indicates that despite three decades of feminism the European citizen is still represented as white and male. Also focusing on advertising texts, Mary Talbot's chapter explores the appropriation of feminist rhetoric by the advertising industry since the impact of the Women's Liberation Movement in the 1970s. Liberal feminism is articulated in the market-place as equality of consumer opportunity; feminism becomes style consumption and empowerment too becomes a commodity, for example, the *prêt à porter* power bestowed by handguns.

Returning to the key medium of television in modern consumer culture, the next chapter explores its impact in the construction of community in the United States. Mary Bucholtz shows that, as callers to shopping channels, women in their own domestic environments participate in the public sphere of broadcast talk. Through discourse analysis of shopping-channel talk, Bucholtz explores the establishment of a sense of shared location and intimacy on the air: a virtual neighbourliness between host and caller predicated on consumption.

The commodification of power is central to the next two chapters. Focusing on self-help books on gender and communication, Deborah Cameron critically examines the 'empowerment' and 'self-realization' offered by the genre. She argues that self-help books offer 'empowerment' as an object for individual consumption, deflecting the project of feminism onto the personal rather than the collective, and that, in any case, actual readers of these books appear to be seeking reassurance rather than any sort of transformation. Similarly, in Joanne Entwistle's chapter, on power dressing, she argues that while it is ostensibly about empowerment, it is in fact deeply conservative. Dressing for work is a source of anxiety for many women; 'power dressing' is a way of dealing with the masculine domain of the workplace by manipulation of dress codes, but it is not so much buying 'power off the peg' as personal safety.

Jane Hobson's chapter looks at 'non-occasion' greeting cards, that is, cards which do not specify any occasion (wedding anniversary, birthday . . .), examining their use, predominantly by women, to do interactional work on relationships. She argues that commodification of intimate relations through these cards both disrupts the inevitability of the personal lifecycle determined by heteronormative discourses and foregrounds the constructedness of 'the couple'. The final chapter explores the place of consumption in relationships within and across generations of women. Maggie Andrews and Rosie

Whorlow argue that relationships between mothers and daughters and 'imagined communities' of both young girls and mothers are formed through shared consumption. The case study used to establish their argument is the 1996 Boyzone concert tour.

In arguing for a wide interpretation of the concept of consumption, we are only too aware of the very many areas of consumer culture which this book is silent upon. These silences should not be seen as a wish by us to marginalize such areas of consumption or, conversely, to indicate the centrality of the status of the areas we are looking at. It is rather, like so much of women's lives, even within the academic sphere, a selectivity which has emerged out of a serendipity of practicalities. We are very aware of some significant areas of consumption that are not here, food, for example. There is little focus on women as the objects of consumption, as in prostitution, as well as other areas of work in the sex industry. But these have been looked at elsewhere (e.g. Dela, 1988). Of more concern to us is that some very significant cultures of women consumers are under-represented or not all, e.g. non-Western women, lesbian women. Moreover, we have perhaps tended to fall into a problem that Angela McRobbie (1997) has pointed to, namely, exploring the cosier issues of women in consumer culture, while ignoring the frequently problematic role they play as underpaid, powerless and exploited workers who underpin and facilitate that culture. The cheaply available clothes through which girls construct their identity, for instance, may well be produced by the alienated labour of other girls. One of our hopes for this volume is that it will function as a catalyst for further research and work on consumption; we look forward, therefore, to these omissions being addressed elsewhere.

References

Atkinson, D. (1992) *Purple, White and Green: Suffrage in London.* London: Museum of London.

Bowlby, R. (1985) *Just Looking: Consumer Culture in Dreiser, Gissing and Zola.* London: Methuen.

Bucholtz, M. (1999) 'Purchasing power: the gender and class imaginary on the shopping channel'. In M. Bucholtz, A. C. Liang and L. Sutton (eds), *Reinventing Identities: The Gendered Self in Discourse.* Oxford: Oxford University Press.

Carter, E. (1984) 'Alice in consumer Wonderland'. In A. McRobbie and M. Nava (eds), *Gender and Generation.* Basingstoke: Macmillan, pp. 185–214.

Davidoff, L. and Hall, C. (1987) *Family Fortunes: Men and Women of the English Middle Class 1780–1850.* London: Hutchinson.

Dela, F. (ed.) (1988) *Sex Work: Writings by Women in the Sex Industry.* London: Virago.

Fairclough, N. (1989) *Language and Power.* London: Longman.

Habermas, J. (1989) *The Structural Transformation of the Public Sphere* (trans. T. Bürger and F. Lawrence). Cambridge: Polity Press (first published 1962).

Johnson, R. (1987) 'The story so far: and for the transformations'. In D. Punter (ed.), *Introduction to Contemporary Cultural Studies.* London: Longman, pp. 277–313.

Latham, R. and Matthews, W. (eds) (1978) *Diary of Samuel Pepys.* London: Bell & Hyman.

Mackay, H. (ed.) (1997) *Consumption and Everyday Life.* London: Sage.

McRobbie, A. (1997) 'Bridging the gap: feminism, fashion and consumption', *Feminist Review,* 55, 73–89.

Miller, D. (1997) 'Consumption and its consequences'. In H. Mackay (ed.), *Consumption and Everyday Life.* London: Sage, pp. 214–44.

Moores, S. (1996) *Satellite Television and Everyday Life: Articulating Technology.* Arcamedia Research Monograph 18. Luton: University of Luton Press.

Nava, M. (1989) 'Consumerism and its contradictions', *Cultural Studies,* 2, 185–214.

Negus, K. (1997) 'The production of culture'. In P. du Gay (ed.), *Production of Culture, Cultures of Production.* London: Sage, pp. 67–119.

Radway, J. (1987) *Reading the Romance: Women, Patriarchy and Popular Literature.* London: Verso.

Talbot, M. M. (1992) 'The construction of gender in a teenage magazine'. In N. Fairclough (ed.), *Critical Language Awareness.* London: Longman, pp. 174–99.

Talbot, M. M. (1995) 'A synthetic sisterhood: false friends in a teenage magazine'. In K. Hall and M. Bucholtz (eds), *Gender Articulated: Language and the Socially Constructed Self.* London: Routledge, pp. 143–65.

2. *'All the World and Her Husband'*: The Daily Mail *Ideal Home Exhibition, 1908–39*

Deborah S. Ryan

In 1908, when there was much talk of the 'new woman', the opening up of professions and civic responsibility to her, and the inevitability of suffrage, the *Daily Mail* reported a 'suffragette invasion' of its first-ever Ideal Home Exhibition:

> A party of suffragettes put in an appearance at the exhibition during the afternoon. Ascending to the second floor, they stood bareheaded[1] and spoke to the large crowd that quickly assembled on the lawn below. The two speakers . . . explained that they came to the exhibition because many women had no homes and because elementary rights were denied to women who made the homes. After a certain amount of oratory the ladies consented to retire. (*Daily Mail*, 15 October 1904, p. 4)

The 'suffragette invasion' was played down in the *Daily Mail*, buried in a column headed 'Ideal Home Record' that reported the attendance of titled ladies at the Exhibition (it was not reported at all in Northcliffe's other paper, *The Times*). Under the sub-heading, 'Growing Interest in the Model Nursery', the 'support and interest of women of all walks of life' was reported (*ibid.*). This was surely a deliberate juxtaposition of honourable, orderly 'ladies' and dutiful mothers, on the one hand, with the unwomanly behaviour of suffragettes, on the other. Furthermore, immediately after the account of the 'suffragette invasion' there was a report of the prize-winners of the 'feminine' competitions for basketwork, wood-carving and embroidery.[2]

At a time when there were enormous changes in the social, economic and political structure of Britain, both the *Daily Mail* and its Ideal Home Exhibition presented a vision of stable femininity and peaceful domesticity that harnessed the latest modern developments, but respected the traditions of the past. With the Empire in decline and anxieties about the future of the race and nation, much importance was attached to the home as a site of citizenship. It was, too, a site of dutiful consumption where women were responsible for the making of the (imperial) citizens of the future.

The picture I have painted thus far is of a newspaper that was hostile to the new rights and opportunities for which women fought so hard in the early twentieth century (Melman, 1988). It is, however, a misleading one. I do not want to paint a picture of suffragettes heroically fighting against the oppressive private sphere of home. Instead, I want to concentrate on the ways in which the *Daily Mail* and its Ideal Home Exhibition reflected women's consumer aspirations for goods and lifestyles, by the display of what Carolyn Steedman calls a 'proper envy' (1986). Cultural critics, particularly those on the Left, have felt uncomfortable with such desires, seeing them as frivolous and empty and a betrayal of working-class communities and cultures (Hoggart, 1957). I would maintain that a study of the *Daily Mail* and its Ideal Home Exhibition gives insights into the neglected history of the hopes, dreams and aspirations of lower-middle-class women – what Valerie Walkerdine refers to as 'conservative, and respectable ordinariness' (1990, p. 162) – in the early twentieth century.

The *Daily Mail* sought to reflect the rapidly changing lives of its women readers. Indeed, its economic survival was dependent upon it so doing. Moreover, since it was founded in 1896 the *Daily Mail* has always been very much a women's newspaper. This chapter explores the ways in which the newspaper's Ideal Home Exhibition reflected the practical concerns and social aspirations of its women readers in a period which saw the rise of new professions and the subsequent expansion of the middle classes. Indeed, class divisions were eroding, shifting and re-formulating. Thus I want to emphasize the temporality of class identities that are under constant renegotiation (Light, 1991). Furthermore, there are particular problems in using as broad a term as 'middle class', especially when applied to women. There is, after all, no fixed division between the lower-middle classes and the middle-middle classes (Jeffrey and McClelland, 1987). Moreover, continually shifting consumer acquisitions and aspirations are used to mark out social identity in the Ideal Home Exhibition. Indeed, it was women's class mobility and their role as consumers that made them such an important target audience for the *Daily Mail*.

Thus, I will examine how the Ideal Home Exhibition educated women with displays of 'suburban modernity' and helped establish a new commercial culture of homemaking. It offered a space for the expression of new forms of feminine expertise which, I would argue, were part of a broader 'conservative feminism'. Its emphasis was not, however, just on rational consumption; it pandered to women's fantasies of modernity and domestic liberation. I also want to blur the imaginary boundaries between public and private, by showing the ways in which the concerns about 'home' as a physical place and emotional ideal were indeed highly visible and public.

The theme of the 'ideal home' appealed to the sentiments of the *Daily Mail*'s readers. The meaning of 'home' is not just confined to shelter and well-being, but to emotional and spiritual values and nourishment (Rybezynski, 1987). Home is and was, as Davidoff and Hall have said, 'as much a social construct and a state of mind as a reality of bricks and mortar' (1992, p. 358). Although few of the newspaper's readers would yet have owned their own homes, as home ownership did not take off until the 1930s,[3] they were fortunate enough to have a roof over their heads. In a world where change seemed to be happening at an alarming rate, an idea of 'home' gave a sense of stability and shelter from constant flux. Furthermore, the idea of 'home' took on a new significance in the early twentieth century when the possibilities of mass democracy citizenship were tied up with the ownership or tenancy of property. Social status was also largely determined by property (Harris, 1993). 'Home' was also the nation at the heart of the British Empire. 'Home' had a particular significance at a time when questions of nationhood, patriotism and race were important and Britain struggled to maintain its economic and military position in the world. Such concerns were highly visible in the pages of the *Daily Mail*.

The audience for the *Daily Mail* was formed by rapid social changes in the numbers and fortunes of the respectable working classes and lower middle classes. At the beginning of the twentieth century there was a real, albeit small, improvement in the living standards of most people, who now had a surplus to spend on needs other than basic subsistence. People exercised choice over how and where to spend their money. Desires were furnished by increasingly sophisticated retailers of products that were the fruits of newly mechanized factories (see Hamish Fraser, 1981). Smaller families were common, perhaps as a result of aspirations towards a better standard of living and the purchase of new consumer goods (Gittins, 1982).

Thus, Lord Northcliffe launched the *Daily Mail* in May 1896 to appeal to the new mass market. Aimed at the newly literate respectable working classes and lower middle classes, the *Daily Mail* played on readers' aspirations for a busy, yet leisured, life. There were new work opportunities in government departments and clerical and managerial work, with the emergence of big business.[4] Although such occupations paid little more than skilled manual work, they brought with them increased expectations and aspirations, which often meant a struggle to keep up appearances, concerns to which the *Daily*

Mail consciously appealed. Therefore, the intended *ideal* audience of the *Daily Mail* was middle class, but the newspaper was calculated to appeal to the aspirations of those lower down the social scale.

The *Daily Mail* was a great success because it saw reportable copy in the mundane features of daily life, extending the concept of news beyond traditional areas of politics and business to what became known as 'human interest' stories. Such concerns were part of a more general 'feminization' of English culture and national life where inward-looking, domestic and private values took on a new national significance (Light, 1991). Domestic metaphors could often be found on the news pages of the *Daily Mail*; for example, a 1930 report on the rapidly expanding civil service was head-lined 'Lavish Politicians: Extravagant National Housekeeping' (*Daily Mail*, 5 April 1930, p. 7). The 'pipe-smoking "little men" with their quietly competent partners' became a powerful symbol for a new private, 'feminized' and home-centred Englishness – 'a nation of gardeners and housewives' (Light, 1991, p. 211). This image provided a model for a companionate marriage where couples worked in partnership as homemakers and consumers.

The *Daily Mail* made calculated appeals to its audience's domestic and consumer aspirations. The choice of the 'ideal home' for the theme of the *Daily Mail*'s exhibition in 1908 turned such concerns into a spectacle. The emergence of exhibitions in the mid-nineteenth century was linked to broader transformations in manufacturing, retailing and advertising (see Briggs, 1988; Richards, 1991). By the turn of the century, retailing had undergone a dramatic transformation. There were now multiple shops, co-operatives, specialist shops and all-embracing department stores. The Ideal Home Exhibition not only functioned as an enormous department store, but acted as a form of publicity for them. Department stores fed off exhibitions and vice versa; a 'dream world of mass consumption' was created by the increasingly sophisticated forms of display that resulted (Williams, 1982). Both department stores and exhibitions, as Rosalind Williams suggests, positioned consumers as audiences to be entertained by commodities: selling became 'mingled with amusement' and the 'arousal of free-floating desire [was] as important as immediate purchase of particular items' (*ibid.*, p. 67). The Ideal Home Exhibition's mixture of consumer desires, retailing, manufacturing and leisure enabled it to explain the 'modern ways of domestic life' to its predominantly female audience (*Daily Mail Ideal Home Exhibition Catalogue*, 1908, p. 7). The Exhibition was, then, a recognition of the importance of the female consumer.

The *Daily Mail*'s Ideal Home Exhibition turned the two-dimensional world of the newspaper's women's and magazine pages into three dimensions. It had a particular appeal to the newspaper's women readers. The Exhibition portrayed a feminine and domestic world of goods, to which, it was claimed in coverage of the third exhibition in 1912, flocked 'all the world and her husband' (*Daily Mail*, 22 October 1908, p. 4). In the uncertainties of modern domestic life, where there was an array of new products and appliances to choose from if one could afford them, the *Daily Mail* claimed that its Exhibition offered a route through the maze of homemaking. The Exhibition, it said, would teach 'easy housekeeping'; 'homemaking and housekeeping were never lighter, pleasanter, or easier' than with a well-designed home and the aid of modern appliances. However, many *Daily Mail* readers could only aspire to the world that the Exhibition depicted. Thus labour-saving advice was offered to middle-class women, who until after World War I largely directed other (working-class) women's labour, but this advice ignored the needs of those who could not afford servants. Nevertheless, the Exhibition offered women who could afford the 6d entrance fee a fantasy of domestic life to which they could aspire.

The Ideal Home Exhibition was a tool with which young women could be educated in the skills of homemaking. Thus mothers were urged to take their daughters and schoolmistresses their female charges. The feminine skills of housekeeping and child-rearing were thought too important to be left to experience, and ought instead to be learned through instruction. Information, in the form of demonstration, instruction and advice, was consumed, in addition to objects. Visitors to the Exhibition were treated to a daily programme of lectures and demonstrations.

Much of the coverage of the Exhibition in the *Daily Mail* concerned the needs of brides-to-be or newly-weds. Moreover the Exhibition was itself a kind of moral training course, producing respectable couples. Thus one journalist described the adventures of Colin and Barbara, the 'ideal couple', at Olympia. At the beginning of their visit they were not engaged; Colin thought matrimony 'a stuffy, dullish institution, which necessitated the tedious process of taking a flat or house and filling it with uninspiring chairs and monotonous tables'. Barbara, however, dazzled Colin with an 'unexpected display of housewifely knowledge', grasping the scientific principles of an advanced curtain-rod design, and proving to Colin that there was more to her than the 'chaffing, sporting, slangy little friend' that he knew. Overwhelmed, too, by Barbara's display of tenderness at 'Babyland', a vision came to Colin as they toured the Ideal House that revealed to him the 'Ideal Life'. On the tube home he proposed to Barbara, asking her to 'live in a house like that' (*Daily Mail*, 16 April 1912, p. 8). A visit to the Ideal Home Exhibition could, then, even result in matrimony. For women, the Ideal Home Exhibition proposed marriage as knowledgeable consumption and dutiful motherhood.

Women were not just educated with housewifely skills by the Ideal Home Exhibition, they were also introduced to new joys of consumption. One woman visitor in 1910 described the 'proper spirit in which to visit an exhibition' thus:

> If you cannot have everything you want in the world, you can imagine yourself having it, and there are so many things here that you do want, or would want if you dared to, that you must have some of them some day, if not all of them at once. (*Daily Mail*, 13 April 1910, p. 7)

This atmosphere of free-floating consumer desire was commonly invoked by women writers in the *Daily Mail*. Thus a 'lady correspondent' described how her visit to the Ideal Home Exhibition in 1913 turned her into 'the slave of the naughty vice of envy' (*Daily Mail*, 11 October 1913, p. 3). The Ideal Home Exhibition, then, pandered to women's rational needs and consumerist fantasies.

In the inter-war years the *Daily Mail* and its Ideal Home Exhibition promoted a 'modern' way of life. It offered new modern identities to con-sumers through a vision of a new home, an imaginary purchase of a new kitchen or living-room suite, or perhaps the most up-to-date and efficient gadgets. In a visit to the Ideal Home Exhibition new identities could be witnessed, forged or merely dreamed about. Aspirations for, and consumption of, objects that represented modernity created a modern identity for the housewife. Indeed, the role of 'housewife' was constantly reformulated in the inter-war years. She could be chancellor of the domestic economy; skilled personnel manager of truculent and lazy servants; and professional home economist using the latest American scientific management techniques and labour-saving technology in her kitchen-laboratory. Most of the women depicted in the catalogues, stands and advertisements of the Ideal Home Exhibition were overwhelmingly middle-class – well-dressed, affluent and glamorous – and, almost certainly, married.

The homemaking discourse of the expanded women's press, the *Daily Mail*, the Ideal Home Exhibition and advertisements for gadgets and appliances, addressed women as professional housewives, as not only managers of their homes, but increasingly as workers. The 'servant problem', which intensified after World War I, changed the relation of the established middle classes to the home forever. Those amongst the middle classes who could still afford to employ servants did so on a daily, rather than a live-in, basis (domestic service did not go into an absolute decline until the mid-1930s). Thus both upper- and lower-middle-class women were addressed as housewives – workers in the home, rather than managers of it. The hard work of housework, it was claimed, could be eased only if the home was a labour-saving one. The modern housewife was both a fiction and an economic reality (Glucksmann, 1990).

The Ideal Home Exhibition educated women in rational consumption and the latest labour-saving appliances. Thus in 1922 it was claimed:

> Since the first Ideal Home Exhibition opened its doors in 1908 the progress of home-making has greatly accelerated. Women's striving for more freedom, for self-expression, has probably been the greatest factor in this speeding up of the march towards the Ideal Home, and nothing has done more to bring the perfect home nearer than women's determination to be freed from the thraldom of domestic duties carried out in archaic and inefficient ways. (*Daily Mail Ideal Home Exhibition Catalogue*, 1922, p. 8)

The *Daily Mail* and the Ideal Home Exhibition presented new role models for women, justified by ideas of 'progress'. Advertisers, as Martin Pumphrey points out, transformed the freedoms that women had gained during World War I, in employment and legal rights, into 'consumer discourse' through the figure of the 'modern housewife', whose life could be liberated by use of the correct household appliance (Pumphrey, 1987). However, despite the claims of the consumer discourse of the *Daily Mail* and the Ideal Home Exhibition, the modern housewife could never achieve her 'ideal home' because technology was constantly improving: each ideal was surpassed by another. Indeed, the 'ideal home' was in a constant state of flux. Each Ideal Home Exhibition promised to surpass the previous one with its labour-saving innovations and the hope of improvement.

Ideas about 'efficiency' were widespread in both the workplace and the home in the inter-war years. Indeed, the application of scientific management techniques and new technologies to the home was an implicit recognition that the home was, too, a site of production. The labour-saving appliance, or gadget, one of the most potent symbols of the Ideal Home Exhibition's suburban modernity, was also represented as a source of pleasure and pride. For example, N. Clifton Reynolds wrote in 'Making housework a pleasant game' in 1929:

> The modern housewife has discovered that, if she uses the correct household appliance for her work, if the right tool is used for every task, she can have a perfect home, and at the same time, plenty of leisure . . . Housekeeping can become a game. It can be played to time, with pauses for rest and periods of effort. (*Daily Mail Ideal Home Exhibition Catalogue*, 1929, p. 195)

Reynolds suggested that scientific principles of household management could be fun, but only if the housewife had purchased the appropriate appliances. 'It can', he said, 'provide endless interest and be the subject of daily experiment but, without the saving help of the correct household appliances it loses its glamour and becomes dull and wearisome' (*ibid*.). The appliance was not, then, just valued for its labour-saving potential. It was also valued for the image that it projected; it could invest a boring and tiresome task with glamour. Thus the modern identity of housewife depended upon the possession of the most up-to-date appliances.

In the inter-war years the Ideal Home Exhibition guided the housewife through the maze of new technology that claimed to offer practical and 'labour-saving' solutions to all her domestic problems. Homemaking was simultaneously constructed as a duty – an expression of love and respect – and a demonstration of professional skill, as well as a source of pleasure and fun. By the mid-1930s a commercial culture of homemaking was firmly established in England, which is perhaps paradoxical given that this is also a time of high unemployment, hunger marches and strikes. Yet for many of the middle classes, life was better than it had ever been, with higher real wages, a lower cost of living (which lowered the price of food and manu-factured goods) and increased leisure time to enjoy cinema and radio. This enabled new levels of consumption of goods upon the production of which Britain's industrial growth was based. Furthermore, the economic climate varied geographically: whilst depression was concentrated in the old industrial areas, the new suburbs boomed in the South. It became possible for the average salaried person to buy a house on a mortgage, own a car and afford consumer durables that would have been quite unthinkable twenty years before (Cook and Stevenson, 1977).

Thus the Ideal Home Exhibition, aided by hire purchase, new manu-facturing techniques and materials, such as plastics, and increasingly sophisticated advertising techniques, both educated and entertained the public in the new ways of consumerism. The 'servant problem' greatly facilitated the growth and success of the Ideal Home Exhibition and was used to underpin the labour-saving discourse used in the selling of new houses and appliances and the concept of 'professional housewife'. The *Daily Mail* and the Ideal Home Exhibition advocated cheap, efficient, labour-saving appliances to aid the harassed middle-class woman. A notion of progress that promised increased efficiency, through new technology, with each purchase fuelled the selling of appliances.

New labour-saving appliances did have the potential to reduce women's work within the home and relieve the drudgery of heavy work such as cleaning carpets and laundry. Homemaking was being elevated to an art and even a glamorous activity. Yet the actual lives of modern housewives differed vastly from that depicted in consumer discourse (Beddoe, 1989). Certainly, the use of appliances was not widespread until after World War II, primarily because of their high cost and the inconsistencies of an electrical supply that was not standardized. It is testimony to the value placed on such objects that they are included in museum collections (Porter, 1988). The appliances that were, in fact, used tended to be the smaller ones such as irons that were little changed in design, other than being wired for electricity, which made them easier to use. And they were often rented rather than purchased (Zmroczek, 1994).

The advertisements and articles of the *Daily Mail* and the Ideal Home Exhibition presented the labour-saving appliances as modern and efficient. Thus the cultural and social meanings that appliances carried could symbolize new consumer identities (Clarke, 1997). The question of whether an appliance actually fulfilled its function of labour-saving was not always the most important consideration. Thus the motive for the acquisition of goods could be to participate in a shared sociability and a collective modern identity. Furthermore, even if appliances did not necessarily save labour, they could enhance the status of the task, by recognizing women's labour in the home as house*work*.

Conclusions: women, suburbia and modernity

I have described in this chapter the ways in which the *Daily Mail* and its Ideal Home Exhibition were associated with a particular form of femininity which, I would argue further, was inherently associated with the modernity of the suburbs. However, cultural critics and Modernist designers and architects saw the suburbs and their inhabitants as either outside modernity or as representing a negative and feminized modernity that they denigrated for its consumer excesses and aspirations. Some critics damned the products of popular taste found in suburbia as retrograde 'bad design'; others condemned the very technological up-to-dateness and newness of popular products (Lloyd Jones, 1979). Such disparaging attitudes were also part of an unease felt about the new estates that reflected a change in lifestyle of the upwardly mobile working classes who entered the ranks of the lower-middle classes and began to experience a more private, home-centred way of life. As John Carey shows, cultural critics and novelists in the inter-war years despised the world of 'the suburbs and the clerks', labelling their aspirational values as trivial and gendering them feminine (Carey, 1992). Many intellectuals saw suburbia as emasculated; to them 'suburban' was a derogatory and disparaging term. Suburbia was also associated with a particular kind of feminized modernity, as Sally Alexander points out: one that embraced the trappings of mass culture, such as magazines, cosmetics and cinema (1994). Furthermore, as Andreas Huyssen shows, women were inherently identified with mass culture, as 'modernism's other' (1986).

Thus, because of their suburban audiences, the *Daily Mail* and its Exhibition provoked disdain amongst intellectuals and modernist critics. For example, despite articles by many well-known journalists and feature writers such as G.W. Steevens and Max Beerbohm (Bourne, 1990), one critic declared that the *Daily Mail*, with its cycling column, fashion page and home hints, 'reeks of the concerns of villadom' (Carey, 1992, p. 58). F.R. Leavis was one of the strongest critics of the *Daily Mail* in the inter-war years. In *Mass Civilisation and Minority Culture* (1930) he made a very personal attack on Northcliffe, whom he held responsible for a general 'overthrow of standards' and a 'process of levelling down'. Leavis declared, 'Lord Northcliffe showed people what they wanted, and showed the Best people that they wanted the same as the rest' (Leavis, 1930, p. 8). Leavis's criticisms were, as John Carey (1992) suggests, motivated by a fear and disdain for the masses.

The Ideal Home Exhibition was, then, despised because of displays which were thought to appeal especially to women's tastes. For example, Thomas Sharp suggested in his 1936 book *English Panorama* that the typical woman

> has a sense of property and a desire to display it . . . that is far more highly developed than his, she is at once more conservative and more open to the appeal of small novelty: aesthetically she has few or none of the makings of a citizen. (quoted in Edwards, 1981, p. 130)

Thus, the combination of conservatism and minor novelty, or tradition and modernity, in the mock Tudor or 'Tudorbethan' houses that were loathed by Modernist critics was thought to be especially attractive to women. Yet, I would argue that it was the modern features – the latest materials, techniques and technologies that aided labour saving – for which women clamoured, rather than the nostalgic. Women were, however, associated with both the 'sham' Modernistic and the 'sham' Tudor and thought to be swayed by artifice. Furthermore, women were thought by many to be outside what Wyndham Lewis called the 'rough and masculine work' of Modernism (Attfield, 1989), yet were condemned for their modernity. But it was their modernity that made them the ideal audience for the *Daily Mail* and its Exhibition.

The organizers of the Ideal Home Exhibition had the confidence not to take the new labour-saving suburban England too seriously. In the 1934 Exhibition, the cartoonist Heath Robinson affectionately lampooned suburban modernity with the creation of a house named 'The Gadgets'. The house was nearly full-size and was peopled by automatons called Mr and Mrs Glowmutton and more than twenty moving figures and animals. The house had an open front, like a doll's house, allowing visitors to see four main rooms, as well as an entrance hall, bathroom, study and attics. All the rooms were fitted with a variety of fantastical labour-saving devices, as were the gardens. Heath Robinson's house signified a specifically suburban form of modernity that did not radically alter the exterior of the home but instead entered through the back door, via the kitchen. Labour-saving appliances were the most potent symbols of modernity in the Ideal Home Exhibition in the inter-war years. The kitchen was shown to be the major site of experimentation and modernization, ruled over by the housewife. To visit the Ideal Home Exhibition was to become part of the progress of homemaking. The experience was a collective one: to be part of the crowd that gathered round Heath Robinson's Ideal Home was to participate in a collective, knowing and joyful experience of consumer culture and modernity.

Notes

1. To be hatless was an act of defiance against feminine conventions that was used as a form of political protest by suffragettes. In March 1912 members of the Women's Freedom League proposed that women should become a 'hatless brigade' and boycott all male makers of hats. See *Daily Mail*, 30 March 1912, p. 3.
2. *Daily Mail* reporting of the suffragettes was, on the whole, negative. For example, on 14 October a *Daily Mail* editorial entitled 'The monstrous regiment of women' described the suffragettes' attempt to rush Parliament as having gone beyond a 'prank'. It roundly condemned the 'disorderly' behaviour of these 'bad citizens' and expressed outrage at the actions of one of the women who had urged the unemployed to arm and attack property in London. See *Daily Mail*, 14 October 1908, p. 6.
3. Two million houses were built for sale in the inter-war years and house prices actually fell. Building societies, which had previously required a 24 per cent deposit, offered 95 per cent mortgages at rates as low as 4½ per cent by 1934. Consequently, by 1939, 31 per cent of houses were owner-occupied: a rise of over 10 per cent in 10 years. See Branson (1975, pp. 93 ff.).
4. In 1911 there were 2.4 million workers in such occupations; in 1931 there were 3.4 million, an increase of 41 per cent. Moreover, 69 per cent of this increase was in relatively humble clerical jobs (*ibid.*, pp. 92–3).

References

Alexander, A. (1994) 'Becoming a woman: growing up in the 20s and 30s', in *Becoming a Woman and Other Essays in 19th and 20th Century Feminist History*. London: Virago.

A. M. (1910) 'Ugly age past: wonders of the modern home', *Daily Mail*, 13 April, p. 7.

Attfield, J. (1989) 'FORM/female FOLLOWS FUNCTION/male: feminist critiques of design', in J. A. Walker (ed.), *Design History and the History of Design*. London: Pluto Press.

Beddoe, D. (1989) *Back to Home and Duty: Women Between the Wars, 1918–1939*. London: Pandora.

Bourne, R. (1990) *Lords of Fleet Street: The Harmsworth Dynasty*. London: Unwin Hyman.

Branson, N. (1975) *Britain in the Nineteen Twenties*. London: Weidenfeld and Nicolson.

Briggs, A. (1988) *Victorian Things*. London: BT Batsford.

Carey, J. (1992) *The Intellectuals and the Masses*. London: Faber.

Clarke, A. (1997) 'Tupperware: products or social relation?', in A. Smart Martin and R. Garrison (eds), *Material Culture: The Stranger in the Field*. London: Winterthur Press.

Cook, C. and Stevenson, J. (1977) *The Slump: Society and Politics during the Depression*. London: Jonathan Cape.

Daily Mail Ideal Home Exhibition Catalogue (1908, 1922 and 1932) London: *Daily Mail*.

Davidoff, L. and Hall, C. (1992) *Family Fortunes: Men and Women of the English Middle Class, 1780–1850*. London: Routledge.

Edwards, A. M. (1981) *The Design of Suburbia*. London: Pembridge Press.

Gittins, D. (1982) *Fair Sex: Family Size and Structure in England, 1900–1939*. London: Hutchinson.

Glucksmann, M. (1990) *Women Assemble: Women Workers and the New Industries in Inter-War Britain*. London: Routledge.

Goodall, P. (1983) 'Design and gender', *Block*, 9, 50–61.

Hamish Fraser, W. (1981) *The Coming of the Mass Market*. London: Macmillan.

Harris, J. (1993) *Private Lives, Public Spirit: A Social History of Britain 1870–1914*. Oxford: Oxford University Press.

Hoggart, R. (1957) *The Uses of Literacy*. London: Chatto & Windus.

Howard, K. (1912) 'The ideal couple at Olympia', *Daily Mail*, 16 April, p. 8.

Huyssen, A. (1986) 'Mass culture as woman: modernism's other', in T. Modleski (ed.), *Studies in Entertainment: Critical Approaches to Mass Culture*. Bloomington: Indiana University Press.

Jeffrey, T. and McClelland, K. (1987) 'A world fit to live in: the *Daily Mail* and the middle classes, 1918–1939', in J. Curran, A. Smith and P. Wingate (eds), *Impacts and Influences: Essays on Media Power*. London: Methuen.

Leavis, F. R. (1930) *Mass Civilisation and Minority Culture*. London: Chatto and Windus.

Light, A. (1991) *Forever England: Femininity, Literature and Conservatism Between the Wars*. London: Routledge.

Lloyd Jones, P. (1979) 'A taste of class', *Architectural Review*, February, pp. 72–9.

Melman, B. (1988) *Women and the Popular Imagination in the Twenties: Flappers and Nymphs*. London: Macmillan.

Porter, G. (1988) 'Putting your house in order: representations of women and domestic life', in R. Lumley (ed.), *The Museum Time-Machine: Putting Culture on Display*. London: Routledge.

Pumphrey, M. (1987) 'The flapper, the housewife and the making of modernity', *Cultural Studies*, 1(1), 179–94.

Richards, T. (1991) *The Commodity Culture of Victorian England: Advertising and Spectacle, 1851–1914*. London: Verso.

Rybezynski, W. (1987) *Home: A Short History of an Idea*. London: Heinemann.

Steedman, C. (1986) *Landscape for a Good Woman*. London: Virago.

Walkerdine, V. (1990) 'Dreams from an ordinary childhood', in *Schoolgirl Fictions*. London: Verso.

Williams, R. H. (1982) *Dream Worlds*. Berkeley: University of California Press.

Zmroczek, C. (1994) 'The weekly wash', in S. Oldfield (ed.), *The Working-Day World: Women's Lives and Culture(s) in Britain, 1914–45*. London: Taylor & Francis.

3. New disciplines for women and the rise of the chain store in the 1930s

Janice Winship

Introduction

In our everyday lives we may shop locally for food at the '7-Eleven' or the village post office, have a weekly outing to an edge-of-town superstore and, in town, frequent markets, specialist food stores, the smaller supermarkets or cut-price stores. A trip to the High Street with its chains and department store (if we're lucky) will provision us with clothes, gifts and home goods. Meanwhile, in the 'bohemian' quarter (now replete with heritage signposts), the well-off browse for the chic fashion garment or the quirky and interesting *objêt* and the poor for necessary items from Oxfam or the flea market. For some there are regular excursions to an out-of-town mall; for many this is a rarer holiday treat (or trial depending on taste), since in Britain full-blown malls are few and recent, albeit the covered town shopping centre is more prevalent and longer established (Marriott, 1981; Guy, 1994). What is also particularly striking, and also lamented (Gardner and Sheppard, 1989), is the dominance of chain stores across Britain: in the High Street, in edge-of-town developments and in the mall. Marks & Spencer, Woolworths, W.H. Smith, Boots and Sainsbury's, together with newer chains, are household names and successful companies (Guy, 1994). Moreover, as the franchised operation – Benetton, The Body Shop and Gap – the chain store has become *the* modern form of retail practice (Ritzer, 1993). It is surprising, then, that it has not been the subject of much cultural debate[1] and that in recent studies of shopping it is the mall which has merited most discussion (Chaney, 1990; Fiske, 1989; Morse, 1990; Shields, 1989).

Accounts of the mall have tended to see its genealogy as rooted in the European arcades and department stores of the nineteenth century and to regard America as its birthplace and 'natural' home. Such a gloss is not wrong but offers a particular angle on the development and experience of shopping. By attending to the chain store we throw up a neglected history and other meanings and practices around shopping which begin to paint a richer picture.[2] In this chapter I focus on one strand of this history: the story of how the chain store as cultural form served the 'social needs' of an emergent class (Williams, 1990, p. 14).

I begin, however, with the experiences most vividly evoked by current theorizations of shopping in order to justify the need for a study of the 'chain-store experience'. In the second part of the chapter I turn to the inter-war years in Britain, the period when the chain store developed as a significant retailing form catering, in particular, to the emerging lifestyle of lower-middle-class women (Beddoe, 1989; Giles, 1995; Gittins, 1982; Light, 1991). In this section I address how women were subject to new disciplines traversing work, home and leisure to produce the female body as 'nice and neat'. In the third section I consider how this body was involved in new (consumer) routines served by the goods and performative space of the chain store.

The missing chain

To carve out a space in which the chain store can be explored I have adopted the device of sketching three motifs for shopping, each of which has been pulled out from a particular theoretical approach and for the purposes of argument simplified and caricatured. The motifs are shopping as *empowerment*, shopping as *flânerie* and shopping as *(self-)discipline*. The key terms of the first are 'resistance' and 'sign wars', of the second 'distraction' and 'phantasmagoria' and of the third 'routine', 'repetition' and 'reassurance'. If the 'guerrilla' is the persona featuring in the first and the *'flâneur/flâneuse'* characterizes the second, the 'wo/man-with-toddler-in-buggy' is the emblematic figure of the third. It is the last, I shall argue, who is most associated with chain-store shopping.

Shopping as empowerment characterized the new-found intellectual interest in consumption in the 1980s (Nava, 1992). It was a reaction to the inadequacies of previous, often Marxist-inspired, conceptualizations which ignored consumption as unimportant (to the class struggle) or, whether from left or right (Hebdige, 1988), posited the consumer as passive cultural dupe buying into capitalism. It was both a response to and an expression of what were dubbed 'new times' (Hall and Jacques, 1989). A politics of consumption was thrown up both by the new social movements – in the form of green issues, feminist, gay and black identity politics – and by the changes wrought by a global capitalism oiled by the deregulation policies of Reagan and Thatcher's 'popular capitalism'. The latter's rhetorics hailed and lauded the consumer at the expense of the citizen (Keat *et al.*, 1994), and their policies redefined the landscape (Zukin, 1991; Corner and Harvey, 1991; Bird *et al.*, 1993): shopping malls, yuppie dockland developments, alongside run-down council blocks and desolated factory sites, were only the most visible and material manifestations of the restructuring of industry and work, and of public and private responsibilities. In the shift from so-called Fordism to post-Fordism, consumption was placed centre stage (Murray, 1988; Harvey, 1989; Slater, 1997) and some intellectual argument followed suit in arguing its political importance.

This was consumption and shopping envisaged as an active and creative engagement. On the model of male youth subcultures ('resistance through rituals', Hall and Jefferson, 1976) consumption is seen to subvert the codes of behaviour in shop or mall and rework the meaning of commodities in a 'sign wars' (Hebdige, 1979; Clarke, 1991). Such a model assumes a panoptical power (Foucault, 1977) which is being resisted or evaded in the making and remaking of identities. John Fiske's motif of 'guerrilla warfare' (1989, p. 14) undercuts any notion of shopping as a seduction in which the (feminine) consumer is the passive, helpless partner overwhelmed by brightly lit window displays and the sexual aura of (department) store ambience (Abelson, 1989; Bowlby, 1985; Morris, 1988; Reekie, 1993; Nava, 1995). It also breaks with those theorists who collapse the cultural into the economic by separating the economic and cultural fields, but in its most banal form those with the fewest economic resources are the most culturally resourceful. In respecting consumption it also heroizes. As Peter Jackson puts it, 'An impression can be given . . . that shopping is a truly subversive activity with revolutionary potential' (1993, p. 216).

By 1998 it is easy to see the several ironies of this formulation. First, that in rejecting seduction as a model for consumption these critics are themselves seduced by a form of commodity fetishism:

> What we see is the excess of signs, not the conditions of production, distribution and exchange which make them available. The effect, ironically, is to replicate that view of capitalism which capitalism would most like us to see: the richness of the market-place and the freely choosing consumer. (Clarke, 1991, p. 85)

Second, consumption is masculinized, at a moment when men are being emasculated by unemployment and restructured work practices are favouring (part-time, low-paid) women workers. As Nicky Gregson puts it, 'Boys go shopping' (1995, p. 136). Even if theoretical scrutiny is not only *by* men or *about* men (Rutherford, 1988; Mort, 1988; Nixon, 1992), the modes of shopping addressed accord with a masculine agenda. In particular, leisure shopping which, with its newly found pleasures for those whom Angela McRobbie refers to as 'the born again shopper' (1991, p. 10), is in sharp contrast with shopping as domestic work. McRobbie also suggests a masculinism in the emphasis put on the 'objects of consumption' rather than on 'the social relationships which entwine themselves' within consumption practices (1991, p. 12). As Clarke nicely puts it, 'These cultural *bricoleurs* do not feel as though they are pushing prams around while trying to keep to the week's budget' (1991, p. 85).

Masculinization is particularly obvious in my second motif: shopping as *flânerie*. The clutch of studies making the imaginative leap from nineteenth-century arcades and department stores to the mall of the late twentieth century (Friedberg, 1993; Langman, 1992; Shields, 1992, 1989) do so via the pioneering work of Charles Baudelaire and Walter Benjamin and the resolutely male (Wolff, 1985) figure of modernity, the *flâneur* (Benjamin, 1973, 1983; Buck-Morss, 1989; Frisby, 1985; Tester, 1994). *Flânerie* emphasizes shopping as a private pursuit, involving the experience of wandering amidst an urban crowd and responding to disparate stimuli. It highlights shop window and mall environment as spectacle to be gazed at and consumed: 'Everyday life has . . . become a realm where ordinariness has been transformed into an unending series of mass-mediated fragmented "spectacles" and carnivals that celebrate the universalisation of consumption' (Langman, 1992, p. 47).

This transformation of everyday life – the creation of 'dream worlds' (Williams, 1982) – induces a fractured identity, which for Anne Friedberg is associated with the panoramic gaze.[3] She suggests that, 'like the panopticon system, *flânerie* relied on the visual register – but with a converse instrumentalism, emphasizing mobility and fluid subjectivity rather than restraint' (1993, p. 16). Where accounts are most celebratory of shopping they tend to adopt shades of this *mobile gaze/mobile subjectivity*.

However, it is interesting that the distracted psychological state – what Margaret Morse describes as 'the phantasmagoria of the interior', a mixture of levels of consciousness and objects of attention (1990, p. 201) – is more usually regarded as a problematic and enervating condition associated with women carrying out their multiple domestic roles – flitting from task to task, unable to concentrate wholly on any of them. Such distraction has also been associated with the experience of working on a fast-moving assembly line where consciousness is only partly focused on the job in hand but cannot properly be engaged elsewhere. Certainly, some commentators have expressed a more general unease, most clearly Frederic Jameson in his pessimistic interpretation of postmodernity: 'schizophrenia' is seen as the characteristic distracted state of cultural life (1984, p. 71). Yet in conjunction with the term *flâneur*, distraction acquires positive and assertive characteristics.

Finally, if the panoramic gaze implies a speeding up of the circulation of commodities and of city life more generally, the *flâneur*, like the tourist, does not heed time but has the opportunity to indulge in the sensory overload. Recent feminist contributors have insisted that *flânerie* can also be the spatial activity of women – as *flâneuses* (Friedberg, 1993; Nava, 1995; Wilson, 1992) – but it remains, I would argue, an activity of the *leisured*.[4]

My third motif, shopping as (self-)discipline, suggests different priorities of time, space and sight/site. Rather than shopping as 'buying out', as in the case of the guerrilla or *flâneur*, it poses shopping as 'buying into' a normative culture. It also returns us to elements of Foucault's panopticon though with the emphasis Mica Nava puts on understanding consumption as part of a new technology of power in which it is 'both a form of subjection to . . . and a form of resistance' (1992, p. 165; see also Slater, 1997, p. 59).

Even Laura Langman's article, on the whole a tribute to shopping as empowerment and *flânerie*, concludes by foregrounding the disciplinary character of shopping:

> Malldom is better seen as a modern 'panopticon' in which the search for subjectivity locks people into 'neon cages' of consumption, sentenced to lifetimes of shopping for subjectivity . . . The mall generations have now eaten almost 100 billion identical burgers and express their pseudo-individuality in the mass-produced fads and fashions of 'The Gap' or 'Limited' brand clothing. They experience not degradation but celebration. They flock to the malls or other carnival sites to seek the surveillance, scrutiny and recognition by the Others who share their tastes. When they grow up and work for the administrative apparatus of amusement society, the corporations, they will have been well socialized, malled, to deny any genuine individuality or any kind of critical consciousness. (1992, p. 71)

Echoing Adorno and Horkheimer's pessimistic views (1977), nevertheless Langman usefully places repetitive chain-store purchases at the centre of malldom. By invoking the 'mass-produced fads and fashions' she is implicitly pointing to industrial production and the economics of Fordism lying behind the cultural experience. She also links work and consumption: the one is not repressive and the other liberating but they are intertwined.

For Margaret Morse 'the mall is a miniature suburbia' (1990, p. 211). It is not a space where the potential for carnivalesque is foregrounded but 'a place to shore up the boundaries of the self (*ibid.*, p. 198). Meaghan Morris also emphasizes repetition and routine:

> The commodities in a discount house boast no halo, no aura. On the contrary, they promote a lived aesthetic of the serial, the machinic, the mass-produced: as one pair of thongs wears out, it is replaced by an identical pair, the same sweatshirt is bought in four different colours, or two different and two the same. (1988, p. 222)

> . . . one of the things that is fascinating about Big W aesthetics is the way that the store provides little more than a set of managerial props for the performance of inventive scenarios in a drama that circulates endlessly between home and the pub and the car park and Green Hills and back again home. (1988, p. 223)

Unlike the male *flâneur* who as a tourist (and stranger) seems always to experience the present as new and different and thus places (of modernity) as curiously the same, Morris's female 'pedestrian' invests time, energy and emotion in shopping places which gain both histories and familiarity. Morris deploys the figure of the pedestrian to argue against the positions I have outlined above. 'Pedestrian' refers literally to someone on foot but also emphasizes the mundane. The pedestrian is precisely not the *flâneur*. Daniel Miller draws on 'the housewife' (1995, p. 34) and McRobbie invokes woman-with-children. 'Wo/man-with-toddler-in-buggy' (a publicity image discussed by Morris) suggests a responsibility for others and routines to be kept to. Suggesting both mobility and non-mobility, such a figure may have arrived to shop by car, public transport or on foot, and observation suggests a purposeful perambulation that is not *flâneuring*: time is of the essence. Barbara Ehrenreich offers an insightful fictional description: 'Della watched a young mother with a tattoo on one bare arm moving furiously ahead; the stroller she was pushing might have been a minesweeper' (1994, p. 204). In keeping with such a figure, McRobbie emphasizes consumption as 'necessary reproduction' (1991, p. 8) which 'does not deny the pleasures of consumerism by replacing them with drudgery, but . . . registers the intersection of social control, state intervention and leisure culture' (*ibid.*, p. 9). It signals the non-individualized nature of much of women's consumption and the anxiety as well as pleasure it involves. In the exercise of her power she does *not* always experience empowerment:

Housewives are given the burden of provisioning for their household. This is a task whose skills are commonly uncredited but whose failures, as in a lack of thrift, or forgetting to replace some mundane item such as toilet paper, may quickly become the source of blame. (Miller, 1995, p. 36)

The term 'thrift' points to the economic and cultural resources that in needing to be managed are also constraining (Lunt and Livingstone, 1992), an issue that accounts of shopping as empowerment and *flânerie* ignore. Thus have *flânerie*, distraction and phantasmagoria been tamed. For the 'wo/man-with-child-in-buggy' there is less a mobile subjectivity and gaze than a constrained subjectivity and a foreshortened gaze. Foregrounding such a figure brings the chain store firmly into the picture. For it is the chain store which is most associated with value-for-money goods, with routine, repetition and convenience, and with the purchase of necessities in daily life.[5]

I turn next to the inter-war period, when chain stores took on their recognizably modern characteristics in Britain and find their place in a cultural field marked by class divisions (Carey, 1992).

'Nice and neat'

Originally rooted in working-class neighbourhoods and in expanding industrial centres, by the inter-war years chain stores had a solid presence in High Streets and suburban Parades. Adopting 'the doctrine of rationalisation' (Hannah, 1983, p. 30) they marked the arrival of Fordist mass distribution practices to match Fordist mass production (Rees, 1969; Fraser, 1981, Strasser, 1989). Marks & Spencer's intimation to customers that it introduced 'the girl who makes the stockings to the girls who wear them' (*The Marks & Spencer Magazine*, Summer 1932) concisely points to the active creation of markets (not least by their magazine); a simplification and speeding up of distribution (partly by excluding the wholesaler); and the retailer's control of distribution *and* manufacture. The upshot was a tendency towards a *standardization* of goods, shops *and* consumers.

Yet standardization and mobility, I would argue, go hand in hand, embodied in the figure of the young woman: 'the young working girl – lipsticked, silk-stockinged'. She is set against 'the cloth cap and spare frame of the unemployed man' evoked in Sally Alexander's characterization of Britain's 'two nations' – south and north, suburb and inner city, in work and out of work, well-off and poor (1994, p. 103). J. B. Priestley, observing English life from the new social space of a cinema café in Boston, also notes how under the influence of models from Hollywood, the young were no longer marked by their market-town roots. But 'it was only the girls . . . who had this cosmopolitan appearance; the young men looked their honest, broad, red-faced East Anglian selves' (1934, p. 376).

The men are still tied to class and place but the young women are the sign of social and industrial transformation. Light industries – electrical goods, synthetic fibres and food-processing – blossomed in edge-of-town locations in the Midlands and South-east, deploying flow and assembly line methods and recruiting cheap, mostly non-unionized, female labour (Alexander, 1994; Glucksmann, 1990). But 'the outstanding change' was in the growth of white-collar workers, including women, particularly in 'retail distribution, local government, transport and entertainments' (Pollard, 1983, pp. 184–5). For all these workers, many of whom moved out to the new – both speculative and council – housing in the suburbs (Abrams, 1946; Glynn and Oxborrow, 1976; Jackson, 1973), standards of living rose.

Alexander's 'young working girl' is echoed in photographs. Women assembling valves for wireless sets have bobbed hair, white, low-belted overalls, probably artificial silk stockings (they have a shiny look) and heeled shoes with ankle strap. Glucksmann describes how such women (at the forefront of the new Fordism) took on the qualities of the work they performed: 'clean, neat and tidy workers', in contrast to workers in the older heavy industries who were seen as 'large, strong, untidy and bawdy' (1990, p. 216). Similarly the term 'white collar' graphically points to *dress*, invoking both the appearance of *this* worker and the worker s/he definitely is not. *The Marks & Spencer Magazine* shows a model standing primly for the camera and captioned 'This neat and attractively dressed girl bought her clothes at a Marks & Spencer Store'. Her demeanour and dress are visible embodiments of an emergent class.

For suburban 'Dunroamin' owners, Paul Oliver suggests that the predominant aesthetic was organized around a combination of 'pretty' and 'nice'. Whereas 'pretty' was 'full of charm, sentiment and sweetness', 'nice' was 'orderly and controlled' (1981, pp. 181–2). 'Nice and clean, nice and neat, nice and tidy, nice and smart, nice and bright' also illuminatingly codes the outcome of new self-disciplines for women. Etched out on the body they can be thought of in terms of the shift in the governance of people towards 'technologies of the self' (Foucault, 1988).[6] The new disciplinary regime was tied to changed work practices and nurtured by a shift of routines at home and at leisure; all served by consumption.

Such a view undercuts the common-sense view (endorsed by more intellectually grounded accounts, cf. 'shopping as empowerment') that sees the workplace as a site of discipline – workers only able to act at the behest of machinery and/or boss – but home and leisure as sites of 'freedom' where workers choose and buy and consume, beholden to no one and constrained only by disposable income.

During the inter-war period Antonio Gramsci (1971), Walter Benjamin (Wollen, 1993) and Siegfried Kracauer (1975) all engaged with the cultural impact of the new workplace represented by Fordism and the discipline it engendered in and beyond the factory gate, envisaging a progressive potential but expressing an ambivalence about modern developments. Kracauer in particular focuses attention on the white-collar worker as the 'product . . . of . . . rationalisation and its victim' (Frisby, 1985, p. 164), and latches on to *women* and the *lower middle classes* as at the heart of Fordism. It was the woman's body ('the mass ornament'), in the form of the dancing troupe The Tiller Girls, which was the most vivid symbol of Fordism:

> When they formed an undulating snake, they radiantly illustrated the conveyor belt; when they tapped their feet in fast tempo, it sounded like, business, business; when they kicked their legs high with mathematical precision, they joyously affirmed the progress of rationalisation. (Witte, 1975, pp. 63–4)

But in Kracauer's account the 'mass ornament' does not quite register as the brilliant mirror of the white-collar worker whose body was materially produced by Taylorism at work and in the consumption practices of 'free time'.

Pierre Bourdieu's study *Distinction* (1984) makes such a connection between work, leisure and consumption. Depending on education, family of origin, job and income, choices are made about consumption which reproduce distinct class lifestyles. These 'become *inscribed*' within different bodies, making them 'fit' for some activities and not others (Shilling, 1993, p. 135). The body is a form of *'physical capital'* (*ibid.*, p. 127) with dominant classes attempting to 'define their bodies and lifestyle as superior . . . and as, metaphorically and literally, the embodiment of class' (*ibid.*, p. 140). Since the body betrays class origins, aspirational classes invest considerable effort in 'remaking' the body: it becomes the site on which class tensions are played out.

According to Bourdieu, the lower-middle-class man, the *petit* bourgeois, is one 'who has to make himself small to pass through the strait gate which leads to the bourgeoisie: strict and sober, discreet and severe, in his dress, his speech, his gestures and his whole bearing, he always lacks something in stature, breadth, substance, largesse' (Bourdieu, 1984, p. 338). It is an evocative description of the lower-middle-class man whose female counterpart is 'nice and neat'. Their bodies express 'cultural goodwill' towards the bourgeoisie and a 'distinction' from the working class. But how does the 'nice and neat' body emerge as a significant classed body in the inter-war period? With its emphasis on 'social reproduction' Bourdieu's account is little help.

Shoshona Zuboff's (1988) analysis of the relation between Taylorist/Fordist practices and the body is pertinent. Taylorism deskilled workers and took away control, but the body was still involved in *acting-on* materials and utilizing equipment (pp. 98–9). On the assembly line the work was lighter and cleaner, the hours shorter and the pay better than in domestic service or retail (Glucksmann, 1990). Yet, there were costs involved with discipline more intense than under older work regimes and a 'collective self-disciplining . . . virtually built into this form of work organisation' (*ibid.*, p. 173). Those not able to 'stand the pace' (*ibid.*, p. 178), whose 'acting-on' was too slow, moved or were sacked. As one woman who had worked in such a factory commented: 'It was awful really – women used to be carried out screaming hysterics' (*ibid.*, p. 177).

In contrast, the white-collar worker uses her body in the service of '*acting-with* people – interpersonal communication and co-ordination' (Zuboff, 1988, p. 99). Nevertheless women's entry into clerical work occurs as it is routinized by scientific management (Braverman, 1974). Lower-grade work loses its *acting-with* qualities (these shift up the hierarchy) to be replaced by tasks more devoted to *acting-on* materials and equipment (e.g. typing). A similar 'rationalization' process occurs in shop work: large numbers of women become shop assistants as expertise shifts into the hands of management, manufacturers and advertising agencies.

Thus the 'mass' intake of women into (new) manufacturing jobs, clerical and service jobs is such that women's bodies are caught on the boundary between being instruments for *acting-on* and instruments for *acting-with*. Those symbolically placed on the side of the latter strive fiercely to protect this class marker and status. It is here that appearances are so important. The 'neat and attractively dressed woman' signifies both the 'lightness' of the work involved in *acting-on* the assembly line – even when self-discipline is intense – and the status of *acting-with* in the office and service industries – even when the content of that work has been downgraded.

Paralleling the classification accorded to women assembly workers, Judy Giles's account of suburban working/lower-middle-class women shows them self-identifying ('some would not have been thus defined by their peers' (1995, p. 27)) as 'respectable' not 'rough', a label more often attached to those still living in the old working-class communities. The battle for respectability was won across several fields including ownership of a council house which 'conferred a certain status as a "good" tenant and housewife' (*ibid.*, p. 88). Yet, home, family, childcare and sexuality in this period were publicly scrutinized by a range of 'experts'. In the face of this 'surveillance' the new suburbanites developed an 'emotional thriftiness'. Those

> who knew how quickly and easily the brutalities and deprivations of poverty could endanger a hard won sense of belonging as a citizen, a tenant, a home owner, were unlikely to squander their inheritance in emotional excess any more than they would be likely to indulge in financial extravagance. (*ibid.*, p. 98)

With contraceptive use, the lower middle class also curbed family size, a further sign of 'respectable' difference from the 'unruly' reproductive patterns of the unskilled working class.[7] In comparison to the emotionally open relationships of inner city residents, those in suburbia also developed a more insular family life and adopted a reserve: they 'kept themselves to themselves' (*ibid.*, p. 94). But this gave them a space, argues Giles, 'in which, rather than finding themselves always already inscribed in the narratives of others, women might resist the inevitable exposure and scrutiny of such inscription' (*ibid.*, p. 101). 'Emotional thriftiness' and Bourdieu's making oneself 'small' are two sides of the same lower-middle-class demeanour. Giles also comments on the transgression of cultural boundaries involved in 'the emergence of respectable working-class women into spaces previously reserved for middle-class men (and their chaperoned wives) – the shopping street, the office, the cinema/theatre, the park' (*ibid.*, p. 104). It is a transgression tempered by the non-threatening (non-sexual) 'nice and neat body'. In this way too is the body made 'small'.

For young women across the classes, the shift from the fashionable Edwardian body – ' "*raide*": taut, stiff, tight' – to the 'modernist' body of the 1920s – 'healthy, intelligible and progressive . . . functioning like an efficient, smoothly running machine' (Wollen, 1993, pp. 20–1) – involved practising new internal disciplines: 'exercise, sports and diet rather than the corset and the stays' (*ibid.*, pp. 20–1). However, the lower-middle-class attachment to 'nice and neat' as a version of the modernist body involved a particular inflection of new routines, including chain-store shopping.

New routines and the performative space of the chain store

Without servants or extended family support, managing a tight budget and keeping up appearances, the lower middle classes were promising targets for the advice from 'scientific management' experts on running a 'rational' home.[8] Advertising fed such routines, but also offered respite: 'Salmon? that's a treat!' *Husband* enjoys the treat, (*house*)*wife* enjoys minimal preparation. Alongside tinned peaches and evaporated milk this reprieve-for-mum/treat-for-family itself became a routine: Sunday tea after the rigours of preparing/eating the Sunday roast. Children were also caught up in regimes proposed by experts like Truby King, who advocated no emotional pampering and feeding baby at regular intervals, never on demand (Hardyment, 1983; Light, 1991, p. 124). Training combined with doses of Syrup of Figs encouraged the self-discipline of obligatory daily bowel movements. As Jackson Lears graphically describes US laxative advertising: 'the pitch for occasional heroic purgation was being streamlined into an emphasis on "regularity" – a more methodical regime better suited to the emerging rhythms of modern life' (1994, p. 165).

Both treat and respectable routine were provided by the expansion of suburban supercinemas: 'going to the pictures' and enjoying 'luncheon or tea' (p. 22) in the café offered a 'brief escape from dull routine at low cost' (Jackson, 1973, p. 176), whilst 'listening-in' to the wireless (affordable by the 1930s)[9] offered entertainment and access to music, plays and discussions, hitherto outside lower-middle-class experience. As a key institution to routinize daily life, the wireless schedules soon fitted around and consolidated women's domestic day-time duties and men's evening return from work (Moores, 1988; Pegg, 1983; Scannel, 1988), with the added 'convenience' of enabling women simultaneously to 'relax' and 'work' – listening-in whilst ironing or darning.

According to Michael Schudson, the 'convenience' product is available to a wider group, is easier to use and has a 'suitability': 'if there is a producer's interest in mild goods to appeal to the widest possible audience, there is also a consumer's interest in developing a taste for mild goods because they *do not offend*' (Schudson, 1993, p. 202; my emphasis). The development of a 'mass, British *middle-brow* culture', epitomized in the BBC's 'light entertainment' output, which offered 'balanced' programmes that were relaxing, 'guaranteed soothing ("wholesome") by . . . exclusion of all excesses' (Frith, 1983, p. 121), can be considered in this context of a 'culture of convenience'. Established during the inter-war period as time becomes a scarce commodity, convenience facilitates a safe 'mobility', so that convenience and democratization go hand in hand (Schudson, 1993).

Schudson's own discussion of 'convenience' centres on the cigarette as a mild good: 'the standardised, reliable, quick and easy smoke' (*ibid.*, p. 199), in comparison to older forms of tobacco consumption – smoking a cigar or pipe, chewing tobacco or taking snuff. Smoking was another repetitive 'leisure' practice which could be enjoyed whilst otherwise engaged, and became 'a symbol of women's renewed demand for equality' (*ibid.*, p. 203).

The newly developed 'roll-on', shaping the body with elastic instead of whalebone, steel and lacings, also had convenience value. Easier to put on, more comfortable, and more 'suitable' for the younger and lighter figure, it erased the unpopular word 'corset' (Ewing, 1978, p. 147).[10] Together with the use of cosmetics – lipstick, powder and rouge – it differentiated a younger generation. No longer the distinguishing sign of the prostitute, make-up by the 1920s was worn and frequently renewed in public: 'Lipstick . . . marks were seen everywhere on cups and handkerchieves' (Jackson, 1991, p. 46). This repetition was echoed in routines associated with haircare. Washed more frequently than long, pinned-up tresses ('Friday night is Amami night'),[11] young women's short hair required regular cutting and a 'Marcel' wave or perm (expensive until the late 1930s) at the hairdressers (Jackson, 1991, p. 138).

Chain stores variously catered to these new routines. With the fashionably shorter skirt-length demanding the display of stocking-clad leg, Etam opened branches in the City of London specifically to sell stockings to office girls (*The Times*, 21 March 1936, p. 13). These cheap rayon stockings easily laddered, but were not easily darned, and had routinely to be replaced to maintain respectability (neatness). But this was only one of the more obvious ways in which chain stores met certain class needs. Whether selling clothes or food, the chain store catered to a different rhythm. The independent grocer might drop round and consume a leisurely cup of tea while the mistress of the house decided on her weekly requirements. Her order would be delivered and she might enjoy considerable credit. Chain-store shoppers did their own shopping, regularly and for cash, and often travelled by bus. Their purchases were in pounds and dozens and goods were likely to be packaged and branded. Shopping was thus neither the bulk-buying of grander households nor the daily ounces and single items resorted to by the poor from nearby corner shops.

Such stores were geared to the anonymous consumer, not to the known customer. Uprooted from inner-city communities and transplanted into the suburbs, suburban women lost their ties with community-based shops and became a 'natural' constituency for the expanding chains (Blake, 1936). Moreover, the shopper did not have to carry her family background into her exchanges with sales staff. She could 'keep herself to herself' in the chain store or, to a degree, construct herself anew. She could afford, if she so wished, the promiscuity of shopping across a range of stores since she did not require the credit offered by the traditional corner shop. She availed herself, however, of hire purchase to manage her tight budget ('easy purchase' was increasingly available in the inter-war period, for buying furniture, for example (Jackson, 1991, p. 48)). There was also an 'anonymity' to goods. The 'simpleness' of women's clothes, the standardization of men's shirts, was partly an economy on the part of the retailer, a means of providing reasonable quality at a cheap price. But such clothes also allowed the consumer to blend in, not stand out from the crowd. As Oliver comments, the ethos in the new suburbs was '"keeping up with" not *"beating"* the Joneses' (1981, p. 191). A magazine article in which 'Mrs Goodwife goes out shopping' vividly illustrates how chain stores facilitated a class mobility and suburban taste. Joining the tennis club ('the principal summer recreation in our suburb') is a necessary but hardly affordable expense, only managed by prudent purchases at M&S: 'It was not a question of buying cheap clothes at low prices, all the things I purchased are in excellent taste' (*The Marks & Spencer Magazine*, Summer 1932).

The space of the chain store, as exemplified in the modernized M&S 'superstore', was also distinctive. The 'chaotic-exotic' (Williams, 1982, p. 71), typical of earlier arcades and department stores which borrowed the 'dangerous' mix of a market culture (Slater, 1993), containing and rendering it safe for shoppers, was absent. Instead of the stimulating visual register, the play of images, light and 'theatrical sets' contributing to the 'ambiguity of space' (Frisby, 1985, p. 241), and the illusion of an exterior space provided by glass and steel roofs, there is (the illusion of) transparency. The shop window does not aspire to the 'modernism of European poster art' (Gaines, 1989, p. 37) as, for example, did Selfridges' admired windows. Rather, it aspires to the kind of window pronounced against by the advocates of the 'show window' or the 'illusion window'. Frank Baum insisted that 'goods can't be made to go if they are *simply and transparently displayed*; they require the supplement of representation' (Culver, 1988, p. 107).[12] To cross the store threshold from the bustle and heterogeneity of the street, albeit one that has been 'rationalized' or 'scythed through' (Osborne, 1981, p. 59) to accommodate modern transport and retail needs, is to step clearly into another plane. Inside, the store is brightly and uniformly lit (resembling daylight as near as possible), signage indicating the type of good and price – 'Wool jumpers 2/11' – is prominent, and at eye height, and (a limited range of) goods are piled up, in an abundance (evidently mass-produced but offering, for example, a range of colours or fabrics) on counters laid out in a symmetrical grid pattern. Goods are at waist height – easy to look at and handle without the intervention of an assistant – with nothing to distract the customer from finding and contemplating the goods she is interested in. The space is an ordered, hygienically clean and visible one, spacious but not so big or spread across floors (ground floor only) that the whole cannot be immediately grasped: it reveals rather than hides, offers the known rather than throws up surprises. Such transparency communicates the accessibility of both space and goods. There is the illusion that the barriers to consumption for those who have hitherto consumed relatively little have been removed.

The basis of the appeal of this design is perhaps similar to that of The Tiller Girls: 'the ornamental structures underlying these revues transform the everyday experience of depersonalisation, drill and routine into aesthetic pleasure' (Berghaus, 1988, p. 213). One might say that the 'ornamental structure' of the chain store transformed the disciplines experienced at home and work into the aesthetic pleasure of consumption. The lower middle class were *arrivistes* but only just; consumption was crucial to their lifestyle but not to be engaged in lightly; and their shops, by today's standards, were austere spaces. Nevertheless, in their uniformity and predictability from store to store, chain stores represented 'oases of order' in a notoriously uncertain world (Sigsworth, 1990, p. 53, on the Montagu Burton chain). Such order was a quality keenly appreciated by the insecure 'lower middles' (Jackson, 1991).

Conclusion

In this chapter I have explored the relation between the rise of a particular class grouping in Britain and an emerging cultural form – chain-store retailing. My argument has focused on new disciplinary modes at work and at home, exercised on and by the lower middle class, especially women, and carrying through into the perfomative space of the chain store. I have placed the 'nice and neat' body centre stage as the site across which new disciplines, with their turn to consumption-led 'technologies of self' are played out, and class and gendered relations are struggled over. Routine, repetition and the consumption of the standardized and 'convenience' commodity are key to holding on to what was, for the lower middles, the proudly won but fragile new social space in which they found themselves. Paradoxically, such routines and the consumption of the standardized commodity facilitate a mobility. They are part of the means by which a young generation of women (and men) take on new modes of femininity (and masculinity). They also contribute to the lower middle class culturally distancing itself from its working-class roots and having opportunity for some cultural manoeuvre in fields where the middle classes hold the ring.

Of course, for the sake of argument I have overstated the links between the lower middle class, the 'nice and neat' body and the chain store,[13] but I make no apology for that. Those links are still evident today and there are aspects of my analysis of this formative period of chain store history that are worth taking up in the present. The disciplinary relation between shopping, and especially chain-store shopping, and the other (home, work and leisure) routines of our lives remains. Here my earlier figure of wo/man-with-toddler-in-buggy is emblematic of such a disciplinary mode. Second, the chain store continues to be the standardized store offering a range of standardized commodities, yet the purchase of these arguably facilitates a (safe) mobility. Potentially open to all, the chain store helps to disguise the obvious marks of class difference, and enables the management of a gendered identity which cannot offend – the modern-day equivalent of 'nice and neat'.

When critics rail against the uniformity of the shops in British high streets and the conservatism associated with a lower-middle-class culture, they are thus denying the history in which such uniformity and conservatism were the means to a more democratic participation in the culture of the nation. It was, of course, not a means that the cultured middle classes much approved of, then as now. These critics are also ignoring the difficulties of the present in which a combination of time, finances, responsibilities for reproducing self and others, the cultural constraints of the workplace, and so on, drive those of us who are responsible for shopping (most especially women?), and whatever our class, to rely heavily on the 'convenience' of the supermarket and chain store rather than on the 'more interesting', but in consumer terms less convenient and more 'risky', independent retailer and market.

Notes

1. Lowe and Wrigley also note the focus on mall and department store and a 'reluctance to carry out research on the (relatively) "everyday" sites of the High Street or supermarket' (1996, p.19). In the British context contemporary chain stores, and particularly the food supermarkets, are discussed in Gardner and Sheppard (1989). Rachel Bowlby (1997) engages with the supermarket as cultural form. Otherwise there are company histories and/or biographies of 'founding fathers' of Marks & Spencer, Sainsbury's, Tesco, Burtons, Boots, and so on (Bookbinder, 1993; Briggs, 1984; Chapman, 1974; Corina, 1971; Sigsworth, 1990; Williams, 1994; Flanders *et al.*, 1968). Jefferys (1954) is a useful and full account of retailing up to 1950 looking particularly at the development of co-operative, multiple shop and department store methods of trading. Mort and Thompson (1994) represent a current ongoing research project to seriously engage with the economic and cultural significance of a particular chain store in Britain (Burtons). In the US context the chain stores are discussed in the literature concerned with changes in American culture between the years 1880 and World War II (Boorstin, 1973; Bronner, 1989; Cohen, 1989; Ewen, 1976; Fox and Lears, 1983; Horowitz, 1985; Leach, 1994; Lebhar, 1959; Strasser, 1989).
2. A more developed history of the chain store would necessitate attention to the processes of modernization producing the form: 'industrialisation, the growth

of science and technology, the modern nation state, the capitalist world market, urbanisation and other infrastructural elements' (Featherstone, 1990, p. 6). But see also Lee (1993) and Slater (1997).

3. Friedberg's use of this term follows Wolfgang Schivelbusch's (1980) coining of the term 'panoramic perception' to describe the way a speeded-up railway system transformed perception of the world beyond the carriage windows: 'speed causes the *foreground* to disappear, it detaches the subject from the space that immediately surrounds him . . . it intrudes itself as an "almost unreal barrier" between object and subject. The landscape that is seen in this way is no longer experienced intensively, auratically . . . but evanescently, impressionistically – panoramically, in fact' (1993, p. 183). In the case of the department store (concerned to speed up the distribution of goods), 'the price tag interposes itself between goods and customers as the railroad's speed interjects itself between traveler and landscape' (*ibid.*, p. 184).

4. Schivelbusch interestingly comments: 'Walter Benjamin has found the one final straggler in the lineage of the old-time grand tourist: The *flâneur's* leisurely experience of the city has not yet been absorbed by circulation . . . the arcades already are refuges from the vehicular traffic on the regular streets' (1980, p. 189).

5. I wouldn't want to suggest that my motif of shopping as (self-)discipline is the dominant one. In reality our shopping practices are complex and certainly not uniform from one occasion to the next. It is possible to conceive of a switching between the motifs of empowerment, *flânerie* and (self-)discipline. It is possible too that other motifs are needed to fully describe and explain (Gabriel and Lang, 1995).

6. 'Nice and neat' was also an externally imposed discipline. Rebecca Preston (1995) points to an East London tenancy agreement advising that 'Neglect of the garden spoils the appearance of any house. It is of special importance that the front garden should be *neat and tidy* throughout the year' (Preston, 1995, p. 86, my emphasis).

7. The lower middle classes were also more likely to use the more reliable cap for contraception, indicating their more 'joint role-relationship and joint decision-making process' (Gittins, 1982, p. 169). Bourdieu also acknowledges the small family size of the *petit bourgeois*, stressing the difficulty of rejecting the extended family support system without yet having alternative protection – the social capital 'needed to make the most of economic and cultural capital' (1984, p. 337).

8. Women's magazines were a prime vehicle for such advice (Braithwaite *et al.*, 1986; White, 1970).

9. Mark Pegg (1983) indicates that the distribution of wirelesses went hand in hand with industrial and suburban developments in the Midlands and the South-east and thus that until the availability of a cheaper 'utility' set in the 1940s audiences were more (lower) middle than working class.

10. Women's magazines, however, still carried corset ads, sometimes diminutized as 'corselettes'. The battle *to be slim* and the 'failure' of relying on the (self-

discipline of) dieting is also revealed in the puff for 'Slymlastik Health Corset', 'Dermina cream', 'Bile Beans' and 'Antifat Tablets' (*Woman's Own*, 8 October 1938).

11. A tag line from a fondly remembered ad from the late 1930s.

12. L. Frank Baum is perhaps better known as author of *The Wizard of Oz* (1900). But he also wrote *The Art of Decorating Goods Windows* (1900) and became editor of *The Show Window*, the trade paper for window-dressers in the USA.

13. Then as now, shoppers at the chain stores would have come from a wider class grouping and different chains targeted different classes. The stores were also more diverse than I have perhaps implied, in the commodities they sold – books and newspapers, toiletries and medicines, clothes, foodstuffs, household goods and knick-knacks – as well as, to some extent, in design (Jefferys, 1954; Chapman, 1974; Sigsworth, 1990; Williams, 1994).

References

Abelson, E. (1989) *When Ladies Go A-Thieving: Middle-class Shoplifters in the Victorian Department Store*. New York and Oxford: Oxford University Press.

Abrams, M. (1946) *The Condition of the British People 1911–1945*. London: Victor Gollancz.

Adorno, T. and Horkheimer, M. (1977) 'The culture industry: enlightenment as mass deception', in J. Curran *et al.* (eds), *Mass Communication and Society*. London: Edward Arnold.

Alexander, S. (1994) *Becoming a Woman and Other Essays in 19th and 20th Century Feminist History*. London: Virago.

Baumann, Z. (1983) 'Industrialism, consumerism and power', *Theory, Culture and Society*, 1(3), 32–43.

Beddoe, D. (1989) *Back to Home and Duty: Women Between the Wars 1918–1939*. London: Pandora.

Benjamin, W. (1973) *Illuminations*. London: Collins.

Benjamin, W. (1983) *Charles Baudelaire: A Lyric Poet in the Era of High Capitalism*. London: Verso.

Berghaus, G. (1988) '*Girlkultur* – feminism, Americanism, and popular entertainment in Weimar Germany', *Journal of Design History*, 1(3–4), 193–219.

Bird, J., Curtis, B., Putnam, T., Robertson, G. and Tickner, L. (eds) (1993) *Mapping the Futures: Local Cultures, Global Change*. London: Routledge.

Blake, A. E. (1936) *Planned Retail Advertising*. London: Blandford Press.

Bookbinder, P. (1993) *Simon Marks: Retail Revolutionary*. London: Weidenfeld and Nicolson.

Boorstin, D. (1973) *The Americans: The Democratic Experience*. New York: Random House.

Bourdieu, P. (1984) *Distinction: A Social Critique of the Judgement of Taste*. London: Routledge.

Bowlby, R. (1985) *Just Looking: Consumer Culture in Dreiser, Gissing and Zola*. London: Methuen.

Bowlby, R. (1997) 'Supermarket futures', in P. Falk and C. Campbell (eds), *The Shopping Experience*. London: Sage.

Braithwaite, B., Walsh, N. and Davies, G. (1986) *Ragtime to Wartime: The Best of Good Housekeeping 1922–1939*. London: Ebury Press.

Braverman, H. (1974) *Labor and Monopoly Capital: The Degradation of Work in the Twentieth Century*. New York: Monthly Review Press.

Briggs, A. (1984) *Marks and Spencer 1884–1984*. London: Octopus.

Bronner, S. J. (ed.) (1989) *Consuming Visions: Accumulation and Display of Goods in America 1880–1920*. New York: W.W. Norton.

Buck-Morss, S. (1990) *The Dialectics of Seeing: Walter Benjamin and the Arcades Project*. Cambridge, MA: MIT Press.

Carey, J. (1992) *The Intellectuals and the Masses: Pride and Prejudice among the Literary Intelligentsia, 1880–1939*. London: Faber and Faber.

Chaney, D. (1990) 'Subtopia in Gateshead: the Metrocentre as a cultural form', *Theory, Culture and Society*, 27(4), November, 49–68.

Chapman, S. (1974) *Jesse Boot of Boots the Chemists*. London: Hodder and Stoughton.

Clarke, J. (1991) *New Times and Old Enemies: Essays on Cultural Studies and America*. London: HarperCollins.

Cohen, L. (1989) *Making a New Deal: Industrial Workers in Chicago 1919–1939*. Cambridge: Cambridge University Press.

Cohen, L. (1993) 'The class experience of mass consumption: workers as consumers in inter war America', in R. W. Fox and T. J. Lears (eds), *The Power of Culture: Critical Essays in American History*. Chicago: University of Chicago Press.

Corina, M. (1971) *Pile It High, Sell It Cheap*. London: Weidenfeld and Nicolson.

Corner, J. and Harvey, S. (eds) (1991) *Enterprise and Heritage: Crosscurrents of National Culture*. London: Routledge.

Culver, S. (1988) 'What manikins want: the wonderful Wizard of Oz and the art of decorating dry goods windows', *Representations*, 21, Winter, 97–116.

Ehrenreich, B. (1994) *Kipper's Game*. London: Virago.

Ewen, S. (1976) *Captains of Consciousness: Advertising and the Social Roots of the Consumer Culture*. New York: McGraw-Hill.

Ewing, E. (1978) *Dress and Undress: A History of Women's Underwear*. London: B.T. Batsford.

Featherstone, M. (1990) *Consumer Culture and Postmodernism*. London: Sage.

Fiske, J. (1989) *Reading the Popular*. London: Unwin Hyman.

Flanders, A., Pomeranz, R. and Woodward, J. (1968) *Experiment in Industrial Democracy: A Study of the John Lewis Partnership*. London: Faber and Faber.

Fox, R. W. and Lears, T. J. (eds) (1983) *The Culture of Consumption: Critical Essays in American History 1880–1980*. New York: Pantheon.

Foucault, M. (1977) *Discipline and Punish: The Birth of the Prison*. London: Allen Lane.

Foucault, M. (1988) 'Technologies of the self', in L. Martin, H. Gutman and P. Hutton (eds), *Technologies of the Self: A Seminar with Michel Foucault*. Amherst, MA: University of Massachusetts Press.

Fraser, W. H. (1981) *The Coming of the Mass Market, 1850–1914*. Basingstoke: Macmillan.

Friedberg, A. (1993) *Window Shopping: Cinema and the Postmodern*. Berkeley and Los Angeles: University of California Press.

Frisby, D. (1985) *Fragments of Modernity: Theories of Modernity in the Work of Simmel, Kracauer and Benjamin*. Cambridge: Polity.

Frith, S. (1983) 'The pleasures of the hearth', in *Formations of Pleasure*. London: Routledge and Kegan Paul.

Gabriel, Y. and Lang, T. (1995) *The Unmanageable Consumer: Contemporary Consumption and Its Fragmentations*. London: Sage.

Gaines, J. (1989) 'The Queen Christina tie-ups: convergence of show window and screen', *Quarterly Review of Film and Video*, 11(1), 35–60.

Gardner, C. and Sheppard, J. (1989) *Consuming Passion: The Rise of Retail Culture*. London: Unwin and Hyman.

Giles, J. (1995) *Women, Identity and Private Life in Britain, 1900–1950*. Basingstoke: Macmillan.

Gittins, D. (1982) *Fair Sex: Family Size and Structure in England, 1900–39*. London: Hutchinson.

Glucksmann, M. (1990) *Women Assemble: Women Workers and the New Industries in Inter-war Britain*. London: Routledge.

Glynn, S. and Oxborrow, O. (1976) *Interwar Britain: A Social and Economic History*. London: George Allen & Unwin.

Gramsci, A. (1971) *Selections from the Prison Notebooks of Antonio Gramsci* (ed. and transl. Q. Hoare and G. Nowell-Smith). London: Lawrence and Wishart.

Gregson, N. (1995) 'And now it's all consumption?', *Progress in Human Geography*, 19(1), 135–41.

Guy, C. (1994) *The Retail Development Process: Location, Property and Planning*. London: Routledge.

Hall, S. and Jefferson, T. (eds) (1976) *Resistance through Rituals: Youth Subcultures in Post-war Britain*. London: Hutchinson.

Hall, S. and Jacques, M. (eds) (1989) *New Times*. London: Lawrence and Wishart.

Hannah, L., (1983) *The Rise of the Corporate Economy*, 2nd edn. London and New York: Methuen.

Hardyment, C. (1983) *Dream Babies: Childcare from Locke to Spock*. London: Cape.

Harvey, D. (1989) *The Condition of Postmodernity*. Oxford: Blackwell.

Hebdige, D. (1979) *Subculture: The Meaning of Style*. London: Methuen.

Hebdige, D. (1988) *Hiding in the Light: On Images and Things*. London: Routledge.

Horowitz, D. (1985) *The Morality of Spending: Attitudes toward the Consumer Society in America, 1875–1940*. Baltimore: Johns Hopkins University Press.

Jackson, A. A. (1973) *Semi-detached London: Suburban Development, Life and Transport, 1900–39*. London: George Allen & Unwin.

Jackson, A. A. (1991) *The Middle Classes 1900–1950*. Nairn: David St. John Thomas Publisher.

Jackson, P. (1993) 'Towards a cultural politics of consumption', in J. Bird, B. Curtis, T. Putnam, G. Robertson and L. Tickner (eds), *Mapping the Futures: Local Cultures, Global Change*. London: Routledge.

Jameson, F. (1984) 'Postmodernism, or the cultural logic of late capitalism', *New Left Review*, 146, 53–92.

Jefferys, J. B. (1954) *Retailing in Britain 1850–1950*. Cambridge: Cambridge University Press.

Kracauer, S. (1975) 'The mass ornament', *New German Critique*, Spring 1975, 67–76 (first published 1927).

Keat, R., Whiteley, N. and Abercrombie, N. (eds) (1994) *The Authority of the Consumer*. London: Routledge.

Langman, L. (1992) 'Neon cages: shopping for subjectivity', in R. Shields (ed.), *Lifestyle Shopping: The Subject of Consumption*. London: Routledge.

Leach, W. R. (1984) 'Transformations in a culture of consumption: women and department stores', *Journal of American History*, 71(2), Spring, 319–42.

Leach, W. R. (1994) *Landscape of Desire: Merchants, Power and the Rise of a New American Culture*. New York: Vintage Books.

Lears, J. (1994) *Fables of Abundance: A Cultural History of Advertising in America*. New York: Basic Books.

Lebhar, G. (1959) *Chain Stores in America 1859–1959*. New York: Chain Store Publishing.

Lee, M. (1993) *Consumer Culture Reborn: The Cultural Politics of Consumption*. London: Routledge.

Light, A. (1991) *Forever England: Femininity, Literature and Conservatism between the Wars*. London: Routledge.

Lowe, M. and Wrigley, N. (1996) 'Towards the new retail geography', in N. Wrigley and M. Lowe (eds), *Retailing, Consumption and Capital: Towards the New Retail Geography*. Harlow: Longman.

Lunt, P. K. and Livingstone, S. M. (1992) *Mass Consumption and Personal Identity: Everyday Economic Experience*. Buckingham: Open University Press.

McRobbie, A. (1991) 'New times in cultural studies', *New Formations*, 13, Spring, 1–17.

Marriott, O. (1981) 'Troubles at the Bull Ring and the Elephant and Castle', in A. Cochrane, C. Hamnett and L. McDowell (eds), *City, Economy and Society: A Comparative Reader*. London: Harper and Row.

Miller, D. (1995) (ed.) *Acknowledging Consumption: A Review of New Studies*. London: Routledge.

Moores, S. (1988) '"The box on the dresser": memories of early radio and everyday life', *Media, Culture and Society*, 10, 23–40.

Morris, M. (1988) 'Things to do with shopping centres', in *Grafts: Feminist Cultural Criticism*. London: Verso.

Morse, M. (1990) 'An ontology of everyday distraction: the freeway, the mall, and television', in P. Mellencamp (ed.), *Logics of Television: Essays in Cultural Criticism*. Bloomington, Indianapolis and London: Indiana University Press and BFI Publishing.

Mort, F. (1988) 'Boy's own? Masculinity, style and popular culture', in R. Chapman and J. Rutherford (eds), *Male Order: Unwrapping Masculinity*. London: Lawrence and Wishart.

Mort, F. and Thompson, P. (1994) 'Retailing, commercial cultural and masculinity in 1950s Britain: the case of Montague Burton, the "Tailor of taste"'.

Murray, R. (1988) 'Life after Henry (Ford)', *Marxism Today*, October.

Nava, M. (1992) *Changing Cultures: Feminism, Youth and Consumerism*. London: Sage.

Nava, M. (1995) 'Modernity's disavowal: woman, the city and the department store', in M. Nava and A. O'Shea (eds), *Perspectives on a Century of English Modernity*. London: Routledge.

Nixon, S. (1992) 'Have you got the look? Masculinities and shopping spectacle', in R. Shields (ed.), *Lifestyle Shopping: The Subject of Consumption*. London: Routledge.

Oliver, P., Davis, I. and Bentley, I. (1981) *Dunroamin: The Suburban Semi and Its Enemies*. London: Barrie & Jenkins.

Osborne, J. (1981) *A Better Class of Person*. London: Faber and Faber.

Pegg, M. (1983) *Broadcasting and Society 1918–1939*. London: Croom Helm.

Pollard, S. (1983) *The Development of the British Economy 1914–1980*, 3rd edn. London: Edward Arnold.

Preston, R. (1995) 'Little English landscapes: developing suburban gardens between the wars', *Things*, 2, Summer, 69–87.

Priestley, J. B. (1934) *An English Journey*. London: William Heinemann/Victor Gollancz.

Reekie, G. (1993) *Temptations: Sex, Selling and the Department Store*. Sydney: Allen and Unwin.

Rees, G. (1969) *St. Michael: A History of Marks and Spencer*. London: Weidenfeld and Nicolson.

Ritzer, G. (1993) *The McDonaldization of Society: An Investigation into the Changing Character of Contemporary Social Life*. Thousand Oaks, CA: Pine Forge Press.

Rutherford, J. (1988) 'Who's that man?', in R. Chapman and J. Rutherford (eds), *Male Order: Unwrapping Masculinity*. London: Lawrence and Wishart.

Scannel, P. (1988) 'Radio times: the temporal arrangements of broadcasting in the modern world', in P. Drummond and R. Paterson (eds), *Television and Its Audiences: International Research Perspectives*. London: BFI.

Schivelbusch, W. (1980) *The Railway Journey: Trains and Travel in the 19th Century* (translated by A. Hollo). Oxford: Basil Blackwell.

Schudson, M. (1993) *Advertising, the Uneasy Persuasion*. London: Routledge.

Shields, R. (1989) 'Social spatialisation and the built environment: West Edmonton Mall', *Environment and Planning D: Society and Space*, 7, 147–64.

Shields, R. (ed.) (1992) *Lifestyle Shopping: The Subject of Consumption*. London: Routledge.

Shilling, C. (1993) *The Body and Social Theory*. London: Sage.

Sigsworth, E. M. (1990) *Montague Burton: The Tailor of Taste*. Manchester: Manchester University Press.

Simmel, G. (1950) 'The metropolis and mental life', in K. Wolff (ed.), *The Sociology of Georg Simmel*. London: Collier-Macmillan.

Slater, D. (1993) 'Going shopping: markets, crowds and consumption', in C. Jenks (ed.), *Cultural Reproduction*. London: Routledge.

Slater, D. (1997) *Consumer Culture and Modernity*. Cambridge: Polity.

Strasser, S. (1989) *Satisfaction Guaranteed: The Making of the American Mass Market*. New York: Pantheon.

Tester, K. (ed.) (1994) *The Flâneur*. London: Routledge.

White, C. (1970) *Women's Magazines 1693–1968*. London: Michael Joseph.

Williams, B. (1994) *The Best Butter in the World: A History of Sainsbury's*. London: Ebury Press.

Williams, R. (1982) *Dream Worlds: Mass Consumption in Late Nineteenth Century France*. Berkeley: University of California Press.

Williams, R. (1990) *Television, Technology and Cultural Form*. London: Routledge.

Wilson, E. (1992) 'The invisible flâneur', *New Left Review*, 191, 90–110.

Witte, K. (1975) 'Introduction to Siegfried Kracauer's "The Mass Ornament"', *New German Critique*, Spring, 59–66.

Wolff, J. (1985) 'The invisible *flâneuse*: women and the literature of modernity, *Theory, Culture and Society*, 2(3), 37–46.

Wollen, P. (1993) *Raiding the Icebox: Reflections on Twentieth-Century Culture*. London: Verso.

Zuboff, S. (1988) *In the Age of the Smart Machine: The Future of Work and Power*. Oxford: Heinemann.

Zukin, S. (1991) *Landscapes of Power: From Detroit to Disney World*. Berkeley: University of California.

4. *Modernity tamed? Women shoppers and the rationalization of consumption in the inter-war period*[1]

Mica Nava

Virginia Woolf and Oxford Street

I was flicking through a coffee-table collection of *The Best of* Good House-keeping *1922–1939* (Braithwaite *et al.*, 1989) in pursuit of personal accounts of consumption in the inter-war years when I came across an article called 'Oxford Street Tide' by Virginia Woolf, first published in January 1932. Could this be *the* Virginia Woolf, I wonder, surprised to find work by her in this context. And, yes, it is. The introductory editorial caption to what *Good Housekeeping* calls a 'word picture' reads: 'in the beautiful precision of its language and thought this reveals the name of its distinguished author – Virginia Woolf'. 'Precision', however, is not what strikes me first about this piece. I read it through, trying to establish what Virginia Woolf's view of Oxford Street and shopping is, but she is elusive, alternately disdainful and sympathetic. Is this one of the 'odd jobs cadged from newspapers in order to make a living' that she refers to in *A Room of One's Own* (Woolf, 1963, p. 39)? Some of the prose seems careless and unedited. The early part of the essay is dominated by an extended and florid metaphor of nature: Oxford Street is 'the pebbly bed of a river whose stones are forever washed by a bright stream . . . [where] slips of coloured paper expand into bristling forests of splendidly tinted flora' (Woolf, 1989, p. 138). Meandering through this allegorical landscape is a drawn-out comparison between the traditional aristocracy 'whose stately mansions lined the Strand in ancient days' and the 'modern aristocrats' – 'the great Lords of Oxford Street' – whose impermanent 'sugar icing palaces' now line the banks of this 'river of turning wheels'. And so it goes.

But there does seem to be an argument here too. Early on in the piece Woolf identifies a set of opinions about Oxford Street, even though she remains reticent about her own:

> Oxford Street . . . is not London's most distinguished thoroughfare. Moralists have been known to point the finger of scorn at those who buy there . . . In Oxford Street there are too many bargains . . . The buying and selling is too blatant and raucous. But . . . the garishness and gaudiness . . . has its fascination . . . Everything glitters and twinkles. (Woolf, 1989, p. 138)

I read backwards and forwards, anxious to pin her down, but can't judge how much irony inflects her comments first about the 'twinkling' street and later the 'new lords of commerce', whose magnanimity she contrasts with that of dukes and earls:

> the largesse [of the new lords] takes . . . the form of excitement, of display, of entertainment, of windows lit up by night . . . They give us the latest news for nothing. Music streams from their banqueting rooms free. You need not spend . . . to enjoy . . . the high and airy halls . . . the soft pile of carpets, and the luxury of gifts, and the glow of fabrics, and carpets and silver. (*ibid.*, p. 139)

Is this a textual strategy – a deliberate technique to represent 'multiple shifting perceptions' (Moi, 1985, p. 3)? Or is Woolf simply uncertain about what she thinks? How significant is it that her voice wavers, that she appears both to disparage and quite like what she represents to us as vulgar and superficial? But then, as she proceeds, her argument firms up and her depiction of Oxford Street ephemera becomes less equivocal, more generous. It is as though she has made up her mind in the course of writing:[2]

> The moralists point the finger in scorn . . . [at] the levity and ostentation . . . of our age. Yet . . . the charm of modern London is that it is not built to last . . . Its glassiness, its transparency, its surging waves of coloured plaster give a different pleasure and achieve a different end from that which was attempted by . . . the nobility of England. Their pride required the illusion of permanence. Ours, on the contrary, seems to delight in proving that we can make stone and brick as transitory as our own desires . . . We knock down and rebuild as we expect to be knocked down and rebuilt. It is an impulse that makes for creation and fertility. Discovery is stimulated and invention on the alert. (Woolf, 1989, p. 139)

Here Woolf shows an unambiguous and, for 1932, a quite unusual, appreciation of the ingenuity and temporality of mass culture and modernity, and I will come back to what it might mean for a distinguished modernist and feminist author of her moment to take up such a position. First, though, a comment on this 'we' she refers to so intriguingly: how should this collectivity be understood? Is it simply a stylistic convention, or should it be read as a deliberate challenge to the reproving moralists and traditionalists of the moment? The latter, I think. In my reading, Woolf's 'we' encompasses those who occupy and live off and through the shopping streets of the metropolis: the shop owners, the builders, the shop assistants, the customers, the onlookers like herself. Implicitly it acknowledges a new alliance of *modernizers*, albeit contradictory, and in this sense is emblematic of the modern democratizing (and largely feminine) consumer culture which, as I will show, becomes increasingly entrenched and at the same time normalized during the inter-war years. In Woolf's final paragraph, the representatives of the new alliance are treated sympathetically by her as they respond to the insistent accusations of the moralists and elitists who cling to the imperatives of an earlier regime:

> True, says the great merchant, I am not thinking of educating the mass to a higher standard of aesthetic sensibility. It taxes all my wits to think how I can display my goods with the minimum of waste and the maximum of effectiveness . . . I grant, says the middle-class woman, that I linger and look, and barter and cheapen . . . But my husband is a small clerk in a bank; I have only fifteen pounds a year to dress on; so here I come; to . . . look, if I can, as well dressed as my neighbours. (Woolf, 1989, p. 132)

So finally Woolf's reflections in this unlikely piece of mass-circulation journalism lead her to invent and defend (albeit not unreservedly) what Marshall Berman has more recently called a 'modernism of the streets' (Berman, 1983). Woolf, the high modernist, also salutes popular pleasures: in this instance, the ostentatious, the magical, the cheap, the fleeting. Like Berman, she gives credit to the everyday processes and visions of modernity which allow ordinary men and women to become subjects as well as objects of their worlds (Berman, 1983, p. 16), to imagine a better future and transform the materiality of their lives – or at least of surface appearances – to improve the *look* of things. There is no doubt that Woolf was ahead of her time in her appreciation of these elements, as prescient, brave and experimental in this little-known, rather clumsy piece as she was in her celebrated fiction and political essays. Indeed, the very act of writing for *Good Housekeeping*, a popular magazine for women, ensured that the divisions between high, middle-brow and mass culture would be challenged and the concerns and pleasures of women foregrounded. Here as elsewhere she wrote against the current: 'I do my best work and feel most braced with my back to the wall. It's an odd feeling though, writing against the current: difficult entirely to disregard the current' (Woolf, 1953, cited in Barrett, 1979, p. 4).

At the centre of the intellectual current against which she was braced were contemporary figures such as F. R. and Q. D. Leavis, among the most scathing and elitist critics of mass culture and popular writing and quite possibly models for 'the moralists' in Woolf's 'Oxford Street Tide'.[3] The Leavises adopted a highly critical and patronizing response to mass entertainment and the 'feminization' of popular culture, and linked these to the expansion of commerce and advertising. Such attitudes were widespread among critics of both the left and right during the 1930s and 1940s, and occurred (with variations) in Germany and the USA as well.[4] Indeed, it was rare to find an intellectual anywhere who was prepared to consider seriously whether there might be positive implications of mass culture; even cinema was disregarded, let alone consumption and the expansion of metropolitan shopping streets.[5] In this sense, then, Virginia Woolf's odd and marginal essay represents a breakthrough. It anticipates the tone of much more recent cultural studies work on popular culture and consumption (indeed, even postmodernism in its appreciation of surface and parody), and appears to belong to a much more modern feminism in so far as it marks out and validates the terrain of everyday feminine experience and pleasures (since, of course, the shoppers on Oxford Street were overwhelmingly women). In its recognition of an alliance of modernizers it contentiously refuses the simple theoretical polarities of class or of 'educated' and 'uneducated'. Implicitly it affirms the notion of a significant popular modernism worthy of the attention of cultural critics.

But this attention is complicated. My aim in this chapter is to explore the widespread normalization of shopping and the consolidation of consumer culture in England in the inter-war period, and particularly in the 1930s. Virginia Woolf's reflections in *Good Housekeeping* are worth looking at in this context, not merely because her concession to the financial, social, aesthetic and libidinous economy of Oxford Street is interesting in itself, but also because it is ultimately part of a much more extensive, albeit contradictory, inter-war discursive network, which includes market research, Marks & Spencer and Hollywood cinema, in which modern consumption is increasingly known, represented, rationalized and managed.

Modernity and department store shopping before World War I

In order to understand how this happens and what the components of this discursive network are, it is necessary to go back to developments at the turn of the century, the period widely accepted as the high point of 'modernity'[6] – a relatively disordered moment in which department store shopping was at its peak in all the major cities of the western world. I have addressed the significance of this for women and for theorizations of modernity and consumption in an earlier piece (Nava, 1996). There I locate women in terms of the conceptual and imaginative features of modernity, and at the same time construct a genealogy of absence – I explore why consumption has been so neglected in the critical literature. This is intended as a sequel and therefore requires a review of the pertinent features of department store consumption for women of the middle classes prior to World War I.

Shopping was, of course, both part of the wider economic process – the development of capitalism – and a leisure activity for upper-middle-class women well before the emergence of the department store in the last decades of the nineteenth century. Nevertheless, the department store marked a significant development. It coincided with improvements in urban public transport, an expansion in the production of ready-made clothes and household goods, new methods of retailing, growing demand from a wider constituency of consumers and a social restlessness among many middle-class women for whom respectable meeting places in the city were limited. In this context the new stores offered much more than the sale of merchandise. They constituted an expansion of acceptable public space for women and provided a luxurious, modern and social venue in which to meet friends and be entertained, to learn about new fashions and commodities, and to develop consumer expertise. Often massive theatrical emporia, they offered a huge range of departments, products, entertainments and facilities (including restaurants, libraries, children's areas and delivery services) and were considered among the great sights of the metropolis which visitors from the provinces and abroad would expect to see. Customers were encouraged to spend the day in the stores without obligation to buy, and in the years before restrictions were placed on hours of opening and the stores stayed open till late at night, and before the advent of radio and cinema, going shopping was certainly an excursion as well as work.[7]

Selfridges of Oxford Street was launched in 1909 by the American entrepreneur Gordon Selfridge and in the first week alone the store had an astonishing one and a quarter million visitors. The opening was a world event, reported on at length by the press throughout the colonies, in South Africa, Egypt, Jamaica and India.[8] The newspaper cuttings do not comment on who the many ordinary visitors were, but everything we know about store customers suggests that they were overwhelmingly women. Indeed almost all of the forty-five different full-page advertisements printed in the national newspapers in the week before the opening specifically address and aim to recruit women.[9] So the stores were widely known for their appeal to women. They were also increasingly associated in the public imagination with hedonism and the jettisoning of conservative values. The most reported event about Selfridges in the period following the launch was a private costume ball occupying three huge ballrooms and the entire roof garden of the store, where '4,000 lamps glittered in luxurious foliage'.[10] The celebrated guests danced the tango to a rag-time orchestra until 5 in the morning when breakfast was served. The fascination with which the press reported the occasion is evidence that the association of the stores with glamour and modernity was established well before Hollywood stars were called on to promote consumption. The stores were also modern and must have been rather threatening in another sense as well, in that several of their owners (Gordon Selfridge in particular) were known to approve of women's emancipation (Leach, 1984; Nava, 1996); some stores loaned their premises for suffrage meetings while many supplied goods in purple, white and green, the symbolic colours of the struggle (Tickner, 1987; Lancaster, 1995). It must be remembered that the women's movement was at its most militant and conspicuous during the years preceding the war, so this unruly point of feminism coincided with the years in which the stores were at their most spectacular, innovative and commercially successful.

The imagined pleasures and dangers increasingly associated with shopping in metropolitan centres during this period were compounded by the public sense of women's growing, and sometimes uncontrolled and irrational, exercise of economic power. Women shoppers were often constructed (particularly in press cartoons at Christmas time; see Hosgood, 1994) as at once gullible, capricious, demanding and absurdly powerful. There were a few well-publicized cases of shoplifting by women from wealthy and respectable families (Abelson, 1989). The fact that department store customers were often treated with extreme deference by male as well as female staff in an ambience of extravagant comfort and visual opulence added to the unease. In general, therefore, the shopping experience provoked considerable anxieties, particularly among husbands and fathers constrained by more rationalized workplaces. So, although the new stores intentionally constituted an expansion of acceptable public space for women, and although essential to economic growth, they were not unambiguously welcomed.

The inter-war period: what did women want?

Store owners and managers were themselves confused about how to understand and treat their customers. What did they want? How could their tastes be catered to? How could they be satisfied? Women shoppers were not sufficiently predictable in marketing terms. This problem was exacerbated after World War I in a context in which women's lives were to change quite markedly. The 1920s saw a 'demographic crisis' of unprecedented proportions in which women of marriageable and working age heavily outnumbered men. Northcliffe (owner of the *Daily Mail*) was to describe this on a visit to America in 1921 as 'Britain's problem of two million superfluous women' and during the years following the war the popular press was full of hostile accounts of the new freedoms acquired and displayed by modern young women (Melman, 1988, p. 19). A number of authors (among them some of the moralists identified by Woolf) are critical of what they perceived as the 'feminization' of England in the inter-war period, when women generally gained greater public visibility and wielded relatively more economic strength both on behalf of their families (real incomes for the employed working class and salaried middle class rose overall in the 1920s and 1930s[11]) and on their own behalf as they were drawn increasingly into new sectors of the labour market and influenced by Hollywood movies and the new women's magazines in their spending patterns and aspirations (Alexander, 1995; Buckley, 1995). One of these magazines was *Good Housekeeping* (aimed at a largely middle-class readership), which during the 1920s frequently published challenging articles about marriage and work.[12] So how did these changes, which occurred across the social spectrum, relate to developments in consumption?

The information about English retailing practices during this period is still fairly sparse. We do know, however, that from the mid-1920s onwards many department stores (in both the United States and Britain) started slowly to decline from their earlier high points in terms of profitability and levels of service, despite an overall increase in consumption which was sustained – if unevenly – right through the Depression (Filene, 1938; Davis, 1966; Porter Benson, 1986; Stevenson, 1984). They were unable to withstand the competition from the emerging chain stores. A number of factors contributed to this situation. First of all the comprehensiveness of merchandise and the convenience and comfort of the department store no longer had the same allure, even for middle-class women, who now had greater personal independence and other sources of entertainment. Chain stores were able to respond to the expansion of consumer demand for cheaper products and could offer goods at lower prices because they could take advantage of mass production, had lower operating costs, and provided fewer services – there were no doormen, roof-garden restaurants, orchestras and home deliveries – so they were inevitably going to be more popular with shoppers whose resources were limited (Rees, 1969). They also offered a narrower range of goods so were less likely to suffer the costs of overproduction and supply. But one of the most significant factors in the transformation of both chain and department store shopping was the knowledgeableness of customers. As Edward Filene, the Boston department store owner, put it, 'consumers are more value conscious and informed than ever before' (Filene, 1938, p. xiii). Women shoppers were increasingly discriminating and business-like, and as a consequence they possessed what Christine Frederick, a keen contemporary advocate of 'efficiency in purchasing', called an 'ominous and ruthless power' (Marchand, 1986, p. 84).[13] They were more likely to shop around for quality and good value, particularly in times of economic instability, as we saw the woman doing in Virginia Woolf's account. They could withdraw their custom and take it elsewhere if they wished.

Another factor which preoccupied shop owners and manufacturers during this period was fashion. The growing emphasis on the importance of new styles, matching colours, regular new clothes for all occasions and seasons at a range of quality and price levels, which was promoted partly by magazines, advertising and cinema and made possible by new fabrics like rayon, was commercially advantageous in so far as it contributed to enhanced production and demand (Lynd, 1933). It was also increasingly widespread:

> The American habit of buying cheap mass-produced goods for short use was a novel one to the British: it was gradually extended from clothes to shoes, handbags and household goods. If the old-fashioned shop assistants still mumbled 'I can guarantee this – it will last a lifetime', the modern come-back was 'Then, for goodness' sake show me something else!' (Graves and Hodge, 1991, p. 178)

Yet although it was profitable, fashion also 'injected a new note of uncertainty and unpredictability into an already volatile retail environment' (Porter Benson, 1986, p. 109). Things went out of fashion as quickly and apparently capriciously as they came in, often despite magazines and advertising. It was difficult to keep track of what sold well and what did not, to supply where there was a demand and avoid overproduction. Retailers often had remarkably little information about customer preferences, what influenced shopping behaviour, and indeed even their own stock levels. Wholesale buying strategies were intuitive and usually based on traditional practices, much to the scorn of Filene, who recommended more of what he called 'scientific fact-finding' (Filene, 1938) in order to understand what shoppers wanted (though his strategy was no guarantor of success either and will be returned to later).

Fluctuations in demand and astute yet fashion-conscious consumers were a concern for chain stores like Marks & Spencer as well. By the 1930s there was a Marks & Spencer selling cheap goods in the High Street of every major town and suburb in England, alongside other multiples like Woolworths, Burtons, W. H. Smith and Sainsbury's. The major innovation of Marks & Spencer was its attempt to gauge the rapid changes in popular taste and aspirations and respond quickly by bypassing wholesalers and ordering directly from manufacturers (Rees, 1969). Simon Marks first visited the United States in 1924 and wrote subsequently about how he encountered 'the value . . . of modern methods of administration and the statistical control of stocks in relation to sales', which enabled him to speed up the computation of necessary information from weeks to hours. The commercial success of Marks & Spencer relied on maintaining low prices, which in turn depended on estimating what the consumer wanted. According to the store historian, this was achieved by what he calls 'intimate day to day contact with the public' (Rees, 1969, p. 100). Marks & Spencer clearly made attempts to know the consumer and predict changes in taste but there is no evidence that their methods bore any relationship to the 'scientific fact-finding' recommended by Filene. Ultimately, despite gestures towards research, the retailing strategy of Marks & Spencer was based (as Rees acknowledges) on intuition and imagination rather than rationality (*ibid.*, p. 78).

On the 1924 trip to the States Marks also learned the importance of 'more imposing commodious premises' even for the sale of cheap goods (Marks's autobiography, cited in Rees, 1969, p. 61). The distinctive green and gold fascia of Marks & Spencer was introduced in 1924, and by the 1930s the stores were becoming increasingly elegant and spacious, with high ceilings, wide aisles, walnut panelling, oak floors and diffused lighting. They 'tried to do for the mass of people what the great department stores had done for the middle classes' (Rees, 1969, p. 85). In 1932, the year Virginia Woolf wrote her *Good Housekeeping* article, the Oxford Street branch of Marks & Spencer was honoured by a visit from the Queen; as a phenomenon it had arrived.

Mass consumption and suburban modernity

The history of Marks & Spencer is interesting because it tells us about the spread of good quality, cheap, ready-made fashion and modern shop design to women of the working class and to the suburbs and the regions.[14] Shopping in this kind of store was more modest than the department store, yet for many women it was popular and exciting nevertheless. Attractive clothes made them feel good, enhanced their self-esteem and enabled them to envisage a better future for themselves and their families: 'to *imagine* an end to domestic drudgery and chronic want' (Alexander, 1995, p. 205). Carolyn Steedman describes her mother's desire for glamour and commodities in these terms also, as a longing for things that a social system had withheld from her (1986, p. 6). The appeal of fashion and make-up for working-class young women – the much-discussed attempts of factory girls to look like film stars – was an important element in the increased visibility of consumption and in the growth of its representation during the inter-war period.

The massive expansion of house-building in the middle- and lower-middle-class suburbs and the development of new High Streets for the new multiple stores was another significant factor in the conspicuous new universe of consumption. Shopping for the self, the family and the home was an everyday activity for a larger proportion of women than ever before. It was part of the new suburban domesticity which went with new houses and cheap mortgages, and was part of the process of becoming middle class. This new 'suburban modernity', as Deborah Ryan has called it, was on display each year at the *Daily Mail* Ideal Home Exhibitions which promoted the most up-to-date goods and instructed visitors not only in the appropriate taste and lifestyle for people of their position, but also in skills of housekeeping and shopping. This purpose was succinctly expressed by Winston Churchill at the 1934 opening of the exhibition:

> This Ideal Home Exhibition . . . [gives] pleasure to countless people, and guidance and instruction to very large numbers . . . It not only guides public thought and taste . . . but . . . also stimulates . . . optimism and progress, and above all expenditure, which must be the most important elements in our social and economic regeneration. (Pleydell-Bouverie, 1944, p. 20)[15]

Thus the Exhibition both incited and contained consumption. The suburban middle-class modernity which it represented was a *tamed* modernity, one regulated by a conservative desire to lead a more comfortable, labour-saving and private family life.[16]

The Exhibition was often ridiculed by English social commentators and intellectuals, along with other aspects of modern mass culture like the movies, variety chain stores, cheap and plastic 'luxuries' and tinned food, for being mass-produced, popular, sentimental and Americanized. What exercised the critics so is not consistent or clear. There was a widespread aversion to the suburbs, which seemed to epitomize English dullness and narrow-mindedness as well as 'bad design'. Orwell in particular was afraid that cheap luxuries for the working class would inhibit the revolution (Orwell, 1937) and the Leavises feared that standards of taste were being 'levelled down' (Leavis, 1932). In this general debate on the popular and consumption, accusations of greed and vulgarity co-existed with others of indolence and lack of control, and with yet others of boring predictability. The contempt and snobbery commonly attributed to the critics of the new mass culture in order to explain the diverse group of responses should perhaps be re-read as anxiety, as fear of being swamped, engulfed by hordes of women, and even consumed along with the cheap luxuries and tinned salmon.

Rationality and irrationality

In any case, what clearly emerges from the responses is a centre-staging of consumption and an unease about its perceived irrationality, even, paradoxically, where it was most rationalized (Woolworths was often singled out as a target – the result of its symbolic positioning in the new order as American, modern, suburban and cheap). Rationality and irrationality were major preoccupations in the commercial and advertising discursive worlds as well as among more literary groups. Most of the work on these sources so far has been done in the United States. Roland Marchand's (1986) extensive review of advertising agency records and trade magazines in the inter-war years presents a fascinating picture of an industry quite unable to reconcile its own utterly distinct images of the women consumer. (It must be said that Marchand himself makes no comment about these different representations which he reports to us in different sections of his book.) Thus, on the one hand, (women) consumers are depicted in these sources – and often in the advertisements themselves – as impulsive, extravagant and easy to persuade, and on the other, as rational, discriminating and astute (see also Bowlby, 1990). The rational consumer is part of a wider discourse of rationality in which the rhetoric of scientific management of the domestic sphere and modern business administration are together evoked increasingly in relation to buying and selling. During this period in America a growing number of advertisements construct the modern woman as the business executive of the home, as 'general purchasing agent' or GPA, with planning and decision-making responsibilities (see, for example, the advertisement entitled 'Little Woman GPA' in which the executive housewife is standing at a modern desk surrounded by graphs, charts and telephones; Marchand, 1986, p. 169). Informed about new products and new technology, an authority on shopping, the housewife becomes the agent of domestic modernization. This is also the image presented to us in women's magazines like *Ladies Home Journal* in America (Stein, 1985) and the British *Good Housekeeping*, which are typically full of rational consumer advice throughout this period and present the woman consumer as a capable and knowledgeable person who derives pleasure from her expertise in shopping; these skills do not, however, preclude a more libidinous irrational pleasure in consumption derived from the physical adornment and nurturing of the self.

The American sociologist of everyday life, Robert Lynd, was one of the few social scientists of the period who showed an interest in these questions. In 1933 he produced a wide-ranging and detailed report entitled 'The People as Consumers' (for 'The President's Research Committee on Social Trends') which looked at issues such as the proliferation of consumer goods, changes in consumer spending and leisure patterns, the problem of overproduction, the development of branding, and so forth (Lynd, 1933). Rationality and irrationality in relation to consumption were among his concerns also and the way in which he makes sense of their co-existence in the realm of shopping is to understand them as outcomes of the insoluble tension between unruly psychic impulses and the social values to which we must all adhere: 'Within each of us this exciting drama is played out in our every waking and sleeping hour until the end of the picture' (Lynd, 1933, p. 867). The tension is not, however, confined to the contradiction between infantile wants and societal expectations. Contemporary American society is also experiencing a conflict of historical significance between 'traditional' and 'modern' values in relation to consumption. Among these Lynd cites:

– The lingering Puritan tradition of abstinence which makes play, idleness and free spending sin; and the increasing secularization of spending and the growing pleasure basis of society.

– The tradition that rigorous saving and paying cash are the marks of sound family economy and personal self respect; and the new gospel which encourages liberal spending to make the wheels of industry turn as a duty to the citizen. (*ibid.*)

The increasing pervasiveness of modern values and the need to be permissive in relation to the old moral imperatives in order to sustain and strengthen the economy create a social problem which requires, according to Lynd, more government intervention and the promotion of widespread consumer education by schools and other agencies. It is in this way, he implies, that the people's irrational impulses will be contained and deployed in a more productive manner:

The primary concern . . . is whether the government is prepared to give
to the spending of the national income the same degree of concern that
it at present bestows upon the earning of that income. Such coherent
leadership is needed if schools and other agencies are to educate the
individual consumer in the practice of the fine art of spending money.
(*ibid.*, p. 911)

So from a much more academic and policy-oriented source we see the
expression of similar concerns about the contradictions that beset
consumption and the proposal of similar solutions. This kind of view also
contributes to what emerges as a highly complex set of representations, in
which elements from apparently distinct discursive fields combine into an
uneasy web and the buying of things is increasingly marked out as an integral
and necessary aspect of the new economic order, yet also unpredictable and
untrammelled – fantasy as much as work. Shoppers (mainly women) are
perceived to be full of contradictory responses and practices: at once irrational,
capricious, pleasure-seeking, and also 'ominously powerful' in their ability
to withhold custom, shop for bargains and not reveal what it is that they want.
It is from this nexus then that we see growing demands for a more disciplined
and educated consumption, for a greater rationalization and modernization
of retailing in order to increase efficiency,[17] and above all, for more knowledge
of the consumer, of what and how she buys, and increasingly of *why* she buys
as she does, in order to develop a predictable and stable market (see, e.g.,
Filene, 1938). It must be remembered that underlying and compounding these
insecurities about the shopper were the serious economic recessions and
political crises of the inter-war years.

Knowing the consumer: market research and Mass-Observation

This is the context in which the new 'discipline' of market research establishes
its agenda. As far as I am aware, there is no authoritative critical historical
account of the development of market and consumer research in America and
Britain. The retailing and advertising histories that I have looked at offer
different versions about when, where and how it started and when the term
became current within the industry. There also are different opinions about
what type of research was introduced and how valid or useful it was:
retrospective readings suggest that most of it, in the United States as well
as Britain, was haphazard, intuitive, and often based on informal chats with
customers or friends – as we saw in the case of Marks & Spencer (Marchand,
1986; Nevett, 1982; Porter Benson, 1986; Rees, 1969). Some claims were made,

as they were in the sociology of the period, to a narrative of scientific truth: Filene, whom I have already mentioned, was a keen believer not only in the scientific management of retailing but also in the possibility of establishing by scientific means the fine detail of what customers really wanted (Filene, 1938, p. 293). However, Marchand argues about the United States that, 'By present day standards . . . the research efforts of agencies were infrequent and often crude'; agencies derived their information about the public from popular cultural sources (such as women's magazines) and sociological surveys (1986, p. 76). According to Nevett, American market research in the 1930s in which researchers started 'to watch the housewife in the process of making purchases and investigated the contents of pantries and bathrooms' was treated by British advertisers with 'a high degree of scepticism' (1982, pp. 150-1).

Overall, then, there has been no more consensus about the effectivity or usefulness of market research than there is about its origins. But the more general and important argument is that during this period we see increasingly organized if still somewhat contingent and often crude attempts by advertisers and retailers to observe and classify the detailed tastes and habits of the consuming population in order to predict sales. The fact that these investigations are frequently haphazard and unreliable does not detract from their significance as constituent parts of a growing regime of knowledge about the consumer. The relationship of this type of information to the regulation of populations must inevitably invoke the theoretical perspective of Michel Foucault (1978; 1980). Erica Carter, in her path-breaking analysis of consumption and femininity in Germany during the period after World War II (1997), has introduced into English the felicitously apposite German term for market research, *demoscopy*. This term immediately makes the connection to surveillance and, Carter argues, drawing on Foucault, is a new 'science of government', part of a wider regime of knowledge–power, through which consumers in the market-place are made subjects of disciplinary control and at the same time produced as citizens, as active subjects of the consumption and political processes.[18]

Importantly, then, Foucault's model is not only about 'disciplining' subjects. It is also about 'producing' them as visible and informed citizens. This extends the span of his regime of knowledge–power so that it encompasses also, for the period that we are looking at, the BBC listener research of the 1930s (Chaney, 1987) and the British social survey, Mass-Observation, which despite its academic provenance in anthropology and the social sciences and its declared political allegiance to the Left, shares with market research the desire to know the thoughts, customs and taste of the people (Jeffrey, 1978; Harrison and Madge, 1986). The intention of Mass-Observation was to render visible the unnoticed accumulated detail of everyday beliefs and practices. Defining itself on the side of 'the people', it used qualitative research which drew on oral histories, private diaries and people's own written accounts, and is therefore to be contrasted with the dominant approaches of market research. Nevertheless, in its scrutiny and recording of shopping habits, it too contributed to the proliferating discourses around consumption. It provided revelations about the practices of consumers which could be appropriated for the purposes of enhancing the stability of the market. These retailing implications, however, seem to have been largely unheeded at the time: in fact, Mass-Observation, perhaps because of its left-wing associations, incurred much criticism from the right-wing press, which accused it of 'prying' and 'eavesdropping' (Graves and Hodge, 1991, p. 402). The critics were right, of course. Both the market researcher and the Mass-Observation scribe were part of what Denzin (1995) has called the emerging cinematic society in which the apparatus of cinema introduces new epistemologies of realism, and the 'voyeur's gaze' becomes increasingly ubiquitous, extending beyond the eye and frame of the camera to the social surveys and ethnographies which during this period remain founded on claims of truth and evidence.

What I have tried to describe in this chapter is a process and period in which consumption spreads increasingly into the employed sectors of the working class and recruits into its orbit larger numbers of people than ever before. It acquires an unprecedented economic, socio-moral and iconographic prominence. My object has also been to register the expanding regime of knowledge about the consumer – that is to say, the growth in the *representation* of shops, shopping, shoppers and commodities – which, although massively dominated by marketing and advertising during this period, also includes contributions from women's magazines, the cinema, fiction and drama, journalism, critical comment and the social sciences. What this amounts to is an odd and often contradictory configuration of diverse imaginings, practices and epistemological frameworks which coalesce none the less into a complex network of knowledge. This set of representations operates, though inevitably in partial and uneven ways, to define and contain the woman consumer. Ideas about rational consumption and the housewife as manager become a means of regulating disorderly shoppers and in effect contribute to the management of consumption. Knowledge of the consumer, of her taste and aspirations as well as what she has to spend, contributes to a more predictable and stable retailing context, to a more domesticated market-place. Yet in conclusion it is important to stress that this process of normalization and stabilization, which gains so much momentum in the inter-war years, is not inexorable. The market and consumption can never finally be contained. They are always precarious, always undermined by the complexity of psychic life, the anarchic nature of desire, the arbitrariness of fashion, the impossibility of market research and the acquisition of new knowledge, and hence power, by the discriminating and sceptical woman consumer. As Porter Benson has succinctly put it: 'Customers, unlike store fixtures and accounting systems, are enduringly resistant to rationalization' (1986, p. 115).

Notes

1. This article was first published in *Australian Journal of Communication*, 22(2), 1995. Some minor changes have been made for this reprint.
2. This was indeed how she operated; see her *A Writer's Diary* (Woolf, 1953). Thanks to Sally Alexander for pointing this out to me.
3. Q.D. Leavis's *Fiction and the Reading Public* was also published in 1932. Both Q.D. and F.R. Leavis write critically of Virginia Woolf in *Scrutiny* (Barrett, 1979, pp. 4 and 29). See also Alison Light (1991, p. 161).
4. See e.g. Adorno and Horkheimer (1973) and Edmund Wilson cited in Leach (1994). For more recent comments on this type of perspective, see e.g. Hebdige (1988), Huyssen (1988), Carey (1992), Alexander (1995) and Nava (1992 and 1996).
5. Walter Benjamin was among the few, see e.g. Benjamin (1973) for cinema and his *Passagenwerk* for shopping, reconstructed by Buck-Morss (1989). See also Nava (1996) for further discussion of his approach to consumption.
6. See Alan O'Shea (1995) for an overview of the debates about this. For the position of women in modernity see Wolff (1985) and Nava (1996).
7. This history is drawn from a number of sources. See in particular Abelson (1989), Adburgham (1989), Bowlby (1985), Callery (1991) and Honeycombe (1984).
8. Press cuttings file, Selfridges Archive.
9. *Souvenir to Commemorate the Opening of Selfridge's 1909*, Selfridges Archive.
10. The ball took place on 1 July 1913; Press cuttings file, Selfridges Archive.
11. These figures are cited by John Stevenson (1984). The trend for the entire inter-war period was up though the pace of increase was uneven and dipped somewhat during the early years of the Depression, particularly in America (Hobsbawm, 1994; Lynd, 1933).
12. For instance, 'Woman earning her own living', 'Should married women work?', 'Should wives have wages?', 'Superwoman in business: why are there not more?', 'To marry or not to marry?', all in Braithwaite *et al.* (1989).
13. Frederick was a well-known writer on 'scientific home management' in the United States. The book referred to here, tantalizingly entitled *Selling Mrs. Consumer* (New York Business Bourse, 1929), is not available in Britain even at the British Library, an indication of how intellectually insignificant consumption has been thought to be.
14. See Buckley (1995) for an account of how it contributed to the erosion of regional identity.

15.   Thanks to Deborah Ryan for alerting me to this apposite quote. See also her
      Chapter 2 in this volume and her PhD thesis: 'The *Daily Mail* Ideal Home
      Exhibition and Suburban Modernity 1908–1951', University of East London,
      1995.

16.   See Oliver, Davis and Bentley (1994) for a defence of the suburban semi.

17.   This period sees a number of significant co-operative ventures (for instance,
      common Christmas publicity campaigns) and mergers between large retail
      organizations (Leach, 1994).

18.   See Carter's (1997) Chapter 3, 'The rationalisation of the consuming woman'.
      I am indebted to her innovative argument for the development of aspects of
      this article.

References

Abelson, E. (1989) *When Ladies Go A-Thieving: Middle-class Shoplifters in the Victorian
      Department Store*. Oxford: Oxford University Press.

Adburgham, A. (1989) *Shops and Shopping 1800–1914*. London: Barrie and Jenkins.

Adorno, T. and Horkheimer, M. (1973) *The Dialectics of Enlightenment*. London:
      Allen Lane.

Alexander, S. (1995) *Becoming a Woman*. London: Virago.

Barrett, M. (1979) *Virginia Woolf: Women and Writing*. London: The Women's Press.

Benjamin, W. (1973) *Illuminations*. London: Collins.

Berman, M. (1983) *All That Is Solid Melts into Air: The Experience of Modernity*.
      London: Verso.

Bowlby, R. (1985) *Just Looking: Consumer Culture in Dreiser, Gissing and Zola*.
      London: Methuen.

Bowlby, R. (1990) 'Soft sell: marketing rhetoric in feminist criticism', *Women:
      A Cultural Review*, 1(1).

Braithwaite, B., Walsh, N. and Davies, G. (eds) (1989) *Ragtime to Wartime: The Best of
      Good Housekeeping 1922–1939*. London: Ebury Press.

Buckley, C. (1995) 'Modernity, femininity and regional identity: women and fashion
      in the north east of England 1914–1940'. In T. E. Faulkner (ed.), *Northumbrian
      Panorama*. London: Octavian Press.

Buck-Morss, S. (1989) *The Dialectics of Seeing: Walter Benjamin and the Arcades Project*.
      Boston: MIT Press.

Callery, S. (1991) *Harrods Knightsbridge: The Story of Society's Favourite Store*. London:
      Ebury Press.

Carey, J. (1992) *The Intellectuals and the Masses*. London: Faber and Faber.

Carter, J. (1997) *How German Is She? Postwar German Reconstruction and the
      Consuming Woman*. Ann Arbor: University of Michigan Press.

Chaney, D. (1987) 'Audience research and the BBC in the 1930s: a mass medium
      comes into being'. In J. Curran, A. Smith and P. Wingate (eds), *Impacts and
      Influences: Essays on Media Power in the Twentieth Century*. London: Methuen.

Davis, D. (1996) *A History of Shopping*. London: Routledge and Kegan Paul.

Denzin, N. (1995) *The Cinematic Society: The Voyeur's Gaze*. London: Sage.

Filene, E. (1938) *Next Steps Forward in Retailing*. London: Sir Isaac Pitman and Sons Ltd.

Foucault, M. (1978) *The History of Sexuality: Volume 1*. London: Allen Lane.

Foucault, M. (1980) *Power/Knowledge: Selected Interviews and Other Writings 1972–1977* (ed. Colin Gordon). Brighton: Harvester.

Graves, R. and Hodge, A. [1940] (1991) *The Long Weekend: A Social History of Great Britain 1818–1939*. London: Cardinal.

Harrison, T. and Madge, C. [1939] (1986) *Britain by Mass-Observation*. London: Cresset Library.

Hebdige, D. (1988) *Hiding in the Light*. London: Routledge.

Hobsbawm, E. (1994) *Age of Extremes: The Short Twentieth Century 1914–1991*. London: Michael Joseph.

Honeycombe, G. (1984) *Selfridges*. London: Park Lane Press.

Hosgood, C. (1994) 'Christmas shopping and middle-class culture in Victorian England', 16th Annual Conference of the Design History Society, 'Design for Selling: The Culture and History of Shops, Shopping and Consumerism', Glasgow, 16–18 December.

Huyssen, A. (1988) *After the Great Divide*. London: Macmillan.

Jeffrey, T. (1978) *Mass-Observation: A Short History*. Birmingham: University of Birmingham Centre for Contemporary Cultural Studies: Occasional Paper No. 55.

Lancaster, W. (1995) *The Department Store: A Social History*. London: Pinter.

Leach, W. (1984) 'Transformations in a culture of consumption: women and department stores 1890–1925', *Journal of American History*, 7(2).

Leach, W. (1994) *Land of Desire: Merchants, Power and the Rise of a New American Culture*. New York: Vintage.

Leavis, Q. D. (1932) *Fiction and the Reading Public*. London: Chatto and Windus.

Light, A. (1991) *Forever England: Femininity, Literature and Conservatism between the Wars*. London: Routledge.

Lynd, R. S. (1933) 'The people as consumers'. In *Recent Trends in the United States. Volume 2* (Report of the President's Research Committee on Social Trends). New York: McGraw-Hill.

Marchand, R. (1986) *Advertising the American Dream: Making Way for Modernity 1920–1940*. Berkeley: University of California Press.

Melman, B. (1988) *Women and the Popular Imagination in the Twenties: Flappers and Nymphs*. London: Macmillan.

Moi, T. (1985) *Sexual/Textual Politics: Feminist Literary Theory*. London: Methuen.

Nava, M. (1992) *Changing Cultures: Feminism, Youth and Consumerism*. London: Sage.

Nava, M. (1996) 'Modernity's disavowal: women, the city and the department store'. In M. Nava and A. O'Shea (eds), *Modern Times: Reflections on a Century of English Modernity*. London: Routledge.

Nevett, T. R. (1982) *Advertising in Britain*. London: Heinemann.

Oliver, P., Davis, I. and Bentley, I. (1994) *Dunroamin: The Suburban Semi and Its Enemies*. London: Pimlico.

Orwell, G. (1937) *The Road to Wigan Pier*. London: Victor Gollancz.

O'Shea, A. (1995) 'English subjects of modernity'. In M. Nava and A. O'Shea (eds), *Modern Times: Reflections on a Century of English Modernity*. London: Routledge.

Pleydell-Bouverie, M. (1944) *The Daily Mail Book of Postwar Homes*. London: Associated Newspapers.

Porter Benson, S. (1986) *Counter Cultures: Saleswomen, Managers and Customers in American Department Stores 1890-1940*. Urbana-Champaign: University of Illinois Press.

Rees, G. (1969) *St Michael: A History of Marks & Spencer*. London: Weidenfeld and Nicolson.

Steedman, C. (1986) *Landscape for a Good Woman*. London: Virago.

Stein, S. (1985) 'The graphic ordering of desire: modernisation of a middle-class women's magazine 1914–1939', *Heresies*, 18, 84–92.

Stevenson, J. (1984) *British Society 1914–1945*. Harmondsworth: Penguin.

Tickner, L. (1987) *The Spectacle of Women: Imagery of the Suffrage Campaign 1907–1914*. London: Chatto and Windus.

Wolff, J. (1985) 'The invisible flâneuse: women in the literature of modernity', *Theory, Culture and Society*, 2(3).

Woolf, V. [1928] (1963) *A Room of One's Own*. Harmondsworth: Penguin.

Woolf, V. [1932] (1989) 'Oxford Street tide'. In B. Braithwaite, N. Walsh and G. Davies (eds), *Ragtime to Wartime: The Best of* Good Housekeeping *1922–1939*. London: Ebury Press, pp. 138–9.

Woolf, V. (1953) *A Writer's Diary*. London: Hogarth Press.

5. 'The greatest invention of the century':[1] menstruation in visual and material culture

Alia Al-Khalidi

Examining Sears Roebuck's 'Catalog Looking Glass' in the 1930s, a cultural critic observed that American sales promotion for sanitary napkins in mail order had rendered the product increased visibility. He remarked on what he believed to be the transformative nature of mail-order consumer culture in the United States:

> Let us take a single article – sanitary napkins – and contrast their method of presentation in a thirty-year period: 1905-35. In the earlier year, these articles were modestly tucked away toward the end of a page in the latter part of the catalog . . . In 1935, sanitary napkins are prominently displayed in large space at the top of a page, with illustrations of the boxes containing them. (Cohn, 1940, pp. 503–4)

Despite the increasing boldness of the catalogue's visual display of menstrual commodities, however, the gendered sales pitch from the resident Sears nurse continued to sanction the benefits of the privacy of catalogue shopping. She stressed the discreetness of shopping through catalogues, urging consumers to 'Order Your FEMININE HYGIENE NEEDS From this Page – Save Money! Save Embarrassment!' (Sears and Roebuck, 1935, p. 439). The continuation of such strategies – emphasizing concealment and user compliance with standardized menstrual etiquette – remains evident in contemporary consumption practices. Rebecca Ginsberg has observed that 'the design of the objects and their packaging can be read as encouraging private, discreet consumption'. She argues that the significance of sanitary products as material culture 'lies in their helping to delineate and affirm the dominant ideology of womanhood'. She identifies the process by which, 'through users' efforts to comply with the apparent necessity of hiding these objects, and their attempts to justify such absences, tampons and napkins participate in the ordering of their worlds' (1996, p. 365).

This 'dominant ideology of womanhood' and the [in]visibility of menstrual products in the ordering of our world appear to be little changed from earlier historical periods. For example, an account of the experiences of women serving in the ATS (Auxiliary Territorial Service) during World War II both illustrates how women negotiated with prescribed menstrual etiquette in the disposal of sanitary products and reflects the manifestation of sanitary towel use as a form of resistance to such structures:

> What came as a surprise to all of us . . . was the extreme reluctance of many women to use either the wrapping paper or the bins provided. Apart from the frequent blocking of the drains caused by ill-advised attempts to put them down the lavatory, the soiled towels, wrapped and unwrapped were found in the most unexpected places – stuffed behind pipes, in the backs of cupboards and drawers, in desks, anywhere but in the right place . . . the only remedy was constant propaganda, with threats of disciplinary action. (Winner, 1947, p. 233)

In addition to the meanings attributed to menstrual objects through consumption, Park (1996) notes that the key themes mediated in contemporary and early advertisements for menstrual products remain virtually unchanged a century after they first emerged. She suggests that current advertisements and packaging for sanitary products which emphasize flight and freedom are evidence of a postmodern marketing strategy. She claims that this strategy was first evident in the marketing of Tampax and their 'initial cries of freedom' in the late 1940s. Such a claim, however, highlights problems in historicizing developments in the promotional and material culture of menstruation. 'Freedom' strategies were in fact evident in Tampax advertisements appearing in the late 1930s.[2] Prior to the introduction of the first commercial tampons, Kleinerts targeted consumers of their sanitary products as 'Free every day to work & play with unequal concern . . . Freed from such irritating restriction forever' (*Good Housekeeping*, November 1928, p. 163). Indeed, *The Family Doctor* (31 October 1896) had commented on the 'freedom from restraint' conferred upon consumers of Southalls' sanitary towels.

This chapter argues, therefore, that, while it is useful to consider the coded classificatory domain of the mail-order catalogue in 1935 and notions of hygiene, freedom, concealment and discretion evident in this period, the context of earlier promotional forms provides a more generic understanding of the historical development of strategies of menstrual communication. Of particular importance are the practices occurring from the late nineteenth century with the inception of industrially manufactured sanitary products in Britain, and the growth of a commercial and material culture of menstruation.[3] The 'business' of bleeding – that is, the development of a corporate body, signifying the industrialization of the menstrual function to the commercial production of objects through which this process is negotiated – marks the transition from an area of private production and consumption to that of the commercial sphere. This transition provides scope for the exploration of the industrial and cultural encoding of menstruation, and the emerging discourses used to advertise manufactured sanitary products.

Through analysis of the commercialization of menstruation and the developing promotional culture of advertising and publicity material for such products, this chapter suggests that the 'origination' of early strategies for menstrual communication can be situated within dominant medical discourses of the female body. Associations with hygiene, freedom and concealment, evident in the visual and material culture of menstruation, are presented as symptoms of these discourses, operating with differing historical specificity from the late nineteenth century and remaining persistent features of menstrual product marketing in twentieth-century consumer culture.

The commodification of menstruation

The objects of early technical invention in the material culture of menstruation constitute a range of 'shadowed' commodities, embedded in the popular and official discourses of nineteenth-century medicine and commerce. They can, however, be traced to 1880: the date of the first sanitary towel patent by Southall Bros and Barclay, and the period during which the firm pioneered production of the first sanitary towel.[4] The medicalization of the female body, along with prevalent notions of Victorian women as being defined by their reproductive capacity, historically located menstruation within the scientific theory of feminine physiology and the prescribed definitions of feminine behaviour and menstrual etiquette.[5] The menstrual function, and particularly the adolescent phase of female puberty in the Victorian period, were paralleled with depictions of female insanity and classifications of menstruation as mental illness (Showalter, 1972; Spiegel, 1988). Indeed, the onset of menstruation marked the beginning of a different and more limited existence for Victorian girls, where 'simply to manage the hygiene of menstruation in a household where it could not be acknowledged or revealed created a sense of anxiety and shame' (Showalter, 1993, p. 57). Popular medical literature, designed to educate mothers to the 'correct' management of the menstrual

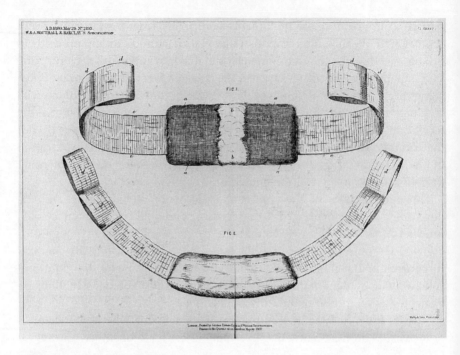

Figure 5.1   Southall Bros & Barclay, patent specification for 'Antiseptic and Absorbent Pads', 1880

function, mediated prevalent ideas concerning the moral- and mental-hygiene imperatives of menstruating adolescents, regulating female performance and activity. For example, in a text entitled *On the Preservation of the Health of Women at the Critical Periods of Life*, Dr E. J. Tilt advised that 'Novels and romances, speaking generally, should be spurned' (1851, p. 40). The feminine character was believed to be flawed by psychological inefficiencies and weaknesses which, through habitual indulgence, 'exert a disastrous influence on the nervous system, sufficient to explain that frequency of hysteria and nervous diseases which we find amongst women of the higher classes' (*ibid*.).

Such beliefs were by no means confined to the treatises of nineteenth-century physicians. The formulation of cultural attitudes towards women in which biological and psychological recognition of female bleeding (as gendered blood, and therefore a signifier of sexual difference) has controlled menstruation by the notion of the menstrual body as unclean. The consequent ritualizing practices of purification and segregation and the mythologizing of menstrual blood and the menstruating woman have been prevalent throughout history (see, e.g., Douglas, 1994; Lupton, 1993; Shuttle and Redgrove, 1994; Weideger, 1978). At the point where Southalls entered into mass production of the first marketable form of commercial sanitarywear, however, theories of sexual difference had emerged in scientific definitions of gender. These had legitimized, within medical discourse, the belief in woman's natural function: a biologically determined reproductive role requiring domestication and motherhood as a prerequisite of femininity (see, for example, Jordanova, 1989; Moscucci, 1993; Oudshoorn, 1994).

Southall Brothers and Barclay's commercial sanitary towel production was not the earliest enterprise of the Birmingham-based company (originally a retail chemist and later a manufacturer of chemist and druggist supplies). Nevertheless, the outcome of their production of cottonwool encased in gauze for surgical use was their invention of the 'sanitary towel' for catamenial (i.e. menstrual) purposes (*British Medical Journal*, 8 June 1895). It was patented as 'Improvements in Antiseptic and Absorbent Pads for Absorbing Discharges in Childbed and Other Discharges': the invention of a pad of a kind 'suitable for general use by women'. The specification enlarged upon the schematics of the towel's composition (see Figure 5.1) and its correct employment on the body:

> In constructing an antiseptic and absorbent pad according to our Invention we form a pad, preferably of an oblong figure, of absorbent wool. This pad we enclose in a casing of absorbent gauze. To the back of the casing of the pad we attach a light band, preferably of absorbent linen, the said band being so long that when passed under the body of the wearer one end of the band will reach the waist in front and the other end will reach the waist behind, the pad fixed to the middle of the band being supported in the required position on the person. (Southall Bros and Barclay, 1880, p. 2)

Impregnated with 'an antiseptic substance, such as, for example, boracic acid, carbolic acid, or thymol, or salicylic acid', the patent specified that 'when thought desirable, a perfume may be added to counteract the odour of the antiseptic material employed', where it 'has an odour it may be disguised by some fragrant material, as oil of lavender' (*ibid.*, p. 2). The cultural emphasis placed on physical and mental hygiene in this period was reflected in the commercial promotion of surgical apparatus and preparations designed to eradicate menstrual odour and contribute more generally to a woman's state of hygiene and health. Vaginal medications and a range of pharmaceutical paraphernalia were widely endorsed in an array of booklets and mail-order catalogues of surgical and birth-control suppliers published in the late Victorian period. In addition to the promotion of a variety of sanitary accessories, such printed materials also provided extensive advice on the menstrual function within the context of marriage, motherhood and contraception.[6] Products for male and female consumption proliferated; douches and syringes were advertised in the light of their cleansing and contraceptive properties.[7] In an advertisement for Lambert's 'Improved Vertical & Reverse Current Syringe' (promising not to 'cause the slightest harm to the most delicate female') internal hygiene was also sold as an antidote to the residual impurities of the menstrual period, in addition to less gender-specific ailments: 'Great comfort and benefit to health is derived by using one with about two pints of slightly warm water after the periodical use of the Sanitary Towels. It is also very useful in cases of obstinate constipation, when an injection affords instant relief' (Warren, 1894, p. 71).

'The "Hygena" Sanitary Towel and Waistband', and 'The "Hygena" Menstrual or Period Protector for Ladies' use' – advertised on further pages in *The Wife's Guide and Friend* (*ibid.*, pp. 118–22) – were not products all women were familiar with. It should be noted that commercial forms of sanitary protection were a luxury few women could afford. Customized sanitarywear was a feature of female menstrual practice well into the twentieth century. Moreover, women who had used commercial products often had to modify their practice in periods of economic hardship, thus alternating between home-made and manufactured styles.[8]

Scientific certification: medical discourse and early menstrual product marketing

Progress of the first patented sanitary towel by Southalls was slow, owing to the difficulty of making the product known to the public. However, by 1949, the Chairman of the company reflected that 'the article was appreciated, once the initial problems had been overcome, and immediately took the pre-eminent position it has occupied ever since' (Southalls, 1949, p. 6). Making the product known inevitably required public promotion, for which the medical, pharmaceutical and trade press were to provide useful endorsements. In their descriptions of new inventions and novelties in 1884, for example, *The British Medical Journal* (15 Nov.) and *The Medical Press and Circular* (26 Nov.) featured tributes to the technical innovations of Messrs Southall and Brothers, of Birmingham.[9] They heralded the pad or towel as 'taking the place of the old-fashioned napkins used by females monthly'. The 'absorbent and antiseptic' qualities of the product were presented as safeguards against not only the site of the female body as a vulnerable source of disease and infection, but also the unhygienic procedure of washing and re-washing sanitarywear (a process necessitated by economic use of materials in home-made forms). Both menstruation and female menstrual practice without the aid of Southalls were thereby presented as implied threats against physiological and domestic purity:

> their softness and convenient shape, which afford increased comfort, and their non-conducting character, which makes them less liable to give rise to chill in delicate health, are obvious advantages; but the greatest advantage of all is that each pad can be burned after use, and that thus they are in the highest degree cleanly, and diminish materially the risks of septic infection. (*The British Medical Journal*, 15 November 1884, p. 969)

Similarly, *The Medical Press and Circular* contrasted the benefits of the product and 'the great increase of comfort derived by the use of the towel for those for whom they are intended' (meaning those who could afford them) with the problems resulting from use of 'ordinary diapers at the monthly period' (by those who could not). The suitability of home-made forms was even further displaced in the context of travel:

> in travelling, particularly, they offer advantages not to be compared with their customary substitutes. Being in the shape of a soft, absorbent, antiseptic pad, they prevent the occurrence of chafing, excoriation and other inconveniences inseparable from the presence of a damp offensive napkin, such as even the most cleanly women cannot prevent from exciting an irritative action . . . their unquestionable hygienic superiority as compared with the latter appliances, will ensure that, as is very desirable, they shall become universally used. (*ibid.*, p. 472)

In the following year, Southalls appropriated these citations. A strategic theme of the product's early promotional culture emerged, evident for many years to come in advertisements for a range of brands. Strategic targeting of the medical press led to resounding endorsements. Combined with 'testimonials from trained medical nurses' reflecting on the personal recommendation of the towel to patients and friends in both Britain and the United States, these were used in circulars introducing 'A Desideratum of the Highest Importance for Health and Comfort' (Southalls, *circa* 1885a). Memorandums were also produced advertising the product, combining medical certification with instructive advice on the product's assemblage (facilitated by additional consumer acquisition of Southalls' Towel Suspender). The towel was marketed as essential for use on long voyages, primarily in terms of its disposable, destructable and hygienic qualities when burnt.[10] This marketing strategy differentiated between the lower orders and upper-class readers, who could not only afford to engage in such pursuits but were also able to employ paid

Figure 5.2   Colour lithograph display card/window bill for Southalls' sanitary towels, circa 1890. Reproduced with the kind permission of the Bodleian Library, University of Oxford, shelfmark JJ. COLL. Medicines 11.

assistance when washing. It also signified the possible impersonal dis-advantages of public exposure accompanying such status. Advertising copy effectively sensationalized the use of customized materials. The message to consumers insisted that the 'carrying of soiled linen in travelling packages, and the keeping it in the house waiting for the laundress, in hot weather, are objectionable' (Southalls, *circa* 1885b).[11]

Associations between commercial sanitary-towel consumption and class, however, were not limited to the choice between either home-made or manufactured forms. Product price and range were to prove a distinguishing feature in the hierarchy of branded protection: 'N.B.- "Southalls' Sanitary Towels for Ladies" are sold in two qualities, marked No. 1 and No. 2; the No. 1 has a larger pad and longer bands than No. 2, and is what has usually been sold. The No. 2 is made in a cheaper form to suit all classes' (*ibid.*)

The important cultural medium of women's magazines provided an appropriate space for the advertisement of menstrual products, reflecting menstruation's shift into consumer culture. Between 1895 and 1902 advertisements for a variety of brands appeared in both launch and first-year publication editions of new women's magazine titles, reflecting the importance of the magazine as a promotional tool and mediator of menstruation in visual culture.[12] The scientific theme was prevalent in such images; for example, 'For Ladies Travelling', Southalls' Sanitary Towels were described as 'the greatest invention of the century for women's comfort at the cost of washing only' (*Home Chat*, 24 August 1895). As reference to 'the laundress' in the previous paragraph suggests, the strategy of 'the cost of washing' invariably reflected the targeting of menstrual products to the wealthy, women who were not only of sufficient economic means to purchase the magazines in which the products were featured, but were also able to incur the added cost of employing someone else to wash their own customized napkins after use. In this sense, the price of the sanitary towel was presented as negligible, an already existing financial feature of the production and consumption of customized forms. Nevertheless, the magazine and mail-order catalogue were not the only contexts in which early menstrual products were advertised and marketed. As early as the 1890s, 'Southalls' "Sanitary Towels" For Ladies', and the 'Improved "Towel" of Downy Softness' were richly featured on colour lithograph window bills or show cards, for possible display on the trade counters or in the windows of shops retailing 'ladies' requirements'[13] (see Figure 5.2). Captioned as 'An article no lady should be without', and operating as point-of-sale promotion, the card featured a decorative depiction of nurse and child, framed by packaged sanitary articles. The iconic use of the nurse, as a symbol of maternal and scientific purity, denoted the transferable quality of the towels and affirmed the trustworthy appeal of the brand.[14]

Modernizing menstrual communication in consumer culture

As the twentieth century progressed, medical certification of the product became an established strategy in advertising copy and in illustration. This certification was presented in the form of testimonials from 'lady doctors' and pictorial representations of nurses.[15] Between 1928 and 1930, photographic and illustrative images of 'Nurse Ashby' appeared in a series of advertisements for Camelia Soluble Sanitary Towels, which introduced instructive text on practical features of the product. Here, menstruation was depicted as an enduring affliction for which 'Science has at last found the solution'. The remedy for 'Woman's most intimate problem' was to be obtained through purchase of 'the new scientific discovery . . . what every woman has wanted since the days of Eve' (*Good Housekeeping*, January 1928, p. 124). The metaphorical fate of Eve's curse had been lifted,[16] through the scientific discovery of the commercial forms of sanitary protection. Advertisements for Lilia Soluble Towels, appearing throughout 1930 in alternate issues of *Good Housekeeping*, implemented a text-based strategy that consolidated the association between authorized, medical prescription and the innovative, hygienic advantages of the product:

> Doctors now condemn home-made washable sanitary towels as being unhygienic and unhealthful. Sanitary towels, they say, are a form of medical dressing – they should be utterly clean and antiseptic and should be discarded immediately they are used. What doctors say in terms of science and hygiene you will confirm by your own personal experience. (*Good Housekeeping*, November 1930, p. 182)

Notions of purifying etiquette – the work of preserving the delicacy of the female anatomy and, by implication, the feminine character – had become reconfigured. By the 1930s, the range of menstrual products on the market had expanded. This led to the development of more considered sales strategies for the promotion of menstrual hygiene applications and, more specifically, for concern with the concealment of menstrual odour. From an early point, Southalls had acknowledged the benefit of the addition of a perfume to their products, primarily to disguise the use of antiseptic chemicals. Later, the use of such fragrant constituents was targeted directly at what was considered to be the predicament of the consumer, in the context of what were deemed the pollutionary characteristics of menstrual blood. In the 1920s, the Camelia sanitary towel was marketed as a product which 'banishes forever that bogey of embarrassment and discomfort that has haunted women at critical periods since the beginning of the world . . . Camelia is exquisitely soft, comfortable, hygienic and deodorant' (*Woman's Friend*, 2 October 1926, p. 19).

With the advent of Tampax in 1936, there were new possibilities for the avoidance of public discovery of 'women's problems on "those difficult days"'. Promoted as 'Good News For Women (Especially those who are married)' in 1950, Tampax was a product which, because it was worn internally, was 'daintier, safer, simpler . . . quite invisible' and, unlike external forms of protection, could not cause 'odour, chafing or discomfort' (*Woman's Own*, 13 April 1950, p. 13). Like the tampon, menstrual odour and, indeed, menstruation had been rendered imperceptible, in both the public and personal domain.

The self-awareness, aspirations and cultural orientation of women and their perception of menstruation were not only represented and mediated by advertisements for menstrual sanitary products in this period. As with the production of popular manuals detailing surgical equipment and advice to female consumers, the increasing prevalence of corporate publications sponsored by manufacturers of menstrual commodities also served to disseminate ideologies of menstruation. Notions of menstrual etiquette were articulated through the certified authorship of many such publications by 'Medical Doctors'.[17] In 1937, the manufacturers of 'Vanderised Camelia Towels and Vanderised Toilet Water' produced the guide, *Feminine Hygiene – Some Remarks and Advice*. Its stated author was Th. H. Van de Velde, MD, a Dutch gynaecologist and sexologist and renowned author of a popular sex manual, *Ideal Marriage* (1928).[18] In the text proclaiming 'The Deodorising Properties of the Vanderised towels and Toilet water', Van de Velde reminded readers of the necessity for precautionary measures to be taken whilst menstruating:

Many women are conscious of an unpleasant body odour and suffer from nervous strain as a result. But we all know women who are afflicted in this way and do not appear to notice it, and would probably emphatically deny that they could cause embarrassment to others. . . . For the menstrual flow, like other bodily secretions, emits its own characteristic smell, and a woman may ignore it, or be quite oblivious to it herself, though to all others it may be obvious. (Van de Velde, 1937, p. 9)

In the same period, new products for use in association with sanitary towels became increasingly prevalent, not only highlighting preoccupations with menstrual odour, but the discomfort which accompanied sanitary towel consumption and wear. Southalls marketed their DEO Powder, alongside their sanitary towels, 'As a deodorant and to prevent chafing'. Used by 'particular' people, both the product and its consumer were credited with qualities of discernment, with the added assurances that it 'neutralises body odour at once' and is supplied in 'dainty tins' (Army and Navy Stores' General Price List No. 9, 1939–40, p. 644). Brand competitor, Quest Deodorant Powder, sponsored by the makers of Kotex, was also advertised in the same period, though at a higher price.[19] The dichotomy between the sales pitch for powder products as safeguards against the effects of towel use, on the one hand, and the identified attributes of the brand performance of industrially manufactured sanitary towels, on the other, was that the latter were most often promoted in terms of the precise qualities which would obviate the necessity of such secondary products. In real terms, however, this was a practice established in the discourses of late-nineteenth-century medicine and advertising through an emphasis on the alliance between scientific invention, hygiene and female comfort, and on the renunciation of the benefits of customized/home-made forms of sanitarywear.

As the commercial culture of menstruation developed and increased product diversity, so did an established discourse of menstrual communication. Reflecting the styles often prevalent in advertisements for domestic and personal products targeted at women, there were shared themes across temporal and product range in the promotional images for commodities linked to menstruation. Representations of work and leisure became increasingly common from the 1920s; these featured graphic images of females engaged in a variety of activities (including those outside of the nursing profession). Though the emphasis on hygiene was retained, science was allied to modernity to promote uninterrupted female pursuits conferred by the product. Through the theme of unification, the concept of the biological universality of the female menstrual experience was also centralized in menstrual product advertisements appearing in the first half of the century. There were three distinct elements involved in this unification: *the familial*, in which menstruation was allied with reproduction to highlight the nurturing role necessitated by motherhood in the instruction of daughters for the efficient management of the menstrual period through an identified product; *the cultural*, in which the experience of menstruation was internationalized across geographical boundaries (or the obverse of this, internalized to promote a specific sense of national identity through the product); *the personal*, through which kindred members of the female sex shared a camaraderie that facilitated sisterly advice in the form of product recommendation. Female intelligence and discernment were also qualities attributed to the consumers' choice of sanitary protection. This was particularly salient from the 1940s onwards, where a singular and informed choice of brand was promoted as an expression of feminine knowledge and essential good taste, paralleling the consumption of sanitary products with other, though deemed less essential, commodities, such as fashion clothes and cosmetics.

Conclusion

As demonstrated here, throughout the late nineteenth and early twentieth centuries, advertisements for female sanitary products continued to operate within the discourses of hygiene, freedom and concealment. This thematic framework developed through the mediation of the ideologies of menstruation, contextualized within the dominant medical discourse of the female body. The origins of the material culture of menstruation and the growth in branded menstrual commodities are of key historical significance if we are to identify developments in the visual and promotional culture of menstruation and women's experience of the developing consumer culture of female sanitary products.

In 1880, Southalls' partner Thomas Barclay Senior had experienced great difficulty placing his product in a suitable retail situation: 'The squeamishness of the draper to stock the goods seemed to be obstinately insuperable' (*Warehousemen & Drapers Trade Journal*, 19 April 1890, p. 347; cited in Peck, 1995, p. 24). This squeamish resistance seems greatly distanced from the events of 1929. It was in this year that the Railway and Tramway Advertising Contractors to the London and North Western Railway approached the manufacturers of the Mene sanitary towel with an unsolicited offer to erect their large-scale promotional mirrors advertising their towels in the ladies' toilets of up to six hundred railway stations.[20] What should remain distinct in the study of menstruation in visual and material culture is that, when the late 1920s traveller looked into the Mene sanitary towel mirror, women had already been in the gaze of the menstrual product mediators for almost half a century.

Notes

1. Advertising pitch for Southalls' sanitary towels from the 1890s. The product was marketed as 'The Greatest Invention of the Century for Women's Comfort at the Cost of Washing Only'. The material presented in this chapter relates to research identified by the author in her PhD thesis 'Menstruation in Visual and Material Culture: A Critical Analysis of the Mediation of Female Sanitary Products 1880-1958'.
2. The advertising message of 'Free from Embarrassment' exemplifies Tampax's earlier marketing technique utilizing freedom (*Britannia & Eve*, August 1939, p. 88).
3. Schroeder, for example, inaccurately states that commercial marketing of sanitary protection prior to the launch of the American Kotex campaign in 1921 was confined to mail-order media in Britain and America (1976, pp. 106–7).
4. It should be noted, however, that at least eleven patents were granted in Britain prior to that of Southalls in 1880. They reflected a diversity of methods designed to impede the emission of menstrual blood, from the Menstrual Receiver or Truss (1859) to a Bandage for Females (1868) (Al-Khalidi, 1999).

5. Extensive work has been carried out in the area of nineteenth-century medical advice to menstruating women; see, for example, Bullough and Voght (1973); Gorham (1982); Lander (1988); Poovey (1986).

6. The titles of publications reflect this, for example, *The Wife's Guide and Friend* (Warren, 1894), and *The Wife's Medical Advisor* (E. Lambert and Son, 1894).

7. *The Wife's Guide and Friend* (Warren, 1894) incorporates products such as 'abdominal and obstetric belts', 'breast relievers', 'chest expanding braces' for men and women, 'Gents suspensory bandages' (for genital support), 'urinals' (for male and female use, echoing the style of sanitary belts and menstrual protector 'slings' in which absorbent material was positioned) and vaginal 'pessaries' for birth control and other sanitary functions. As Porter and Hall (1995) note, the coded promotion of abortifacients appeared in such publications.

8. According to visitors at a day centre run by Age Concern in Southampton, whom I interviewed as a group in 1995. As one interviewee (born in 1924) commented: 'You just bought them according to your money, 'cos you didn't get much money and your husband didn't earn much money. Sometimes I didn't even buy any and I just used a bit of towelling.'

9. Though advice in late nineteenth-century popular guides addressed to women can be found continuing to promote the use of customized home-made forms of sanitary protection, and offering detailed specifications as to their construction (see, for example, Wood-Allen, 1898, pp. 144–5), product endorsements were also featured in popular medical guides produced in the early 1900s. *The Home Doctor* contains an entry listed under Sanitary Towels, identifying key brands (Walters, 1909, p. 295). This practice also extended to the endorsement of menstrual medications, *Everyman In Health and In Sickness* recommends Blaud's pills for menstrual pain relief (Roberts, 1935, p. 283).

10. Shelley Park argues that Southalls' appeal to female voyagers extended from medical prescription, where one of the ways in which upper-class ladies were urged to convalesce from their periodic wound, in addition to bed rest, was by extensive travelling (1996, p. 152).

11. By the 1890s, the promotion of Southall's portable 'cremator' (*The Nursing Record and Hospital World*, 23 October 1897) for the destruction of sanitary towels had sought to alleviate such concerns. Further to this development, the magazines *Madame* (7 August 1909) and *Woman* (December 1909) featured tributes to the benefits of Southalls' 'gusset envelope', a product designed to facilitate female travellers' convenient retention of used towels in the absence of practical disposal facilities. Despite the earlier enterprise of their sanitary towel, which had claimed to alleviate the involvement of hired help, however, it was the introduction of the 'towel container' in 1910 which made the handling of soiled towels acceptable. The editorial columns of *The Draper* (Autumn 1910) advised that the container (bearing the directions 'To be burnt' in three languages) could be 'left with the chambermaid', an alternative preferable to the previously denigrated predicament of the laundress.

12. Indicative representations appeared in *Home Chat* (1895), *The Ladies Home* (1898) and *Chic*, a 'High-Class Illustrated Paper' (1902).

13. By 1911, Southalls' modern pharmacy, for example, contained a number of specialized departments for the merchandising of such products, including the 'Toilet and Fancy Showroom', incorporating the 'Ladies' Department', and the 'comfortable and well-appointed Ladies' Fitting Room', described as 'A feature greatly appreciated by ladies requiring Requisites for the Nursery, Sick Room, or Private purposes' (Southall Bros and Barclay, 1911, pp. 10–11).

14. Depictions of nurses caring/holding small children can be paralleled with the photographic tradition representing nursing in this period, see Fox and Lawrence (1988, pp. 42, 45, 48).

15. For example, an advertisement for Lilia, captioned 'Lilia British and pure as a Lily', exemplifies this theme, its copy prioritizes a message of confirmation to magazine readers: 'A lady Doctor attached to a famous London hospital personally supplies the medical information contained in each Lilia announcement' (*Good Housekeeping*, November 1930, p. 182).

16. See Shuttle and Redgrove (1994) for interpretive discussion of the curse on Eve and mythological narratives of the origins of menstruation.

17. A corporate advice booklet sponsored with the 'Compliments of Kotex Ltd' in 1933 was certified through the identified professional medical status of the author. The publication issued by Kotex, refrains from citing the brand throughout the text, though consisting of contents which reflected the theme of its title: 'Health Facts on Menstruation'; it broadly refers to sanitarywear, emphasizing the advantages of disposable napkins and other features associated with the properties of Kotex evident in advertising campaigns for the product in this period.

18. Though the text *Ideal Marriage* is not cited in the booklet, its subheading, 'The Aims of Ideal Hygiene' (p. 6), echoes the title of the publication. For discussion of Van de Velde's work see, for example, Porter and Hall (1995).

19. The advertisement for Quest deodorant powder (D. H. Evans *Mail Order Catalogue* 1938-39, p. 51) advertises the product at 1/6d in comparison to Southalls Deo Powder at 6d and 1/-.

20. Correspondence from Frank Mason & Company, Limited, Railway and Tramway Advertising Contractors, to Messrs. Robinson & Sons Limited, dated 7 January 1929.

References

Al-Khalidi, A. (1999) 'Menstruation in Visual and Material Culture: A Critical Analysis of the Mediation of Female Sanitary Products 1880–1958'. Unpublished PhD thesis, Southampton Institute.

Bullough, V. and Voght, M. (1973) 'Menstruation and nineteenth-century medicine', *Bulletin of the History of Medicine*, 47 (Jan/Feb), 66–82.

Cohn, D. L. (1940) *The Good Old Days: A History of American Morals and Manners as Seen Through the Sears, Roebuck Catalogs 1905 to the Present*. New York: Simon and Schuster.

Douglas, M. (1994) *Purity and Danger*, 9th edn. London: Routledge.

Fox, M. and Lawrence, C. (1988) *Photographing Medicine: Images and Power in Britain and America since 1840*. Contributions in Medical Studies no. 21. London: Greenwood Press.

Ginsberg, R. (1996) '"Don't tell, dear": the material culture of tampons and napkins', *Journal of Material Culture*, 1 (November), 365–75.

Gorham, D. (1982) *The Victorian Girl and the Feminine Ideal*. London: Croom Helm.

Jordanova, L. J. (1989) *Sexual Visions*. Hertfordshire: Harvester Wheatsheaf.

Lambert, E. and Son (1894) *The Wife's Medical Advisor*. London: R. Forder.

Lander, L. (1988) *Images of Bleeding: Menstruation as Ideology*. New York: Orlando Press.

Lupton, M. J. (1993) *Menstruation and Psychoanalysis*. Chicago: University of Illinois Press.

Moscucci, O. (1993) *The Science of Woman: Gynaecology and Gender in England 1800–1929*. Cambridge: Cambridge University Press.

Oudshoorn, N. (1994) *Beyond the Natural Body: An Archaeology of Sex Hormones*. London: Routledge.

Park, S. (1996) 'From sanitation to liberation? The modern and postmodern marketing of menstrual products', *Journal of Popular Culture*, 30(2), Fall, 149–68.

Peck, J. (1995) *Smith & Nephew in the Health Care Industry*. Hants: Edward Elgar.

Poovey, M. (1986) 'Scenes of an indelicate character: the medical "treatment" of Victorian women', *Representations*, 14, Spring, 37–68.

Porter, R. and Hall, L. (1995) *Facts of Life: The Creation of Sexual Knowledge in Britain, 1650–1950*. London: Yale University Press.

Roberts, H. (1935) *Everyman in Health and in Sickness*. London: Dent.

Schroeder, F. (1976) 'Feminine hygiene, fashion and the emancipation of American women', *American Studies*, 17, 101–10.

Sears and Roebuck (1935) *Mail Order Catalogue*, Spring.

Showalter, E. (1972) 'Victorian women and menstruation'. In M. Vicinus (ed.), *Suffer and Be Still: Women in the Victorian Age*. Bloomington: Indiana University Press.

Showalter, E. (1993) *The Female Malady: Women, Madness and English Culture, 1830–1980*. London: Virago.

Shuttle, P. and Redgrove, P. (1994) *The Wise Wound: Menstruation and Everywoman*, 3rd edn. London: HarperCollins.

Southall Bros and Barclay (1880) Antiseptic and Absorbent Pads, Patent Specification A.D.1880, 29 May, No. 2193..

Southall Bros and Barclay (1911) *Pioneers in Pharmacy: A Comprehensive Book of Reference and Pricelist*. London.

Southalls (*circa* 1885a) Circular advertising Southall's Sanitary Towels for Ladies/A Desideratum of the Highest Importance for Health and Comfort, John Johnson Collection, Bodleian Library: Patent Medicines Box 11.

Southalls (*circa* 1885b) Memorandum advertising Southalls' Sanitary Towels for Ladies, John Johnson Collection, Bodleian Library.

Southalls (1949) 'The Chairman tells you about our history', *Southalls' Magazine*, Winter, 6.

Spiegel, A. D. (1988) 'Temporary insanity and premenstrual syndrome: medical testimony in an 1865 murder trial', *New York State Journal of Medicine*, 9 (September), 482–92.

Tilt, E. J. (1851) *On The Preservation of the Health of Women at the Critical Periods of Life*. London: John Churchill.

Van de Velde, Th. H. (1928) *Ideal Marriage: Its Physiology and Technique*. (Trans. F. W. Stella Browne). London: Heinemann, (first published in Holland 1926).

Van de Velde, Th. H. (1937) *Feminine Hygiene: Some Remarks and Advice*. London: De Vere Press Ltd.

Walters, F. (1909) *The Home Doctor*. Bloomsbury: Swan Sonnenschein & Co.

Warren, S. (1894) *The Wife's Guide and Friend*, 3rd edn. London: Lambert & Co.

Weideger, P. (1978) *Female Cycles*. London: The Women's Press.

Winner, A. L. (1947) 'Public health problems in the ATS', *Public Health*, September, 232–5.

Wood-Allen, M. (1898) *What a Young Women Ought to Know. Purity and Truth: Self and Sex Series*. Philadelphia: The VIR Publishing Company.

6. Georgette Heyer: the historical romance and the consumption of the erotic, 1918–1939

Sallie McNamara

Introduction: consuming eroticism

Attitudes towards women's consumption of popular fiction have invariably been negative. Germaine Greer, for example, attacks romantic fiction, stating that 'the titillating mush of Cartland and her ilk is supplying an imaginative need but their hypocrisy limits the gratification to that which can be gained from innuendo' (1970, p. 189). In the inter-war period, Q.D. and F.R. Leavis, in particular, voiced their criticism of what they saw as mass culture, with Q.D. Leavis referring to 'a drug addiction to fiction', which for readers of romantic fiction can lead to 'a habit of fantasising [that] will lead to maladjustment in actual life' (1932, p. 54). However, recent feminist work on women's genres has done much to challenge these views (e.g. Geraghty, 1991; Radway, 1987; Modleski, 1982). In *Reading the Romance*, Janice Radway argues the act of romance reading is oppositional because it allows the women to refuse momentarily their self-abnegating role, while at the same time stating the romance's narrative structure embodies a simple recapitulation and recommendation of patriarchy and its constituent social practices and ideologies (1987, p. 210). This chapter looks at the historical romances of Georgette Heyer written in the 1920s and 1930s; my intention is to consider readings which are 'against the grain', to consider other possible pleasures offered by consumption in relation to sexuality and sensuality.

Heyer published fourteen historical romances between 1921 and 1938; they were popular at the time and still are. Their popularity indicates their importance in women's lives when set alongside the rise of Mills & Boon, and other popular texts, although Heyer's readers included women *and* men – and her biographer refers to dons and journalists as part of her readership. I would argue that, through the tensions between the characters, the settings and their coded language, the act of reading them can be seen as offering sensual and erotic pleasures beyond what is socially acceptable. I will therefore examine these novels in the context of the historical construction of gender, sexuality and the conflicting discourses of sexologists and the fiction industries. Furthermore, the chapter draws on some oral history relating to women's consumption of leisure in the period, both from personal interviews and those of others. Initially, I will briefly discuss histories of the 1920s and 1930s, and explore some contemporary theories in relation to popular culture and sexuality.

Historical context and theoretical approaches

Histories of the inter-war period emphasize the role of duty and domesticity, the dominant discourses in relation to women's lives being those which focused on the construction of identity in relation to the domestic sphere. Deirdre Beddoe argues the stereotypical image that emerges is that of motherhood, claiming women were 'manipulated to embrace the role of housewife and mother' (1989, p. 9). Judy Giles refers to dominant discourses of medicine, science and psychology as positing a '"modern" women, freed from the restraints of Victorian repression, whose apparently newly acquired robustness and common sense were to be at the service of marriage, housewifery and motherhood' (1995a, p. 21). Alison Light argues that emotional restraint characterized representations of identity, marking a 'private and retiring' people (1991, p. 211). Anti-romanticism is a feature of the period and a cultural space existed in which it was expedient for women to construct themselves as prudent, realistic and restrained (Giles, 1995b, p. 289). Histories, therefore, construct a sense of calmness, composure and quiet, of rigid boundaries, a concentration on family, house and garden, with power and choice confined to servicing the needs of others.

At the same time there was increased access to the consumption of a wide range of leisure pursuits, including the cinema, dancing, popular fiction and mass-produced fashion. Nicola Beauman's analysis of the woman's novel between the wars reveals many overt and covert references to sex and sexuality (1989, p. 9). The publication of the historical novel introduced the development of a new market of erotic literature by women for a female audience (Light, 1991, p. 256). The cinema, with the constructed glamour and sexuality of its male and female stars, packaged eroticism for the mass audience (Costello, 1985, p. 10). The proliferation of discourses on sexology indicates a preoccupation with sex and sexuality, e.g. Marie Stopes's *Married Love* (1918), Theodor Van de Velde's *Ideal Marriage* (1928), H. Havelock Ellis's *Psychology of Sex* (1933), and the writings of Freud. These discourses reinforced binary oppositions of gender.

Heterosexuality was defined as the norm, with an emphasis on sexual difference and the necessity for men to initiate women into sexual responsiveness within marriage (Segal, 1994, p. 86), men active, women passive. Jeffrey Weeks states that '*theoretical* developments reinforced *social* tendencies . . . what sexologists could provide were apparently scientific definitions which could be used to justify social differences' (1985, pp. 87, 88 (emphasis in original)).

However, what interest me are what I see as the tensions between these histories which emphasize the construction of restraint and the dissemination of discourses relating to sexuality and the erotic – specifically those constructed by popular texts such as Hollywood films and popular fiction. Male and female stars were eroticized: consider the sexuality of figures like Mae West, Jean Harlow, Greta Garbo, Marlene Dietrich, and the numbers of women swooning over the highly eroticized figure of Rudolph Valentino. While histories construct one version of sexuality and sensuality, audiences' consumption of popular culture texts is complex, suggesting they provide possible sites of contradiction and transgression of boundaries.

Although Heyer's novels were mass-produced for a large fiction-reading audience, and in many ways follow genre conventions with standardized features and established formats in terms of romance, it is not my intention to follow analysts such as Adorno and Horkheimer (1979; Adorno, 1976), who argue that consumers are passive and manipulated by cultural producers and capitalism. However, neither do I see consumption as solely celebrating the creativity of consumer practices and its subversive possibilities as in some postmodern approaches. While pleasure and empowerment may well form part of a reader's personal experience, if there is an element of subversion, this is at the level of fantasy and daydream where the texts can offer scope or material as the basis for transgression and/or a challenge to gender roles and moral codes.

The approach here is informed by Stuart Hall's work, arguing that popular culture is a site of contestation. He states that people are not cultural dupes, the cultural industries do not work on us as if we were blank screens, rather,

> there is a continuous and necessarily uneven and unequal struggle, by the dominant culture, constantly to disorganise and reorganise popular culture; to enclose and confine its definitions and forms within a more inclusive range of dominant forms. There are points of resistance, there are also moments of suppression. (1981, p. 233)

Popular culture is, he argues, a sort of battlefield (*ibid.*, p. 233), the ground on which transformations are worked (*ibid.*, p. 228).

The historical romance offers distance from the period in which it is written. Anxieties or tensions in relation to the contemporary society (of gender and sexuality) can be reworked within a constructed historical setting, also allowing for conduct which may transgress or challenge existing boundaries. Rosemary Jackson's work on fantastic literature argues that fantasy attempts to 'compensate for a lack resulting from cultural constraints: it is a literature of desire which seeks that which is experienced as absence or loss' (1981, p. 3). Further, it can be seen as transgressive as 'it opens up on to disorder, on to illegality', tracing that which has been silenced (*ibid.*, p. 4). Similarly, in the historical romance setting boundaries on what is permissible raises the spectre of discussing what is *not*, what is forbidden, in the creation of disorder before the status quo is restored. Thus, in speaking of desire, of absence or loss, texts can also offer space for personal fantasy for their readers.

Finally, it is worth briefly referring to other work on the historical romance, notably that by Helen Hughes (1993). She argues that the language used, details of clothing, and so on, relating to the period, create a sense of verisimilitude, with devices which interpolate or address the reader to draw them in. According to Hughes, the historical romance exalts individual prowess and English liberal virtues and offers resolutions for contradictions. Fulfilment for women is through romantic love, and the 'past' remains a site for traditional values: 'the traditional relationship between the sexes is by implication necessary for the continuance of a civilised society' (*ibid.*, p. 37). The supposed foppishness of the male protagonist is a cover for a 'real' English manliness (*ibid.*, p. 89) wherein masculine strength and vigour are still apparent. Essentialism is apparent in the constructions of masculinity and femininity and for the male, 'masculine Englishness and feminine "Frenchness" are . . . presented as coming together to form a well-balanced personality' (*ibid.*, p. 89). At the end, the formerly outspoken and active heroine is quite happy to fall into the arms of her love.

I would argue here that Heyer's novels indicate the transgression of boundaries, the possibility of playing with an apparently fixed identity within the parameters of daily routine and in leisure activities, offering the space for private fantasy. They appear to indicate points of resistance in relation to dominant forms of gender roles. What they also suggest is a merging or collapsing of boundaries in relation to the public and private spheres.

'The red heels of his shoes were very high': gender-benders in Heyer's fiction

With her meticulous research into the period of which she writes, Heyer's novels include lengthy and detailed descriptions of dress – those set in the seventeenth and eighteenth centuries dwell on the silks, lace, velvet, fur, jewels, high heels and make-up worn by the protagonists, sometimes not out of place in the pages of *Vogue*. What is interesting here, and diverges from Hughes' arguments, is that in Heyer's novels these descriptions relate predominantly to the clothing worn by the men. What is termed 'foppishness' can be seen in relation to a kind of 'feminization' of masculinity. A fluidity exists in relation to gender and sexual identity. The first consideration is that it is the *male* body that is offered for display and consumption, as the following examples demonstrate:

A gentleman was strolling down a side street in Paris . . . He walked very mincingly, for the red heels of his shoes were very high. A long purple cloak, rose lined, hung from his shoulders and was allowed to fall carelessly back from his dress, revealing a full skirted coat of purple satin, heavily laced with gold, a waistcoat of flowered silk, faultless small clothes; and a lavish sprinkling of jewels on his cravat and breast. A three-cornered hat, point-edged, was set upon his powdered wig, and in his hand he carried a long beribboned cane. (*These Old Shades*, 1926, p. 5)

Mechelin ruffles and cravats adorned one chair, silk hose another, gorgeous coats hung on their backs; shoes of every description, red heeled and white, riding boots and slippers, stood in a row awaiting attention; wigs perched coquettishly on handy projections. (*The Black Moth*, 1929, p. 144)

Carstairs left off polishing his nails . . . a slim graceful figure in cambric shirt and apricot satin. (*ibid.*, p. 24)

The Apparition wore a coat of palest apricot cloth, with a flowered vest of fine brocade, and startling white small-clothes. Red heeled shoes were on his feet, and his stockings were adorned by sprawling golden clocks . . . He minced down the street. (*Powder and Patch*, 1923, p. 24, 25)

Into the room came Philip, a vision in shades of yellow. (*ibid.*, p. 62)

The language used in these passages is familiar from descriptions of female adornment and perhaps scathingly of homosexual mannerisms. Flugel refers to 'The Great Masculine Renunciation', that is, the adoption of clothing for men from the nineteenth century onwards which precludes any element of narcissism (1930). However, the descriptions here run counter to dominant dress codes for men in the period. In some ways, the familiar male body is made strange and, like the concept of the uncanny in fantastic literature, it 'uncovers what is hidden and by doing so, effects a disturbing transformation of the familiar into the unfamiliar' (Jackson, 1981, p. 65). It is this suggestion of cross-dressing that will be explored further.

This element of cross-dressing is a feature of *These Old Shades*, where the Duke of Avon discovers and 'buys' Leon from his bullying brother. Leon is later revealed to be Leonie, who, having aristocratic lineage, was exchanged at birth for a boy to ensure a claim to a title. Leon/Leonie spends most of the time dressed as a boy, initially acting as Avon's page, and preferring the freedom offered by adopting a male identity. A more complex working of this theme is in *The Masqueraders* (1928) where Robin and Prudence Merriot enter polite society as Kate (Robin) and Peter (Prudence). Kate/Robin is a flirt; his/her unseemly ogling of an elderly gentleman is remarked upon, alongside lengthy descriptions of his creamy white skin, clothing and make-up (*ibid.*, pp. 38–42). There are also references to his almost instinctual ability to use a fan and to curtsey: 'he might have been born to it. His curtseys were masterpieces of grace; the air with which he held out a hand to young gallants so consummate a piece of artistry that Prudence was shaken with silent laughter' (*ibid.*, p. 42).[1]

While both texts remind the reader that the protagonists are cross-dressing (and the heroes *always* know/guess the gender identity of the female object of their desire), there is a sense of gender roles not being as rigid as other discourses of the period might suggest. As Epstein and Straub argue, there are possible challenges to binary oppositions in terms of sexuality:

> since gender definitions offer one of the primary differentiating principles by which binary structures are socially initiated and maintained as hierarchical relations, ambiguous gender identities and erotic practices such as those manifested in transvestism, transexualism, and inter-sexuality offer a point at which social pressure might be applied to effect a revaluation of binary thinking. (1991, p. 4)

There is an element of gender as performance, or as parody. Certainly, in order for the protagonists to act their parts, they have to negotiate and challenge the male active/female passive opposition, thus blurring boundaries further.

Narrative closure inevitably restores the status quo, however. Moreover, Strayer does argue that cross-dressing is not automatically a radical stance 'since the device may be used to confirm the most conservative conviction that gender identity should correspond with biological body'(Gaines and Herzog, 1999, p. 26). Socially defined characteristics relating to masculinity and femininity are constructed and reconstructed via the protagonists, but, as Place comments in relation to women in *film noir*, 'it is not their inevitable demise we remember but rather their strong, dangerous, and above all, exciting sexuality' (1978, p. 36; see also Harper, 1987). Further, if foppishness conceals an essential masculinity, some characteristics are also indicated as being learnt – the character Leon/Leonie, having spent most of her life dressed or masquerading as a boy, has to be taught how to behave as a lady; Kate/Robin is instructed by his sister; Prudence/Peter is initiated into the 'male arts' by her father and brother.

I would argue, therefore, that there is a fluidity in relation to gender and sexual identity in these narratives. Clothing can be used to disguise and conceal biological characteristics, allowing for both the parodying of, and performance of, other gender identities. This concealment does, of course, draw attention to that which is being hidden: the physical or biological characteristics of the hero/heroine. In reading both *These Old Shades* and *The Masqueraders* I spent much of my time wondering and worrying how the female characters coped in the world of the 'other' handling basic functions, dealing with menstruation, etc. It may be that our greater familiarity today in terms of the more readily available display and consumption of cross-dressers, transvestites and drag queens (in films like *Tootsie, Birdcage* (*La Cage aux Folles*), and the infamous Levi's advert with Ru Paul changing in the back of a taxi, etc.) may have deconstructed some of the mystery, but it gives me pause for thought as to its possible consumption in the period of publication.

This fluidity in relation to gender and sexual identity, with gender as performance, is further exemplified by masking (at for example the masked ball) and other acts of concealment in various texts. In *The Masqueraders* Robin, against his sister's wishes, adopts his male identity to attend the masked ball as 'The Unknown' in order to flirt with his daytime friend, Letty, who is unaware of his 'true' identity, transgressing moral codes by kissing her. Horatia in *The Convenient Marriage* (1934) attends a ridotto at Ranelagh, aware that public ridottos 'were looked upon by the select as very vulgar masquerades' (p. 116). She conceals this from her husband, unaware of his knowledge of her attendance. He impersonates another character, plays cards with her in a closed room for a lock of hair, and steals a kiss.

These activities relate to those of carnival, analysed by Bakhtin in *Rabelais and His World* (1984), where he refers to images of inversion and of world-upside-down. Bakhtin argues for the importance of masking in carnival, to 'loosen any fixed daily identity, to enjoy identity as fluid and open, changing and changeable' (Docker, 1994, p. 179). It rejects 'conformity to oneself' and permits 'a play with identities' (*ibid.*, p. 180). Thus in *The Convenient Marriage* Horatia can challenge both the social mores of the society she lives in, and the expressed wishes of her husband who refused to escort her with the warning 'it won't be a very genteel affair you know' (p. 116).

Bakhtin notes that following rites of carnival and masking, hierarchy is restored. However, he also argues that what has been seemingly out of control remains disturbed and changed.

Forbidden places

Thus whilst Heyer's texts indicate points of resistance to dominant forms in relation to gender roles, they also suggest a merging or collapsing of boundaries in relation to the public and private spheres. This issue of women and space in relation to the transgressive possibilities the texts construct ties in with the oral history interviews I conducted with women now in their seventies and eighties, about their lives in the inter-war period.

Nava has argued that women in this period had increased access to public spaces through consumption (1996). Elizabeth Wilson refers to the existence of ladies-only dining-rooms: 'rest rooms and refreshment rooms in department stores had all transformed the middle and lower-middle class woman's experience of public life' (quoted in Nixon, 1996, pp. 66, 67). My own interviewees placed greater importance on the consumption of leisure activities *outside* the home: the most popular activity cited was dancing (cinema, music hall, theatre and reading followed). Whatever the circumstances at home, these offered the opportunity to move outside of both the domestic and work routine. Their comments also suggest, as in masking, that other aspects of their identity could find expression in such leisure activities.

One of my interviewees, Peggy, informed me that her love of dance, particularly tap, was reinforced or developed by seeing Fred Astaire and Ginger Rogers in *Top Hat*. She would often imitate them and subsequently put on a show for family and neighbours. Other interviewees spoke of the opportunity to escape. Dorothy recollected that 'we used to go to the Regent in Hove . . . all lit up and that, sparkling. We used to go every Tuesday.' She added that, later, it was her only opportunity to be alone with her fiancé. It was a source of wonderment, fantasy, escape and glamour. Like the department store it was 'an anonymous yet acceptable public space [which] opened up for women a range of new opportunities and pleasures' (Nava, 1996, p. 52). The dance hall offered a similar space, regulated and unsupervised, a place to meet friends. Giles refers to the enjoyment reported by one of her interviewees: 'it was a mixture of excitement, danger, the pleasures of potential romance and the glamour of the dance hall' (1995a, p. 126).

Similar opportunities are offered within Heyer's texts, and take the idea of access to public space further to explore its transgressive possibilities. What the examples of masking indicate is a space where dominant moral codes might not be strictly adhered to, places which are vulgar and not genteel. The texts also extend this to explore areas of female and male sexuality. In *These Old Shades*, Leon/Leonie when masquerading as the Duke of Avon's page (and before the Duke states his knowledge of her sex) is taken to places I can only describe as brothels (Heyer, 1926, pp. 33, 34). In terms of public/private space, the brothel is an area of the private domain. Although much of the private is usually defined as the woman's sphere, the brothel can be seen as a private male sphere that is unavailable and taboo for many women but is also a female space and a place of work, and a site of both female and male sexuality. The following is a discussion of places Leon is taken to, deemed as being 'not fitting':

> Leon's eyes sparkled mischievously.
> 'Last night I went with Monseigneur to the Maison Chourval', he said demurely.
> 'What!' Madame sank back in her chair. 'It passes all bounds!'
> 'Have you been there, madame?'
> 'I? *Nom de Dieu*, what next will you ask? Is it likely that I should go to such a place?'
> 'No, Madame. It is for the nobles, is it not?'
> Madame snorted.
> 'And for every pretty slut who walks the streets!' she retorted.
> (*ibid.*, pp. 33, 34)

While the language is coded, it quite clearly indicates areas that cannot be spoken about in wider society; but, of course, this discussion in the text of *These Old Shades* (and there are similar references in other texts) does place it within the public sphere, generating knowledge and awareness – and works to reconfirm the double standard in relation to female and male sexuality. Interestingly, there is no condemnation of either party for attending these establishments (Leon/Leonie takes great pleasure in telling her story, to provoke the more staid housekeeper) which perhaps indicates some acceptance of this area of sexuality. The way Leonie's innocence is consistently reinforced (she is usually referred to by Avon as 'child' or 'mon enfant') makes her access to this area even more transgressive of moral codes.

One further point to note, that men will be sexually active is taken for granted in the texts, with references to previous mistresses, children born 'the wrong side of the blanket', and other euphemisms. These are areas acknowledged by the heroines in the texts – whilst their actual sexual (virginal) innocence is assured, their knowledge and awareness are also made explicit. The desire is for a sexually experienced man – there is often a younger, inexperienced suitor who is rejected – as the women in the novels, many in their teens, marry men much older than them, men with a past. Sexologists in the period were arguing the need for men to have the skills to initiate women into sexual responsiveness, for example, Van de Velde (1928) thought it up to the man to 'woo' his wife into sexual responsiveness, urging men on to ever greater virtuosity and resourcefulness in manipulating women to 'concert pitch' in pre-coital 'preliminaries' (Segal, 1994, p. 86). Evidently it is the man with a past who has the prerequisite skills.

There are further examples within Heyer's novels of the inversion of public and private space. Care of the clothes worn by the male protagonists and maintenance of the male body are invariably undertaken by the valet:

> Jim Salter folded one of my lord's waistcoats and placed it carefully in an open valise, then he picked up a coat and spread it on the bed preparatory to folding it in such wise that no crease should afterwards mar its smoothness . . . [he] laid the coat tenderly in the valise, coaxing it into decorous folds. (*The Black Moth*, p. 144).

The language again is that of the feminine, and there is a sense of pleasure in his duties, hinting at a wifely concern. As stated earlier, this caring role is a feature of the period, though the stress on home and domesticity was not necessarily seen as confining (Light, 1991, p. 113). However, while in some ways perhaps an instructional voice, that the carer here is a man is an interesting inversion, and may also offer space for other pleasures and desires in terms of personal fantasy. In this respect, and using Chodorow's psycho-analytic theories of female development, Radway argues that the romantic narrative articulates the reader's desire for nurturance, it legitimizes her pre-Oedipal wish to recover the primary love of her initial caretaker (1986). Through narrative strategies and the actions of the hero she states, 'the romance's conclusion promises her that her needs for fatherly protection, motherly care, and passionate love will be satisfied perfectly' (*ibid.*, p. 149). Here the fantasy for nurturing is not solely placed on the hero but is also transferred on to other (male) characters, and extends further into the private sphere.

Feel me, see me, touch me . . . ?

Sally Alexander argues that in this period there is an 'emotional economy' in respect of women's discussion of sexual knowledge and discussion of their own bodies and sexuality (Alexander, 1996). I would argue that this is displaced and finds some expression via the articulation of desire through other sensual pleasures. Returning, therefore, to the detailed descriptions of fine dress, fabrics, furs and jewels, there is a further area of fantasy and consumption which could provide another source of erotic pleasure, one which is specifically tactile. Beatrice Faust argues that women have a highly eroticized sense of touch, referring to women's fashion as serving both epigamic display (that is to attract a mate) as well as meeting a more personal, almost narcissistic hunger – women's pleasure in haptic stimulation: 'fashions are for men to look at and women to feel' (1980, p. 53). She states that 'perfumes, slinky underwear, furs and rich fabrics, corsets and shoes probably give women as much erotic charge as pornography gives men' (*ibid.*, p. 51), and that these may even have been fetishes for some women (*ibid.*, p. 48).[2] When discussing the Bon Marché department store in Paris, Miller refers to a woman alleged to obtain more 'voluptuous sensations' from the feel of silk than her lover (Miller, cited in Nava, 1996, p. 59). Nava also comments on the 'sensuous' display of goods within the store (*ibid.*, p. 59). Women I interviewed referred to their love of fabric and fashion: Joan would dream of working in a local department store amongst the fabrics (and not going to business school as her father wanted) liking the organdie used to make her clothes, while June enjoyed working in Webb & Walker's fabric shop in Colchester 'because it [the material] was soft and lovely I suppose. I never thought of it as being harsh. Always soft, not like now in leathers'.[3]

Faust's suggestion that fabrics, etc., may have been fetish items for some women is an interesting one, but not one to investigate further here. However, what I do want to develop is the idea of fetishism, fetishism as disavowal. Fetishism in relation to representation involves the substitution of an 'object' for what cannot be seen, 'for some powerful but forbidden force', Hall stating 'disavowal is the strategy by means of which a powerful fascination or desire is both *indulged* and at the same time *denied*. It is where what has been taboo nevertheless manages to find a displaced form of representation' (Hall, 1997, p. 267; emphasis in original). While reference is made in Heyer's texts to the body of the hero, his physical size (broad shoulders, fine legs, etc.), attention is displaced on to their clothing, this becoming eroticized, and invested with a desire which cannot find expression elsewhere. It is also displaced on to other objects such as fans or snuff boxes, attention being drawn to the male protagonist's fine white hands, dextrous manipulation of the fan, snuff box or other object – which could, of course, be the source of erotic pleasure.

An example from *Devil's Cub* (1932) illustrates this idea of displacement and disavowal. The text also involves concealment and deception. The heroine Mary Challoner impersonates her sister Sophia, who had planned to run away with Lord Vidal, believing that when he discovers the substitution he will lose interest:

> She [Mary] glanced up at him fleetingly, but dared not keep her eyes on his. 'You need not think, my lord, that you can seduce Sophia so easily. She led you on finely, did she not? But when she found you'd no thought of marriage, she determined to teach you a lesson!'
>
> 'Marriage!' he said, and threw back his head and laughed, 'Marriage! By God, that's rich!'
>
> Her cheeks were stained crimson. His laughter had a jeering, wicked ring; he looked like a devil, she thought.
>
> He let her go all at once, and cast himself down in a chair by the table. The murderous look had left his face, but in his half-closed eyes was a gleam that alarmed her more. The man meant mischief. His glance stripped her naked. Her cheeks grew hotter, and she saw then an ugly smile had curled his thin lips. His very attitude, while she stood, was an insult. He lounged at his ease, one leg stretched out before him, a hand driven deep into his breeches pocket. (Heyer, 1932, pp. 91, 92)

It is interesting to consider where the gaze is invited to rest in this extract – in relation to both male and female protagonists – but denies or avoids actual focus: her 'crimson cheeks', his lounging, 'one leg stretched before him', etc. This section also goes on to say:

> she had an impulse to run from him, and curbed it. She was swept off her feet and dumped down, none too gently, on a chair by the table. A heavy hand on her shoulder kept her there. 'You elected to come with me,' the Marquis said, 'and by God you'll obey me, if I have to lay my whip about your sides!' (*ibid.*, p. 92)

This particular plot also raises one further and final issue. Like Leon/Leonie in *These Old Shades*, the heroine is here placed in a situation where sex is a possibility (Vidal makes advances and is shot by Mary). Although the plot returns the participants to the status quo, without a direct challenge to the direct moral codes (they marry, of course), it does once more, returning to Jackson's comments, indicate a point of absence or loss, or disorder and possible illegality. It offers the frisson of danger, the possibility of what Erica Jong refers to as the 'zipless fuck' – sex (with a stranger) free from the restraint of social codes (Jong, 1967). That both these particular examples take place in

France (associated in popular discourses with more relaxed moral codes, or as a site where these can be expressed) adds, I would suggest, to both the disavowal and distancing of sexuality. It is both indulged and denied, particularly in a period when more explicit references to sexuality in popular texts were not a feature. Once again, it can open up a space for fantasy for the consumer, one, however, which she controls.

Conclusion

As previously stated, women's consumption of popular fiction has been viewed in negative terms. However, following Radway and other feminist writers on women's genres, I have argued that the act of reading for women can be seen as both an everyday activity, and as part of their 'escape' from routine, sometimes a 'snatched pleasure'. Further, following Light, within a period where emotional restraint characterizes representations of identity, with anti-romanticism being a feature, I have argued that Heyer's texts can offer a space for private consumption which could be transgressive and/or challenging to moral codes. Heyer's texts place women in spaces/situations outside the norm with the possibility of playing with identities outside the domestic sphere. Further, while histories argue it was expedient for women to construct themselves as prudent, realistic and restrained, and the writings of sexologists (amongst others) reinforce binary oppositions of gender and sexuality, within popular culture it is possible to see sites of challenge and contradiction to the stereotypes being represented. The references to cross-dressing can present scope for different readings: the adoption of male attire by women, certainly in *These Old Shades*, extols the freedoms this male identity offers, while the richness of detail in relation to male attire suggests a range of sensual pleasures. Gender in these texts is not fixed and suggests performance, parody and fluidity, whilst fetishism manages to embrace the contradictions of denial and indulgence, acknowledging the absent, the disordered and the illegal, and allowing the space for personal fantasy. It is also interesting to speculate how far and indeed whether the status quo is totally restored following disturbance and disorder.

Notes

1. Kathleen Bell refers to *These Old Shades* and *The Masqueraders* as examples of female cross-dressing, and to other novels and instances of cinematic cross-dressing in the period (Bell, 1995, p. 153). My thanks to jay Dixon for

providing references for further research in Mills & Boon which also include examples of both female and male cross-dressing.

2. That these pleasures solely apply to women I think is extremely debatable, but there is not the space to pursue this here. It is interesting to speculate on this aspect in relation to male readers.

3. Joan's body language and hand movements when describing her wish to work amongst fabrics I would also describe as quite sensuous.

References

Adorno, T. (1976) *Introduction to the Sociology of Music*. Translated by E. B. Ashton. New York: Seabury Press.

Adorno, T. and Horkheimer, M. (1979) *Dialectic of Enlightenment*. London: Verso (first published 1947).

Aiken Hodge, J. (1985) *The Private World of Georgette Heyer*. London: Pan.

Alexander, S. (1996) 'The mysteries and secrets of women's bodies: sexual knowledge in the first half of the twentieth century'. In M. Nava and A. O'Shea (eds), *Modern Times: Reflections on a Century of English Modernity*. London: Routledge.

Bakhtin, M. (1984) *Rabelais and His World*. Bloomington: Indiana University Press.

Beauman, N. (1989) *A Very Great Profession*. London: Virago.

Beddoe, D. (1989) *Back to Home and Duty: Women Between the Wars*. London: Pandora.

Bell, K. (1995) 'Cross-dressing in wartime: Georgette Heyer's *The Corinthian* in its 1940 context'. In P. Kirkham and D. Thoms (eds), *War Culture: Social Change and Changing Experience in World War Two*. London: Lawrence & Wishart.

Bourke, J. (1994) *Working Class Cultures in Britain 1890–1960: Gender, Class and Ethnicity*. London: Routledge.

Costello, J. (1985) *Love, Sex and War 1939–1945*. London: Collins.

Docker, J. (1994) *Postmodernism and Popular Culture: A Cultural History*. Cambridge: Cambridge University Press.

Epstein, J. and Straub, K. (eds) (1991) *Bodyguards: The Cultural Politics of Gender Ambiguity*. London: Routledge.

Faust, B. (1980) *Women, Sex and Pornography*. Melbourne: Melbourne House.

Flugel, J. (1930) *The Psychology of Clothes*. London: Hogarth Press.

Gaines, J. and Herzog, C. (1990) *Fabrications: Costume and the Female Body*. London: Routledge.

Geraghty, C. (1991) *Women and Soap Opera: A Study of Prime Time Soaps*. Cambridge: Polity.

Giles, J. (1995a) *Women, Identity and Private Life in Britain 1900–1950*. London: Macmillan.

Giles, J. (1995b) '"You meet 'em and that's it": working class women's refusal of romance between the wars in Britain'. In L. Pearce and J. Stacey (eds), *Romance Revisited*. London: Lawrence & Wishart.

Greer, G. (1970) *The Female Eunuch*. London: Pandora (1972 edition).

Hall, S. (1981) 'Notes on deconstructing the popular'. In R. Samuel (ed.), *People's History and Socialist Theory*. London: Routledge & Kegan Paul.

Hall, S. (1997) 'The spectacle of the "Other"'. In S. Hall (ed.), *Representation: Cultural Representations and Signifying Practices*. London: Sage.

Harper, S. (1987) 'Historical pleasures: Gainsborough costume melodrama'. In C. Gledhill (ed.), *Home Is Where the Heart Is*. London: BFI.

Havelock Ellis, H. ([1955]1933) *Studies in the Psychology of Sex*. New York: London House.

Hughes, H. (1993) *The Historical Romance*. London: Routledge.

Jackson, R. (1981) *Fantasy: The Literature of Subversion*. London: Methuen.

Jong, E. (1967) *Fear of Flying*. London: Panther.

Leavis, Q. D. (1932) *Fiction and the Reading Public*. London: Chatto & Windus (1978).

Light, A. (1991) *Forever England: Femininity, Literature and Conservatism Between the Wars*. London: Routledge.

Modleski, T. (1982) *Loving with a Vengeance: Mass-produced Fantasies for Women*. London: Methuen.

Nava, M. (1996) 'Modernity's disavowal: women, the city and the department store. In M. Nava and A. O'Shea (eds), *Modern Times: Reflections on a Century of English Modernity*. London: Routledge.

Nixon, W. (1996) *Hard Looks*. London: UCL Press.

Place, J. (1978) 'Women in film noir'. In E. Ann Kaplan (ed.), *Women in Film Noir*. London: BFI.

Radway, J. (1987) *Reading the Romance*. London: Verso.

Segal, L. (1994) *Straight Sex: The Politics of Pleasure*. London: Virago.

Weeks, J. (1985) *Sexuality and Its Discontents*. London, Routledge.

Primary sources

Heyer, G. (1923) *Powder and Patch*. London: Pan (1959).

Heyer, G. (1926) *These Old Shades*. London: Pan (1956).

Heyer, G. (1928) *The Masqueraders*. London: Mandarin (1991).

Heyer, G. (1929) *The Black Moth*. London: Pan (1965).

Heyer, G. (1932) *Devil's Cub*. London: Pan (1979).

Heyer, G. (1934) *The Convenient Marriage*. London: Pan.

Hughes, H. (1993) *The Historical Romance*. London: Routledge.

Stopes, M. (1918) *Married Love*. London: A. C. Fifield.

Van de Velde, Th. (1928) *Ideal Marriage: Its Physiology and Technique*. London: Heinemann.

Interview with June Coe, 16 February 1995.

Interview with Peggy Hyde, 19 January 1995.

Interview with Joan Mackney, 4 January 1995.

Interview with Dorothy Smith, 24 February 1995.

7. 'A Material Girl'? Adolescent girls and their magazines, 1920–1958

Penny Tinkler

In 1959 Mark Abrams (1961) heralded the emergence of the 'teenage consumer' as a by-product of the economic climate of post-war Britain.[1] Post-war teenagers, he argued, were more affluent than their predecessors and constituted a special group of consumers with particular leisure and spending habits. This assumption has been challenged in recent years as historians and sociologists have begun to investigate the consumerism of young people prior to 1950 (Alexander, 1989; Tinkler, 1995). In an exploration of the lifestyles of young wage-earners in Britain, David Fowler (1995) points to continuities in the consumerism of young wage-earners pre- and post-World War II and argues that the teenager and a youth market actually emerged in the inter-war period. Fowler points to the production and circulation of films targeted at youth, the opening of dance halls catering exclusively for the teenage worker, and the appearance and proliferation of magazines for young wage earners that 'brimmed' with advertisements. Although Fowler attaches significance to magazines and advertisements as indicators of the emergence of a youth market, he actually says very little about them and he does not differentiate between magazines produced for girls and for boys.

This chapter aims to shed further light on this matter by addressing the ways in which magazine publishers and editors constructed girls as consumers and attempted to establish a youthful female market in the period between 1920 and 1958. Although publishers and editors worked hard to create specific consumer identities for adolescent girls, it would be wrong to present girls as passively accepting them. Reading patterns suggest that girls had their own consumer agendas which editors were compelled to address. Although, as I shall argue, Fowler is right to emphasize continuities and to stress the significance of girls' magazines as markers of youthful female consumption in the inter-war period, a close examination of girls' magazines and their readers reveals a more complex and interesting picture of youth markets and the construction of girls as consumers than he suggests.

Money to spend

Publishers of periodicals exhibited an early appreciation of the consumer power of adolescents. They were amongst the first to recognize the commercial possibilities of 'girls' as distinct from 'children' or 'women' (Tinkler, 1995). Between 1920 and 1958, periodical publishers were one of the most enthusiastic and persistent wooers of girls as consumers. This fact is reflected in the proliferation of magazines targeted at working-class and middle-class schoolgirls, as well as young workers in factories, business and professional training.

The emergence of the adolescent 'girl' as a consumer identity within the periodical press can be attributed to a number of inter-related factors, most notably publishers' recognition that girls had disposable income; the spending power of working girls had been acknowledged from the 1890s, but that of schoolgirls was not tapped until the 1920s.[2] Whilst it was the norm to pay 'keep' once earning, young workers usually had some pocket money or 'spends'. In contrast, 'stay-at-home' girls, who did not go out to work, remained dependent on parental generosity for their 'spends', although boyfriends usually financed joint leisure activities. It is difficult to generalize about the amount of spending money which girls received as it varied considerably, even amongst girls in similar circumstances. Moreover, the level of disposable income was not equivalent to levels of spending; once girls started courting seriously they often started to save for getting married and setting up a home (Rowntree and Lavers, 1951, pp. 112, 118). Joan Harley's survey of young people's leisure in Manchester in the 1930s found that amongst a group of 108 girls aged between 14.5 and 19 years, drawn from a predominantly working-class area, the level of weekly 'spends' ranged from 6d to 6s.6d; on average, girls received roughly 2s.3d pocket money (cited in Davies, 1992). Considerable variation also characterized the pocket money of a group of Birmingham girls surveyed by Reed in the late 1940s (Reed, 1950, p. 38): 16-year-olds received 5s to 35s pocket money a week, roughly 11s on average, and 18-year-olds received 3s to 50s and an average of 21s 6d. According to Abrams (1961, p. 3), teenage girls spent an average of 54 shillings a week in 1954. However, as Reed's figures suggest, one needs to be cautious of generalizing about teenage spending from this average, particularly as it incorporated young women aged between 15 and 25 years. Age was an important determinant of disposable income: girls of 14 and 15 might hand over their wage packets to their mothers in return for a few pennies, but girls of 16 and older were more likely to insist on keeping more of their earnings (Fowler, 1995, p. 98). The period between leaving school and getting married was, nevertheless, a relatively prosperous stage in the life course for most young women in paid employment pre- and post-World War II (Fowler, 1995, pp. 94–8).[3]

While numerous contemporary surveys cited evidence of the spending money available to working girls, less information is available about the pocket money of schoolgirls. This was because schoolgirls' consumption practices were not seen to constitute a social problem as was the case with their wage-earning sisters. Evidence does, however, confirm that schoolgirls of all ages had small amounts of pocket money but that schoolgirls of 14 years and over received significantly less than their working counterparts. For example, in contrast to the average 11s 'spends' of young working girls aged 15 to 17 years recorded by Reed in the late 1940s, the average pocket money of Birmingham schoolgirls aged 15 to 17 was roughly 4s a week (Reed, 1950, p. 38).

Attention to working girls and schoolgirls as consumers was also related to the development of commercial publishing and the increasingly competitive pursuit of new markets. Inter-related with this, however, was the emergence of a recognizable 'girl' with interests distinct from children and women. The introduction and extension of compulsory schooling during the late nineteenth century and early twentieth century, and the increased prevalence of paid work before marriage for adolescent girls from all social classes, were important factors. Publishers were, however, implicated in the construction of the 'girl'.

Reader identities

Periodical publishers constructed 'girls' as consumers by first demarcating them as a group of readers with separate needs from 'children' and 'women'. By 1920, most publishers had segmented the girl market and acknowledged two key categories of 'girl' consumer – the 'schoolgirl' (10/11–15 years) and the 'working'/'modern' girl (15–20 years); the latter was more commonly described as a 'teenager' after 1950. Key to the differentiation and segmentation of publishing for 'girls' was the creation of a range of youthful female identities and, implicit in these, different types of consumers. These identities were conveyed through the texts but also, importantly, through visual images which were a staple of girls' magazines throughout the period but of particular import in 1950s magazines which featured comic-strip fiction.

Papers which targeted schoolgirls prior to 1950 divide into two types along social class lines – elementary schoolgirl papers and secondary schoolgirl papers. Elementary schoolgirl papers clearly conveyed the schoolgirl identity of their intended readership in their titles – *Schoolgirls' Weekly, Schoolgirl, School Friend*; in their editorial addresses such as 'Notes in Class' (*Schoolgirls' Weekly*); and in their regular articles such as 'Out of school hours' (*Schoolgirl*). Fiction dominated these magazines and reinforced this identity; the most popular stories were set in schools featuring 13- and 14-year-old heroines. Although these papers principally addressed working-class readers, who constituted the bulk of schoolgirls, it is likely that, in view of commercial objectives, publishers sought to attract as wide and large an audience as possible. Secondary schoolgirl papers similarly heralded the schoolgirl status of their readers. Their schoolgirls were presented as interested in entertainment as well as education and they were depicted as having the inclination and the access to resources necessary to pursue a broad range of hobbies and physical activities both inside the home and outdoors. A clearly demarcated schoolgirl identity differentiated by class remained a feature of post-war papers for schoolgirls such as *School Friend, Girls' Crystal* and *Girl*.

Working girls' identities were similarly cross-cut by class. Prior to 1945 there were three types of paper which explicitly addressed adolescent working girls – business girls' magazines (working-class/lower-middle-class), millgirl papers (working-class) and monthly magazines (upper-working-class/middle-class). Readers of all these papers were usually described as 'modern girls'; they were assumed to have traded full-time schooling for (temporary) paid employment, and replaced girl friends with boyfriends. Paid work was key to reader identities, and this was conveyed through articles on how to behave and dress for work, fiction which featured romantic encounters in the workplace, descriptions of readers and heroines as workers and occasional editorial addresses: 'Not so very long ago', claimed the editor of *Peg's Paper*, 'I was a millgirl, too' (5 May 1919, p. 1). Although young wives and 'stay-at-home' girls were occasionally mentioned, it is clear that these readers were not the magazines' primary concern. Modern girls occupied a twilight zone between child and woman. On the one hand, the modern girl was expected to aspire to marriage and motherhood, but this was not presented as her current reality. On the other, she was deemed too old for the tomboyish romps of childhood.

Following World War II, publishers and editors continued to work with two principal consumer groups – the schoolgirl and working girl, but post-war papers increasingly referred to working girls as 'teenagers'. *Woman's* 'Teen Page', which principally addressed upper-working-class and lower-middle-class readers, offers an illuminating insight into teenage identity. Interestingly, the paper both welcomed teenagers into the world of women using the analogy of female kinship, while at the same time it described them as constituting a special interest group:

> We don't like the idea of the under-twenties being bundled off to a paper of their own – any more than we'd like the idea of our teenage sisters at home being excluded from the living-room where the grown-up world of family life goes on.
>
> Teenagers live in the world like the rest of us, and are always warmly welcome to the pages of this magazine, which seeks to reflect and share the interests, problems and ideas that go to make the grown-up world of women.
>
> But since *Woman* likes to make a special corner for specially absorbing interests of womanhood – like marriage, babies, cookery and clothes – we are now . . . glad to start TEEN PAGE – the special section for those absorbed in becoming women. (2 July 1949, pp. 14–15)

Woman was quite clear that teenagers required special treatment because of their age, and in its first 'Teen Page' it promised to discuss 'the teenage angle on beauty, clothes, boy friends and personality' (2 July 1949, p. 15). Teenage readers were even allocated a 'personal friend and adviser' to whom they could write. This 'teenage angle' was necessary because the reader was 'Not a child, too young for make-up. Not a grown-up woman, who needs a full range of cosmetics – but Miss Teenager, a very special, very individual person' (*ibid.*, p. 14). Helen Temple, the magazine's beauty adviser, further explained that 'teenagers need separate beauty articles because their problems are quite different from those of their older sisters' (*ibid.*, p. 14). Pursuit of an identity was another defining feature of the teenager and psychological insights into the transitions of adolescence were drawn upon to explain aspects of the reader's needs and behaviour including her desire to experiment with lipstick: it's 'marvellous to feel that you're expressing yourself as a person in your own right'. Self-discovery was also presented as a teenage characteristic:

> Learning about your self . . . is three-quarters of youth. It is usually only at the very beginning of growing up that we look closely and critically at ourselves; because at this time nature forces us to realize that we are changing from children into women. (2 July 1949, p. 15)

Growing up was defined as the 'special job' of the teenager, turning girls 'into first-class women'.

The new teenage magazines of the late 1950s, which were aimed principally at working-class readers, were less articulate about the specific characteristics of teenagers than was *Woman*. It is clear, however, that teenagers were still expected to be working and courting like their pre-war counterparts. Leisure dominated the fiction and articles, and dancing and listening to pop music were particularly visible markers of female youth. Whereas pre-war magazines usually presented young women alone or in male company, these papers placed greater emphasis on girls' friendships although the role of these was largely one of an aide in the task of finding a man.

Courting the youthful consumer

The construction of different reader identities was one way in which publishers aimed to target specific audiences and win their loyalty. Various strategies were also employed to make papers both appealing and as cheap as possible. Developments in printing technology enabled publishers to use more sophisticated colour; publishers of the quality monthly magazines usually had a wider palette of colour from which to adorn their covers. Free gifts of colour photographs, jewellery and various knick-knacks were also offered. The first editorial of *The Schoolgirls' Weekly* (21 October 1922, p. 2) illustrates the range of strategies which editors employed to win reader loyalty. Particular emphasis was placed on the paper meeting the readers' needs:

> Well, here we are, girls, here with a new and champion paper for all of you . . . a paper that has set itself out to entertain and keep your closest attention, to cater for your every want as regards stories.

The editor went on to reassure readers that the paper would only feature the very best of fiction and, moreover, stories 'that can apply to the lives of most of us':

> There will be thrills galore, for life is full of them; there will be the pathos that is part of our existence; there will be the dramatic moments that we either have or will have to experience.

To consolidate these promises and extend the hand of friendship, the editor encouraged girls to offer feedback on the paper and suggestions for its development:

> I want loyal readers to flock about our banner, and I want their help and advice as well as their support. . . . I am not so old-fashioned that I cannot take advice and accept help.

Typically, the editor also announced 'a magnificent free gift' – a real photo of Edward, Prince of Wales.

Consolidating consumption

While editors worked to secure the sale of their own particular magazines, they also promoted the sale of sister papers and novelettes. In this way, publishers set out to utilize specific magazine loyalties to diversify and expand their publishing markets; indeed, readers were encouraged to enlist friends into the world of magazine reading and consumption. Publishers and editors also sought to foster consumer careers. This involved establishing magazine reading habits and introducing girls to papers which they could purchase when they were older. For example, magazines for mothers often incorporated sections devoted to children's interests and girls' papers frequently appealed to readers to enlist their younger sisters. In 1949, Mary Grieve, editor of *Woman*, introduced 'Teen Page' in a bid to secure the loyalty of a new generation of women readers:

> Teen Page started in the early fifties when paper was decontrolled and new readers could be gained. During the war, circulation was severely curtailed – magazines passed between friends, younger girls seldom saw it. Teen Page was there to introduce them to the habit of magazine reading. (Correspondence, Grieve to author, 18 March 1986)

Another aspect of attempts to foster consumer careers involved introducing girls to the broader realms of consumption.

Schoolgirls, as we have seen, had very little disposable income. Editors acknowledged this and devoted space to suggestions on how to make things from a rope ladder to a comb case. Nevertheless, the middle-class monthly *Girl's Own Paper* also featured advertisements for a range of goods; the April 1941 issue featured adverts for books and booksellers, cocoa, Ovaltine, Bovril, a bike pump and headlamp shield, stamps and stamp shops, a knitting pattern, permanent wave potion, embroidery thread, skin ointment and teeth-cleaning preparations. It also featured many advertisements for various forms of further education and training which were clearly aimed at girls' parents. Schoolgirl papers for mainly working-class readers attracted much less advertising, but even in 1920 *School Friend* featured a full back-page advert for Beechams plus a small section of adverts selling patterns, leather, stamps and clothes as well as promoting a catalogue. Even if advertisers did not figure largely in working-class schoolgirls' papers, schoolgirls were nevertheless depicted in magazines as consumers of sweets, magazines, books and film. During the 1930s in particular, magazines included regular and extensive coverage of the latest films and film gossip. This served the same purpose as advertisements in that it introduced readers to the thrilling features of the latest releases and cleverly conveyed to readers that seeing these films enabled them to partake of girls' culture and, more specifically, the culture of their girls' magazine. The focus and limits of at least some of the schoolgirls' consumption are suggested by the following extract from an article entitled 'Saturday Shopping':

> When all the shopping has been completed, you can then have your look around.
>
> . . . After looking to see what's on at the cinema, perhaps you may decide to explore your local bazaar or sixpenny stores.
>
> . . . If you've been told to 'buy yourself some sweets', you'll probably be popping one or two into your mouth just now. But watch out, won't you? Don't get through them all . . . for the people at home do like just to have a glimpse of the 'little present' they gave you – and to be offered one! (*Schoolgirl*, 2 March 1940, p. 13)

It was not until the eve of World War II that the Institute of Independent Advertising Practitioners showed a specific interest in the consumption of adolescent workers; it is from this time that circulation surveys record the age composition of magazine readership. Nevertheless, prior to 1940 a number of small adverts appeared in magazines for working-class working girls. Medicinal products were commonly promoted including the infamous 'pink pills' for periods, and antiseptic/healing creams such as Zambuk which, readers were assured, would soothe their piles! Adverts for beauty enhancers were also prolific and included various facial creams, also slimming aids, nose straighteners and hair and body growth stimulators. Magazines for middle-class workers were, in contrast, crammed with advertisements. The October 1930 issue of *Miss Modern*, for example, featured 13 pages of adverts. Although working-class girls in employment were not heavily targeted by advertisers prior to 1940, editors nevertheless constructed young women as consumers in their articles and fiction; make-up, magazines, novels and the cinema all featured as important aspects of youthful female consumption. Clothes were particularly important because they embodied layers of meaning. Numerous sources testify to the change in a girl's appearance once she left school and started her first job; many women fondly remember the items of clothing bought with their first wage-packet (Alexander, 1989, pp. 256–8, 263–6). Clothes were visible markers of growing up and of becoming a woman. Dress signified sexual difference and, as girls sought to progress in the heterosexual career, this visible difference which underpinned and rationalized hetero-sexual relations became particularly pressing. Fantasy, desire and social class were also embodied in dress. Through her clothes, the young worker could identify with 'a graceful or beautiful self which both anticipated the woman she would like to become, and transcended the hard work and poverty around her' (Alexander 1989, p. 257).

Acknowledging girls' purchasing power, magazines set themselves up as consumer guides. Articles abounded on all aspects of a woman's wardrobe from how to choose the appropriate shape and colour of a hat to the details of office wear. Considerable attention was directed at educating girls to dress in appropriate ways for their employment and, in particular, persuading office and business girls to forego the pleasures of fussy clothes and jewellery in the workplace: 'Never adopt fluffy frocks or your employer may think your mind is on par with your dress' (*Girls' Favourite*, 1 April 1922, p. 194). Glamorous clothes were associated with leisure; they were also, in some cases, associated with styles of femininity which transgressed restrictive British norms. The purchase and application of make-up were another matter upon which editors felt compelled to comment. Prior to World War I make-up was primitive and improvised and widely perceived as the mark of a prostitute. Meanings shifted during the interwar years as lipstick became increasingly equated with modern femininity. However, in a manner typical of inter-war magazines, the readers of *Girls' World* were advised to use make-up sparingly; 'But girls, if you don't really need a lipstick, *don't use one*. . . . The colour of a lipstick should be the colour of the lips, then its use will not be seen' (7 March 1927). Consumer guidance was not always so explicit. Visual images of the paper's heroines, the representation of the editor and replies to readers' letters all contributed information which fostered a specifically feminine type of cultural competence – an eye for detail and for style, 'touches that tell' (*Pam's Paper*, 12 March 1927).[4]

The appearance of the 'teenager' in the late 1940s did not herald an immediate expansion of young women's consumerism although *Woman*'s 'Teen Page' explicitly related the interests of young working women to the consumption of beauty products and clothes. Post-war magazines do suggest a greater consciousness of youthful consumption, but overall these papers indicate shifts rather than transformations. Whereas pre-war magazines for young working women were ambivalent about make-up, 1950s magazines suggest that this had become more acceptable, even for young women. *Woman*'s 'Teen Page' went so far as to proclaim that the first purchase of lipstick was symbolic in gender and age terms: 'There's a certain fine, independent gesture which none of us can make more than once . . . it's the moment when we hand our money over the counter and rush home with our first lipstick' (2 July 1949, p. 14). The significance of this purchase lay in the central place it was accorded in the current construction of femininity. Ironically, this gesture was defined as a sign of independence and maturity and as an expression of individuality.

Compared to *Woman*, the new 'teenage' magazines of the late 1950s were less forthcoming about the specific consumer characteristics of young women. However, visual representations of the teenager and her lifestyle offered a graphic display of youthful female consumption and stories typically portrayed girls dressed in the most up-to-date of fashions while dancing or listening to music on the radio or record player. The proliferation of small adverts selling a range of products, especially clothes, records and record players, jewellery and cosmetics, also signalled the importance of consumerism as did the appearance in the late 1950s of a range of credit options for young readers. The odd editorial also provided explicit statements on this matter. *Valentine*, the paper which 'brings you love stories in pictures', clearly delineated the consumer identity of its readers in its opening editorial:

> The keynotes of VALENTINE are Romance . . . Youth . . . Excitement!
> Romance which lies deep in the heart of every girl. *Youth* which makes her fresh and lovely – glad to be alive and to be loved. Excitement which comes from the thrill of music, dancing and song.
>
> These are our keynotes. You will always find them in VALENTINE. Every week I will bring you lovely picture-stories inspired by the titles of the loveliest tunes in the world – the tunes we hum, that set our feet a-dancing – the tunes that bring memories of love and romance, of joy and sweet heartache. (19 January 1957, p. 13)

As the term 'keynotes' suggests, music was the organizing theme of this magazine and of other 'love comics' produced at this time. Popular 'songsters', featured in articles and photo spreads, replaced film stars as the focus of interest. The fiction, which dominated these papers, was also inspired by current hits. For example, Doris Day's 'Whatever will be, will be' provided the starting point for a two-page romance. Stories of real-life courtship and marriage featuring music stars and their partners were also regular comic strip features and contributors to these magazines were commonly associated with the music industry.

Valentine and *Roxy* offer good examples of the relationship between 1950s periodical publishing and the music industry and of what Charles Eckert

(1978, pp. 9–10, cited in Stacey, 1993, p. 182) has described as 'cycles of influence'. The link between magazine and music consumption was promoted in a number of ways. These two forms of leisure consumption were also linked via Radio Luxemburg. In 1957, for instance, *Valentine* included a regular feature by Dennis Lotis, a Radio Luxemburg broadcaster, who offered to sing requests sent in to *Valentine* on his radio programme. *Roxy* similarly included a music feature entitled 'around the turntable with Lonnie Donegan' in which Lonnie promoted 'Roxy Time', a half-hour radio slot on Radio Luxemburg which prioritized reader's interests (compèred by David Jacobs). While the shape of magazines was greatly influenced by the music industry, this was to their advantage; editors utilized the glamour and success of cultural commodities such as music to boost the appeal of their magazines.

The inter-relationship of magazines and other leisure products fostered cycles of consumption which consolidated youthful consumption. This was not specific to the 1950s (the inter-relatedness of consumption was also a feature of magazines from 1920 to 1945), but whereas the music industry dominated magazines of the 1950s, the film industry assumed centre stage in the inter-war and the war years. Cinema was a major leisure interest for girls at school and at work in the 1920s and 1930s and girls' magazines were clearly influenced by this popularity in several ways. The content of girls' magazines was affected by editors' attempts to pander to readers' interests by providing features on film and film stars (on cinema attendance, see James and Moore, 1940); *Schoolgirl*, for example, introduced a regular film gossip feature in 1931 and a 'special Schoolgirl film service, which will answer all your questions on film topics' (1 August 1931, Editorial). Editors were also compelled to offer guidance and tips on emulating Hollywood fashions. *Polly's Paper*, for example, ran a series entitled 'Fashions on the film' (1919) and the *Girl's Own Paper* (January 1940) included a feature starring Deanna Durbin, the young Hollywood singing star, modelling various outfits including her trademark, the bolero jacket. Editors also utilized the actual or perceived influence of screen idols to prescribe certain types of behaviour or demeanour and to confer status on their moral guidelines.

While consumption was consolidated in this way, it would be misleading to present magazines as only concerned with readers' purchasing power. A noticeable theme of continuity between pre-war and post-war magazines was the attention devoted to ways of 'making do'. Indeed, the role of magazines in fostering cultural competence was as important in facilitating production as it was consumption. Recognizing the limits of girls' purchasing power, magazines for working girls in the inter-war years, particularly those for working-class readers, featured regular advice on how to be fashionable on a small income, encouraged girls to budget carefully and offered tips on how to replicate the latest 'look' using initiative and domestic skills.

Like their pre-war counterparts, many readers of 1950s teenage magazines were also assumed to have limited, if regular, spending money. This was probably because these magazines principally targeted younger wage-earners rather than their older sisters. Credit options, which proliferated in 1950s magazines, were particularly suited to the teenager's purchasing power: Curry's 'handy gram' (portable record-player), for instance, could be purchased for 20 shillings plus 36 weekly instalments of 7/6. Teenage magazines also stressed the art of making do. In 'Be pretty and smart with "*Valentine*'s" fashion and beauty page', readers were told that a 'well-spent pound can look a million dollars'. Acknowledging the cost of looking modern, the author offered advice tailored to the 'teenage purse':

> We rate a clever girl as one who doesn't splurge everything on one exciting coat or dress, but remembers that she has also to wear shoes and gloves, and carry a handbag. She collects her wardrobe on a 3-year plan – buying one major item a year and leaving the rest of her clothes allowance for smaller, more frivolous things.

The author further suggested that teenagers buy adaptable clothes such as a 'black jewel-flecked pinafore' which can be worn over a shirt for work and on its own, jazzed up with beads, for social occasions (31 August 1957, p. 19).

A mind of her own

Fowler argues that the ways in which leisure entrepreneurs targeted young wage-earners during the inter-war years signalled the emergence of a youth market. The proliferation of girls' papers and the portrayal of the adolescent as a consumer within the pages of these magazines do suggest that there was a widespread appreciation of adolescents as a viable market for goods. Editors were conscious of girls as consumers. This is evident in the ways they fostered consumer careers and set out to educate girls as to the skills and knowledges of consumption, particularly with regard to leisure and dress (what clothes and shoes were available and desirable, how to prioritize shopping needs, how to choose between the variety of goods on offer, fostering an eye for detail). Although editors attempted to operate within their own frameworks of what constituted appropriate material for different groups of girls, this was always with an eye to meeting the needs of their audience, and this meant that editors were compelled to adapt their products to their readers' consumption in other areas. Crude market research based on readers' letters, sales and overheard conversations were utilized as indicators of what girls wanted. Girls' interests in the stage, film and music were all, at different times, influential in determining the content of magazines even if editors then fostered these interests and appropriated them as the business of 'schoolgirls', 'modern girls' and 'teenagers'.

However, the existence of girls' papers and representations of girls as consumers is not in itself evidence of a youthful female market. This can only be ascertained by looking at whether girls actually purchased these commodities. Readership statistics do, however, confirm that both schoolgirls and working girls were avid readers of girls' magazines prior to, and after, the war (Tinkler, 1995, pp. 59–64). However, a closer examination of the reading patterns of adolescent girls and attention to the form and fate of individual magazine titles also suggests that a youthful female market was neither stable nor clearly delineated in the inter-war years.

Reader identities in the period 1920 to 1958 were constructed along two principal axes: in relation to occupation – whether at school or in full-time paid work, and with regard to the heterosexual career – whether too young for relationships with boys, or at an age where these were paramount as a prelude to marriage and then motherhood. Although the category of 'girls' embraced a diversity of experience, they were clearly differentiated from 'women' by the fact that they were usually assumed to be unmarried, even if on the brink of marriage. Although publishers were relatively successful in establishing specifically youthful magazines, those which addressed working girls often encountered difficulties in defining their boundaries. Indeed, many of the working girls' papers which were launched in the 1920s were subsequently amalgamated into 'women's' magazines. This was partly a rationalization exercise, particularly on the eve of World War II, but it also signals that editors found it difficult to sustain a specifically youthful wage-earning identity for girls. Although the reader's status as a paid worker was distinct from that of the wife and mother who rarely engaged in full-time paid work after marriage, her perceived preoccupation with romance and heterosexual fulfilment through marriage was seen to overlap with that of older, and especially married, women. It is perhaps unsurprising that the fiction in papers for working girls and for 'women' was often very similar.

Although publishers were relatively successful in constructing a youth market, young readers were not contained by it. Girls were not passive recipients of identities constructed by editors and they refused to be defined or constrained by them. Reading surveys indicate that schoolgirls did not restrict their reading to schoolgirl papers and, in fact, regularly read magazines for working girls. This was particularly true of working-class girls (see Table 7.1).

Table 7.1 Working girls' papers and women's romance magazines read by schoolgirls in 1939 expressed as a percentage of the total number of magazines read by the age group.

Age in years	Secondary schoolgirls	Elementary schoolgirls
12+	2.3	27.1
13+	3.4	23.9
14+	3.2	30.6
15+	3.3	—

Source: Jenkinson, 1940, p. 218.

This transgression was significant because in reading working girls' magazines, schoolgirls challenged the definition of themselves as too young for heterosexual interests. Although in this respect schoolgirls pursued interests defined as inappropriate for their age, the distinction between schoolgirl and working girl was nevertheless an important one for them. Schoolgirls may have read papers for working girls, and wage-earners may have read papers for their younger sisters, but this did not mean that their interests were synonymous. Indeed, papers which attempted to cater for both groups together were rarely successful. A primary reason for the failure of these papers seems to be that they could cater sufficiently neither for the desired freedoms associated with being schoolgirls nor the passion and romance that were the usual fare of working girls. Working girls, and their schoolgirl sisters, also read magazines for older women and boys. Studies indicate, however, that girls avidly read everything in the home, but that they only regarded 'girls' papers and some women's romance magazines as their own (Jenkinson, 1940). Girls' reading patterns suggest that for most girls there were *at least* two agendas which constituted their identities – *being* a 'girl' (either at school or in paid work, involved in friendships and/or courtships), and *becoming* a woman (destined for monogamous marriage, motherhood and domesticity).

Conclusion

An examination of popular girls' magazines and their readership indicates that a youthful female consumer was around and recognized prior to 1950. However, the relationship between magazines and girls' consumption was not straightforward and the consumer characteristics of girls cannot simply be assumed from the success of girls' magazines or magazine representations of girls. Girls' magazines also reveal that there were important continuities in the construction and courting of the young consumer between 1920 and 1958. Prior to, and following, World War II, for example, magazines were shaped by an appreciation of girls as consumers of magazines and other commodities. Indeed, the promotion of cycles of consumption, spurred in part by readers' interests, was a common feature of magazines throughout the period and one which consolidated youthful consumption and the identification of consumption with girlhood. While there were continuities in the form and content of girls' magazines and their construction of the young consumer from 1920 to 1958, there were also differences; a detailed review of these is, however, beyond the scope of this chapter.

Notes

1. Abrams defined a 'teenager' as an unmarried person aged 15 to 24 years. He argued that teenage spending in the late 1950s constituted a significant proportion of total spending on certain leisure goods and services. In some markets (records, record players, cinema and other entertainments, bikes, motor cycles, cosmetics, toiletries), teenagers accounted for over 25 per cent of all consumer expenditure. In others (confectionery, soft drinks, clothing, footwear, magazines, cigarettes, books, recreation and sports goods), the teenager contributed 10 to 20 per cent of total national expenditure.
2. Fowler (1995, p. 102) erroneously claims that magazines for wage-earners 'first appeared' in the 1920s. In fact working girls' magazines were first published in the 1890s.
3. Studies suggest that on marriage, and especially after the birth of children, working-class women in particular had little, if any, personal disposable income or, indeed, leisure (Beddoe, 1989; Spring Rice, 1981).
4. Winship (1981, p. 16) discusses the role of women's magazines in cultivating the skills and knowledges of consumption in the 1950s. See also Stacey (1993), Chapter 6.

References

Abrams, M. (1961) *Teenage Consumer: Part II*. London: London Press Exchange.
Alexander. S. (1989) 'Becoming a woman in London in the 1920s and 1930s'. In G. Feldman and G. Stedman Jones (eds), *Metropolis London: Histories and Representations since 1800*. London: Routledge, pp. 245–71.

Beddoe, D. (1989) *Back to Home and Duty: Women Between the Wars*. London: Pandora.

Davies, A. (1992) *Leisure, Gender and Poverty: Working-class Culture in Salford and Manchester*. Buckingham: Open University Press.

Eckert, C. (1978) 'The Carole Lombard in Macy's window', *Quarterly Review of Film Studies*, 3, 1–21.

Fowler, D. (1995) *The First Teenagers: The Lifestyles of Young Wage-earners in Interwar Britain*. London: Woburn Press.

James, H. E. O. and Moore, F. T. (1940) 'Adolescent leisure in a working-class district', *Occupational Psychology*, 14, 132–45.

Jenkinson, A. J. (1940) *What Do Boys and Girls Read?* London: Methuen.

Reed, B. H. (1950) *Eighty Thousand Adolescents: A Study of Young People in Birmingham*. London: George Allen & Unwin.

Rowntree, B. S. and Lavers, G. R. (1951) *English Life and Labour*. London: Longmans, Green & Co.

Spring Rice, M. (1981) *Working-class Wives, Their Health and Condition*. London: Virago.

Stacey, J. (1993) *Star Gazing: Hollywood Cinema and Female Spectatorship*. London: Routledge.

Tinkler, P. (1995) *Constructing Girlhood: Popular Magazines for Girls Growing up in England, 1920–1950*. London: Taylor & Francis.

Winship, J. (1981) *Woman Becomes an 'Individual': Femininity and Consumption in Women's Magazines 1954–69*. London: Centre for Contemporary Cultural Studies: Women's Series Occasional Paper, No. 65.

8. 'Mrs Housewife and Her Grocer': the advent of self-service food shopping in Britain

Barbara Usherwood

The early growth of self-service retailing in Britain took place mainly in the food sector from the late 1940s and contributed to a minor revolution in social behaviour, most particularly amongst women, who formed the majority of customers. However, while self-service is often mentioned in overviews of post-war change, little has been done to explore the subject in depth. This chapter begins to address this neglected aspect of post-war retailing which, although rooted in the specific circumstances and rhetorics of the period, helped to establish expectations, protocols and norms which inform current shopping practices. The period examined is from 1947, when there were only 10 self-service shops recorded in government statistics and the system was likened to 'a cloud no bigger than a man's hand' (*The Grocer*, 1947, p. 5), to 1964, when there were around 13,000, selling around 30 per cent of the nation's food. The aim is to examine what the gradual move to self-service food shopping might have meant for women as consumers; it looks at how women were represented in discourses of the period, and reflects upon the extent to which this new retailing system and its associated changes could be seen as either enabling or constraining at both a personal and collective level.

The spread of self-service

American origins

Although self-service was a novel concept in post-war Britain, the act of self-selection, or choosing from an open display without the help of a shop assistant, has a much longer history. With roots in the practices of market traders, booksellers and ceramics showrooms, this method was used in the late nineteenth century as a cost-cutting alternative to counter service, notably by Frank Woolworth in the United States from 1879 and by Michael Marks in England in 1891. The term 'self-service', however, refers to a system where self-selection takes place in a much more controlled environment, one we're very familiar with today. Customers are channelled through aisles of goods, where they select items, put them into baskets or trolleys belonging to the shop and pay for them at the exit. American in origin, this system was reputedly first used in California from 1912 and, perhaps most memorably, by a shopkeeper called Clarence Saunders in his first 'Piggly-Wiggly Store' of 1916 (Towsey, 1964). It was also used in discount food warehouses during the Depression of the 1930s and, by 1946, it is said that 80 per cent of US food was sold in this way (Corina, 1948).

The adoption of self-service in Britain

Britain, along with some other European countries, followed this American example in the post-war period, although it must be stressed that the adoption of self-service was slow, highly contested and inflected by local circumstances. This shift in retailing, which helped to reshape the social practices of women as consumers, occurred as a result of negotiations and decision-making in which they played no active part. Men were talking to men in terms of *economic* investment and return, weighing up the pros and cons of change in attempts to increase sales and reduce costs.

The British government played a facilitating role in this by supporting fact-finding missions to the United States, in addition to a visit by the official 'Productivity Team' organized under the terms of the Marshall Aid agreement of 1947. As a result, 100 special building licences were offered to retailers who wanted to experiment with major structural changes to existing shops, although only 60 of these were taken up and most early conversions were on a much smaller scale. Initial conversions were more numerous in London and the south-east, although the practice was geographically widespread. The tentative nature of the shift to self-service can be partly ascribed to the economic difficulties of the post-war period and partly to the fact that many retailers were simply not convinced of its benefits. The Co-ops were the pioneers and most enthusiastic early users of this new kind of food retailing, but the well-established multiple chains[1] such as Sainsbury's, Tesco and Home & Colonial showed a varied response. New multiple chains such as Fine Fare were set up specifically to take advantage of the system in the mid-1950s when economic conditions improved and the lifting of building restrictions meant that larger 'supermarkets' could be purpose-built.[2] Meanwhile, the independent small traders who ran the bulk of British food shops were the least

Figure 8.1 The male 'expert' in a 1959 advertisement for 'The National Self-Service Advisory Bureau', a specialist section of 'The National Cash Register Company', an American firm which played an important role in persuading British grocers to convert to self-service. Reproduced with the kind permission of NCR Ltd.

enthusiastic group of all and some were positively hostile. The great majority of conversions in this sector were by members of the new voluntary alliances, such as Spar, Londis and Mace, which began to form from the mid-1950s. So if the government was taking a softly-softly approach and retailers themselves were divided on the issue, who were the prime movers in the early stages?

It was certainly in the food manufacturers' interests to have an efficient distribution system, but they weren't particularly active in the promotion of self-service, with the exception of producers of frozen foods. The people who were really *pushing* the idea were mainly American manufacturers of shop equipment who were anxious to find international markets in their own productivity drive after the war: companies such as Frigidaire, Hussman Refrigeration and, most particularly, the National Cash Register Company (NCR) (see Figure 8.1).

These firms played key proselytizing roles in the emerging discourse of persuasion circulating in the grocery trade. They were joined later by energetic managers from some of the multiples and the voluntary groups. So, while self-service may have had advantages for consumers and the larger retailers, it was certainly not promoted in response to consumer demand. Shopkeepers and shoppers alike had to be persuaded of the benefits of the new system.

Discourses of persuasion

In advertisements, booklets, trade journal articles, lectures, films and face-to-face sales pitches, retailers were given advice from 'experts': men who had been to America to see how the system worked, or men with the facts and figures, the 'know-how' and the well-designed products. They were told how to redesign their selling spaces and arrange their goods and fittings to maximize profits and minimize risks: a rational, progressive vision in which women as consumers were positioned as the irrational 'other' against which the modern, future-orientated grocers were defined. For although many shop assistants and some shop owners were women, the majority of those who made decisions about whether to convert to self-service were men. The representation of gender in the growing rhetoric of persuasion within the grocery trade both reflected and helped to perpetuate these divisions. In text and image, the power of male retailers and the male experts who advised them derived from their ability to understand and control female customers, whose supposed impulsiveness and uncertain behaviour had to be managed with care.

Meanwhile, the discourse on self-service available to consumers was rather different. There was little coverage of the topic in newspapers and women's magazines. What there was tended to be critical (e.g. *The Times*, 27 May 1964). Its representation in advertisements appeared as backdrop rather than centre stage. As for the publications of women's associations and guilds, these gave the impression that this major shift in shopping practices was hardly taking place at all: in the 1950s, the manipulative effects of advertising and the introduction of frozen foods were discussed (e.g. *The Townswoman*, July 1951), but self-service and even supermarkets were ignored. Although some retailers did carry out local opinion polls to help them decide whether or not to convert to self-service, they were discouraged by the 'experts' who thought it 'quite impossible to make customers conscious of the benefits without their having actually experienced this new way of shopping' (Towsey, 1964, p. 19). So for consumers the rhetoric of persuasion was mainly to be found inscribed in the newly designed environments of the shops themselves. Overnight or weekend conversions were common and store managers sometimes engaged in a weaning process where they would stand at the entrance to hand out baskets and explain the new system personally. A few of the larger firms also made use of printed publicity in the form of local news-sheets or leaflets.

But, if women as consumers were reactive rather than pro-active in the move to self-service, actual evidence of their reactions is fragmentary. It mainly takes the form of a handful of market research studies carried out between 1957 and 1963 on behalf of companies who sought to sell goods within the self-service system.[3] These studies give us some insight, however partial and biased, into what self-service might have meant for some women at the time, although what emerges is a highly differentiated response: something which is hardly surprising, given the wide variety of preferences and priorities motivating different people, and even the same people at different times. Although there is no space here to consider the nuances of these surveys, some of the main issues arising from them are used, along with evidence from other sources (such as trade journals and retailers' archives) to build up a picture of the rhetorics, practices and reception of self-service food retailing in which, it will be argued, the concept of choice played a significant role.

The concept of choice

The power of choice

The very term 'self-service' encapsulates something of the complex nature of the power relations within the new system. In fact, this label was patently inaccurate in that there was no service involved at all! During the inter-war period, all grocers had little choice but to compete on the basis of their levels of service because so many prices were fixed under 'resale price maintenance' regulations. A move to *self*-service challenged this painstakingly constructed service ethic; the whole point was to make shoppers do the work which had once been done by shop assistants, thereby freeing them for other tasks such as shelf-stacking and pre-packing. Customers and goods were meant to flow freely in and out of shops in a highly efficient way to save time and maximize profits. There was no place for credit facilities, time-consuming deliveries or conversations. A survey by the British Market Research Bureau indicates that some women were relieved that they 'didn't have to bother with assistants', but that others (mainly middle-class shoppers) resented the loss of status that this implied (1964, pp. 23–5).

Other women welcomed the freedoms associated with the new system. For them, self-service mobilized ideas about consumer power: the autonomy and, by implication, the personal choice involved in the act of self-selection. They could choose to shop at their own pace according to their inclination and the time available: they could speed through the aisles and gain more time for other things, or they could browse and inspect goods more carefully without the sales pressure and potential embarrassments inherent in dealing with a shop assistant (*ibid.*, p. 20).

Indeed, this notion of personal choice lies at the very heart of consumer culture. Zygmunt Bauman goes so far as to say that 'individual freedom is constituted as, first and foremost, freedom of the consumer' (1988, pp. 7–8). Certainly, links between consumer choice and individual freedom would have had a particularly emotive appeal in the West during the 'Cold War' conditions of the post-war period, when lack of political freedom in communist countries was conflated with a relative lack of choice in the shops.[4] But if this was part of the broader context within which the idea of consumer choice had currency, and if the self-service system appeared to offer choice and autonomy, it must be said that the actual scope for this was subject to limitations.

Limitations on choice

In spite of the implicit promise of autonomy, the freedom to choose was subject to a number of practical, economic and possibly psycho-social constraints. In the first place, the ability to choose between self-service and counter-service was determined by the availability of shops in any one locality and, as we have seen, this changed quite dramatically over the period in question. Second, by the mid-1960s the choice of counter-service would probably have involved a higher grocery bill and this in itself might well have reduced the options of some people, although those who could only afford very small quantities of goods were more likely to be able to buy them from counter-service shops. Third, once inside the shop, just as with counter-service, choice was limited to the availability of goods, although the number and variety of products expanded alongside the development of self-service during the 1950s as rationing was progressively abolished and production was increased. Even the smaller self-service shops could display more of these goods, giving the impression of greater choice, but the main point of difference with counter-service shops was that the selection process was apparently a *personal* one. Shoppers were on their own, locked into an individual relationship with the visual identities of goods and their environments, responding to the messages these visual cues helped to conjure up, and here the possible psycho-social limitations on choice come into play.

Shopping for food, perhaps more obviously than many other kinds of shopping, is directly related to the 'use-value' of goods in that people do need to eat. But although the use-value of commodities has played a central role in the thinking of political economists since Marx coined the term in 1857, it is their *symbolic* value which has been of central concern to those interested in consumption. Anthropologists such as Douglas and Isherwood, for example, emphasize the role of goods in 'making stable and visible the categories of culture', thereby diminishing the role of individual agency.

The housewife with her shopping basket arrives home: some things in it she reserves for her household, some for the father, some for the children; others are destined for the special delectation of guests. (Douglas and Isherwood, 1978, p. 57)

Here, different foods can be used to indicate different occasions: the birthday cake, the roast meat for Sunday lunch and the breakfast marmalade. From this perspective, the room for individual manoeuvre is limited, as the structures within which shoppers operate are culturally preordained.

Other writers emphasize the *display* function of goods and their role in communicating ideas about 'identity': this is described by Gabriel and Lang as 'a story which a person writes and rewrites about him- or herself, never reaching the end until he/she dies, and always rewriting the earlier parts, so that the activity of writing becomes itself part of the story' (1995, p. 86). However, if people use goods to tell stories about themselves, there is some disagreement about the extent to which symbolic meanings are determined by existing social structures or by the creative use of goods by individuals.

Pierre Bourdieu (1984), for instance, believes that 'taste' in food and other things not only derives from the life experiences afforded by a person's social class, education and occupation but also becomes a marker of these things. There is some scope for individual action, but only within a field of possibilities beyond which lies the unknown or unthinkable. Seen from this perspective, women as consumers and housewives were not only charged with the responsibility of feeding their families but also with the management of important cultural signifiers over which they had limited control, in spite of the apparent choices opened up by the advent of self-service.

However, there are some theorists who emphasize the potential power of individuals to appropriate and transform the symbolic meanings of goods as they buy and use them (e.g. Miller, 1987). Such a view opens up the possibility of a more active engagement with the process of shopping and calls the idea of 'consumer as victim' into question: something which has been examined in relation to feminine culture by Hilary Radner (1995).

Managing choice

Ideas about the relationship between shoppers and goods were of central concern to those who sought to predict and manage consumer choice within the self-service system. To varying degrees, their methods can be related to the theories of psychologists from two different schools of thought: the behaviourists, who assume that behaviour patterns are learned and can be changed by altering conditions or stimuli; and the psychoanalysts (the 'depth-boys' or 'motivation researchers' as they were called at that time), who believe that behaviour is informed by unconscious desires which can be understood and then connected with products in appealing ways. Both approaches were harnessed to the needs of commerce in the post-war period and helped to inform some of the practices of those who converted to self-service and the beliefs of their advisors. So how did retailers seek to control the shopping process and yet appeal to their customers? I will argue that this was done through a combination of ideas about the rationality, hygiene and modernity of these new self-service environments which helped to create subject positions for both sellers and buyers.

Rational spaces

The replanning of shop layouts was the essential first step in any conversion. Unnecessary counters[5] and fittings were replaced by wall shelving, while free-standing shelves or 'gondolas' were arranged so as to create a smooth and efficient customer flow. 'Magnets' such as frozen food cabinets or attractive displays were judiciously placed at the back and centre of shops where research studies indicated that people were reluctant to go. Some equipment manufacturers (notably NCR and Frigidaire) even offered retailers little models of shelving, fridges and checkout counters to help them redesign their interior spaces. This practice, with its very obvious connotations of power and control over customers, can be seen in relation to the planning ethos of the post-war period or, indeed, likened to the 'rats in a maze' experiments of behavioural psychologists.

With easy and full access to goods, the potential problem of shoplifting became an issue. Some retailers used low gondolas so that customers could be monitored via the manager's office or the watchful eyes of the shop assistants; others used two-way mirrors for surveillance. Most self-service grocers insisted that customers used a special open basket to collect their shopping and it was this *overt* manifestation of retailer power which appears to have been particularly badly received.[6] Indeed, one woman is even reported to have thrown her basket at Alan Sainsbury at the opening of a new

Sainsbury's branch in the early 1950s (Williams, 1994, p. 129). The basket or trolley with its open mesh not only physically allowed but also *symbolized* surveillance by implying a lack of trust, particularly when shoppers were asked to leave their own bags at the entrance, and by, as it were, thrusting an individual's private purchases into the public realm.

While shoppers were scrutinized to ensure they didn't steal goods, some retailers and their consultants also sought to monitor the ways people interacted with goods on the shelves. Product positioning and the design of packaging were, and continue to be, matters of great concern in the ongoing attempt to maximize sales. The Metal Box Company even opened its own experimental supermarket in London's Baker Street in 1957 to gather first-hand information about how customers behaved in a 'scientific' way so as to improve their own packaging design and provide a service for other interested companies (McLean, 1959). This early example of a practice which is now commonplace was very much in the manner of the American motivation researchers whose ideas were beginning to have an impact on British advertising and marketing at the time (Henry, 1958).

If customers were being encouraged and coerced to adapt to the new material conditions in self-service shops, they were also expected to adapt to new social relations. For the system to work effectively, people had to be discouraged from using self-service shops as places to stand and chat and this meant controlling the behaviour of shop assistants as well as the shoppers. In their research for a BBC series on 'Working Lives', Pagnamenta and Overy quote a shop assistant in one of the early conversions in Hull as saying, 'When self-service really got going I didn't feel such a complete person. I didn't have the job satisfaction that I'd been having as a counter assistant.' Speaking of the customers, she says, 'People didn't feel they'd done a proper morning's shopping if they hadn't had all these conversations which took up the assistant's time' (1984, p. 116). Such a loss of social interaction is likely to have contributed to the isolation of those 'non-working' women in the increasing numbers of new housing estates built in the 1950s and early 1960s where self-service grocery shops were the norm.

So here we see that the drive for rational efficiency so essential to the smooth running of the self-service system required a large measure of customer control which, in turn, reshaped the social practices of shoppers: something which was particularly significant for women, given their traditional nurturing role where food shopping plays an important part. With the self-service system, grocers were offered an image of themselves as rational beings who sought to use modern methods to increase profits, and women as consumers were offered the prospect of a rational shopping system which could increase their own efficiency as housewives. Such ideas can be related to the productivity ethos of the post-war years which encompassed the domestic sphere (Haslett, 1951; Partington, 1987) as well as the world of commerce.

There is evidence that some women responded favourably to the rational appeal of time-saving, convenience and clear price-marking (see for example British Market Research Bureau, 1964). However, the idea of the *irrationality* and impulsiveness of shoppers is mentioned frequently in the contemporary trade literature (see, for example, *The Grocer*, 1950, p. 34; *Stores and Shops*, 1954, p. 33; *Self Service Times*, 1959, p. 5). Retailers both expected and, as we have seen, sought to encourage a certain amount of impulse-buying and some women accepted this image of themselves as prone to temptation:

> You sort of learn what to get and not to get as you go. When I first went I bought more than I should, but now I get what I want and only sometimes buy an extra. Most people seem to believe you spend more and it is easy as everything is laid out . . . because they look so nice and tempting and make you want to buy. (British Market Research Bureau, 1964, p. 21)

In short, the serried ranks of accessible, neatly organized and judiciously placed goods positioned the customer as someone who was faced with visual seduction but who could learn to exercise self-control. In these new food-shopping conditions, women had to find ways of negotiating self-denial, and one possible means of doing this was to relocate the pleasures of immediate purchase offered by the self-service system around the pleasurable idea of themselves as housewives who could balance their budgets.

Hygienic spaces

If rational, orderly, scientific planning was supposed to mean the eradication of woolly thinking and cluttered shops, connections could also be made with the desire to eradicate dirt. This desire was certainly not new, but it intensified in the late 1940s, when there was a new legal dimension to issues of hygiene. Cases of dirty food shops were discussed in Parliament in 1949, leading to a new system of local inspection. Ironically, but perhaps predictably, the focus of attention was quickly transferred to women when this was reported in the trade press and beyond. Grocers were no longer presented as the offenders, but as front-line troops in the fight against grime: people who could and should educate the British housewife in matters of hygiene. As one Medical Officer of Health put it: 'The housewife is educated by the grocer. If she sees food properly taken care of, she will do the same' (*The Grocer*, 1949, p. 15). Here again we see women shoppers presented as being in need of control:

the messy, dirty 'other' against whom shopkeepers were encouraged to define themselves.

Conversion to self-service presented opportunities for retailers and customers alike to align themselves with the idea of an ongoing process of improvement by demonstrating their commitment to hygiene. Retailers began to use new fittings designed for easy cleaning and made of metal or one of the new plastic laminates rather than wood, which was thought to harbour germs. They wrapped perishables in transparent plastic to keep different kinds of food fresh and, importantly, *looking* fresh. They also altered their shop fronts to encourage public inspection. Large plate-glass windows were recommended, unobscured by posters or window displays so potential customers could see 'the clean interiors with their bright fixtures, well-lit equipment and attractive stocks on the shelves' (Hedges, 1959, p. 27). Significantly, the statement 'everything in supermarkets is very hygienic' was the one most frequently endorsed by women in the British Market Research Bureau's survey (1964, p. 58). To be hygienic was to be modern.

Modern spaces

If rationality and hygiene were elements of the version of modernity offered to consumers, so too was aesthetic change. Self-service shops were to be their own advertisements: clean, bright and orderly. A trend towards simplicity was considered at the time to be particularly appropriate for self-service shops, but it was of course part of a much wider aesthetic shift in the post-war period. Retailers were urged to abandon the flaking, 'gold-leaf glamour' of their old-fashioned lettering and include the term 'self-service' or 'supermarket' on a new, simple fascia in clear, bold lettering to suggest modernity and progressiveness (Hedges, 1959, p. 27). Such new façades provided a startling contrast to older shops on Britain's high streets but were very much in keeping with the Modernist-inspired, functionalist aesthetic of new housing estates and shopping precincts erected during the post-war building boom.

In early conversions, rational problem-solving in the Modernist mode was matched by a fairly austere aesthetic effect, partly in response to the need to suggest cleanliness. But by the mid-1950s, writers began to plead for a version of modernity which was less clinically white and impersonal (e.g. Pilditch, 1956). They suggested the judicious use of lighting, colour and decoration to evoke moods, and stressed the need to create different environments attuned to the character of each shop's neighbourhood or likely clientele: all trends which were well established in American supermarkets of the time. Indeed, there is evidence of a wide spectrum of 'buying atmospheres' as the multiple chains increased their conversion rates in the 1950s. Sainsbury's, for instance, retained a rational, simple, Modernist approach to its interior decor and no manufacturer's publicity was allowed to interfere with the orderly nature of its shop interiors. The aim was to suggest quality through its approach to design. Anthony Jackson's Foodfare, on the other hand, aimed for what was called a 'bazaar' effect, with jumbled displays of goods in 'dump baskets' and the sound of music interspersed with advertising slogans. Premier Supermarkets also opted for what was described critically as American-style showmanship: lots of manufacturers' displays, special promotions and demonstrations, music playing continuously and the inclusion of coffee bars where space allowed, 'encouraging customers to regard shopping with them as an outing' (*Sales Appeal*, May 1959, p. 41). In both practice and rhetoric, assumptions were being made about the preferences of shoppers in relation to class differences as retailers struggled to find the right kinds of atmosphere for selling their wares. For instance, in a report of the opening of a shop in a working-class district it was claimed: 'In an area of this type, there is a danger that people will shy away from a store that is beautifully decorated and scrupulously orderly' (*Self-Service*, 1954, pp. 24–5).

Modern goods on the shelves

If the symbolic meanings of shopping spaces had changed with the advent of self-service, what of the goods themselves? In the first place, there was a need for more pre-packaging of commodities such as bacon, cheese and butter to speed up the selection process, and manufacturers were quick to develop different kinds of transparent wrappings to help retailers to negotiate customer anxiety about freshness. As for branded goods, advertisers had long been weaving positive associations around branded foodstuffs via posters, magazine adverts, point-of-sale material and packaging with the aim of conjuring up appealing ideas about specific products. With self-service, there was an even greater need for 'pre-selling' goods, as the shopkeeper or assistant was no longer the end-point in the selling process. Enormous amounts of effort were put into designing packs with 'eye appeal' which would 'speak for themselves' and court the consumer by using appeals such as 'mouth-watering', 'fresh', 'food which will bring about domestic harmony', and so on. The advent of commercial television in Britain in 1955 was particularly significant here, although its audiences were relatively small in its early stages and its scope for advertising was considerably less than in the United States. TV campaigns were organized to 'turn the relaxed viewer of yesterday evening into this morning's purposeful and brand-conscious customer' (*Sales Appeal*, 1955, p. 26), perhaps most overtly through the visual prompt on packaging: 'As seen on TV'. Meanwhile, some multiple chains used more elaborate point-of-sale material or played advertising jingles to emphasize links between the TV screen and the shelf (*Sales Appeal*, 1959, p. 48).

The demise of rationing, an increase in international trade and new production methods all contributed to changes in the number and kind of foodstuffs on sale during the 1950s and early 1960s. Although not confined to self-service shops, many of these new products could be connected with the particular versions of modernity offered by these shopping spaces. For example, there was an increasing range of frozen foods, including the 'TV dinner', whose links with the new (or at least, more readily available) technologies of television and refrigeration might also have had positive connotations for some people. These products offered an image of the modern consumer as someone interested in speed, convenience and hygiene, although manufacturers had to counteract negative wartime experiences and explain the connection with hygiene in some detail (e.g. Hammond, 1951, pp. 106–7). Other convenience foods such as pre-packed and dehydrated mixes for cakes and puddings offered an 'unusual promise' to the modern woman according to the motivation studies expert, Ernest Dichter, allowing her to 'bake at home, but in an easy fashion which assures her success' (quoted in Marling, 1994, p. 227). In addition to newly designed products, customers were also introduced to a number of unfamiliar foodstuffs such as garlic, aubergines, spaghetti and pizzas as well as an increasing variety of cheeses (Ryan, 1957, p. 1). In short, women were encouraged to become more adventurous in their habits: something which Mollie Tarrant, the Head of Advertising and Research in the J. Walter Thompson Company, believed to be much easier to achieve in self-service conditions:

> the housewife can examine new or unfamiliar products without displaying her ignorance . . . she can also build up a satisfying image of herself as a housewife . . . a taste for the experimental is encouraged; the housewife can (and does) choose more lavishly as she learns to back her own judgement. (British Market Research Bureau, 1964, p. 16)

Modern skills

This aspect of food shopping has links with the concept of the consumer as an 'explorer', something which is discussed in some detail by Gabriel and Lang (1995). Writing of the 1990s hypermarket they note that:

> This jungle of consumption offers a bewildering array of goods . . . shopping for groceries turns from a habit or a rational choice into an exploration . . . of minute variations, of infinitesimal idiosyncrasies of

At Sainsbury's Self-service shopping is EASY and QUICK

1 –As you go in you are given a special wire basket for your purchases.

2 –The prices and weight of all goods are clearly marked. You just take what you want.

3 –Are you a fast shopper or a slow? You can be either when you shop at Sainsbury's!

4 –Dairy produce, cooked meats, pies, sausages, bacon, poultry, rabbits and cheese—all hygienically packed.

5 –Meat is served from Sainsbury's special refrigerated counter. Or you can serve yourself from the cabinet.

6 –Pay as you go out. The assistant puts what you have bought into your own basket and gives you a receipt.

Figure 8.2 This comic-strip guide aimed to persuade women of the ease and convenience of self-service shopping. It appeared in a free local news-sheet advertising the opening of a new branch of Sainsbury's in Lewisham in 1955. Reproduced with the kind permission of J. Sainsbury plc.

style, products, brands, signs and meanings. This type of exploration is the discourse of difference, discovery of difference, the establishing of difference and the appropriation of difference. (1995, p. 72)

Although these shops with their 40,000 products and their cavernous spaces are a far cry from the tiny self-service conversions of the early 1950s and the modestly sized supermarkets of the late 1950s and early 1960s, the skills required to negotiate them are similar. One of the characteristics of the newly designed self-service shops was an emphasis on the act of inspection: people were encouraged to look through the large windows at the visual splendour of the interiors; they could see, but not feel or smell, the quality of pre-packed goods wrapped in transparent plastic; they were hailed from all directions by signs which told them how to behave ('collect your basket here', 'pay at the checkout desk') and which directed them to various commodities; they deciphered the visual messages on packaging, specially designed for these new conditions (see Figure 8.2).

Of course, skills of inspection were by no means confined to self-service food shopping or to this period, but what self-service did help to bring about was a new intensified reliance on the visual, particularly in the form of graphic and typographic messages. Food shopping was becoming increasingly *spectacular*, akin to the experiences afforded by other kinds of shopping. The visual replaced the verbal in these environments and this in turn helped women in particular to acquire a new set of skills and competences with which they could negotiate the fast-changing world of consumption.

Conclusion

When considered in relation to the empowerment of women as consumers, the advent of self-service presents a complex picture. The agenda for change was set at a macro-economic level where the concept of productivity informed post-war business practices. Food retailers of various types were faced with difficult choices in increasingly competitive conditions and adopted self-service methods in progressively large numbers until, by the mid-1960s, the trend was perceived to be unstoppable. It has been shown how these self-service food shops were highly designed spaces, constructed in self-conscious ways following American models of practice and often in response to the well-organized marketing drives of shop equipment manufacturers. Retailers became consumers of ideas about how to manage the new system as well as consumers of material goods such as cash registers, packaging equipment, price labels, baskets, shelving systems, new lighting, flooring and decoration schemes, not to mention the increasing range of goods to put on their shelves. Within the discourse of persuasion aimed at mostly male decision-makers (i.e. the independent grocers and managers of larger firms), 'expert' advisers offered a vision of rational modernity in which the identity of 'progressive' grocers was often defined in relation to those whose behaviour they sought to manage: impulsive female consumers whose spending patterns could be controlled.

We have seen how two, sometimes conflated, models of consumption informed this discourse: a behaviourist model which positions the consumer as someone who will respond to stimuli and therefore ascribes a good deal of power to retailers; and a psychoanalytic model which requires an understanding of the motivations of consumers in order to connect these with products and their conditions of sale. The latter model assumes a slightly more balanced relationship, at least at the collective level, where assumptions about the behaviours, attitudes and taste preferences of consumers inform the decision-making process. Indeed, retailers, manufacturers, advertisers, market researchers and designers alike struggled to find the right buying atmospheres, the right kinds of packaging, the right visual tones in which to create environments where shoppers would feel comfortable.

At a personal level, the advent of self-service can also be seen as both enabling and constraining for women as consumers. On the one hand, they were required to change their shopping habits, to subject themselves to higher levels of scrutiny and to conform to a new set of expectations where the scope for social contact was greatly reduced. On the other hand, they were offered a number of practical advantages such as speed, cleanliness, convenience and lower prices which contributed to a new set of symbolic meanings centred on the concepts of improvement and a rationalized modernity, allowing women to build up 'satisfying' images of themselves as housewives (Tarrant, 1964, p. 16). The traditional nurturing role of women was not challenged but was recast for modern times. Faced with more and more goods from which to select, the modern shopper was expected and enabled to negotiate an increasingly spectacular, information-laden visual environment and to exercise self-control and judgement: in other words to become a more efficient consumer and an 'expert' in her own right.

Notes

1. 'Multiples' were defined at the time as chains of more than ten shops.
2. 'Supermarketing' originally referred to the practice of selling different kinds of food in one shop, although it soon came to mean self-service food shops of over 2000 sq. ft.

3. Surveys entitled *Mrs. Housewife and Her Grocer* were carried out for the food manufacturer, Alfred Bird & Sons Ltd., in 1957 and 1960. Southern Television published a survey entitled *The Southern Shopper* in 1963 and the findings of the British Market Research Bureau's 1961 survey for Premier Supermarkets Ltd., W.H. Smith & Son Ltd. and the advertising agency J. Walter Thompson Co. Ltd. were published as *Shopping in Suburbia* in 1964.

4. See, for example, the account of President Nixon's visit to Moscow in 1959 in Marling, 1994, pp. 243–83.

5. Counters were still needed until the final abolition of rationing in 1954, but some retailers used (and continue to use) a combination of selling methods so as not to alienate those who preferred counter-service for some items.

6. An early report in *The Grocer* (23 July 1949, p. 16) noted that while women were 'nervous' about using baskets, men were not.

References

Bauman, Z. (1988) *Freedom*. Milton Keynes: Open University Press.

Bourdieu, P. (1984) *Distinction: A Social Critique of the Judgement of Taste*. London: Routledge.

British Market Research Bureau Ltd. (1964) *Shopping in Suburbia: A Report on Housewives' Reactions to Supermarket Shopping*. London: J. Walter Thompson Ltd.

Corina, J. (1948) *Spotlight on Self Service*. Manchester: Co-operative Union.

Douglas, M. and Isherwood, B. (1978) *The World of Goods: Towards an Anthropology of Consumption*. London: Allen Lane.

Gabriel, Y. and Lang, T. (1995) *The Unmanageable Consumer: Contemporary Consumption and Its Fragmentations*. London: Sage.

Grocer, The (1947) 'Self-service trading', 18 October, p. 5.

Grocer, The (1949) 'The housewife is educated by the grocer', 22 October, p. 15.

Grocer, The (1950) 'New methods in retail trade', 12 August, p. 34.

Hammond, W. (1951) 'What are quick-frozen foods?' *The Townswoman*, July, p. 106.

Haslett, C. (1951) 'The changing attitude of the homemaker to science and scientific management', *The Townswoman*, April, pp. 58–60.

Hedges, H. J. (1959) *This Way to Self-Service*. London: Piscatorial Press.

Henry, H. (1958) *Motivation Research*. London: Crosby, Lockwood & Son.

Marling, K. A. (1994) *As Seen on TV: The Visual Culture of Everyday Life in the 1950s*. Cambridge, MA: Harvard University Press.

McLean, J. W. (1959) 'This store is a test-house', *Sales Appeal and Packaging Technology*, October, pp. 42–4.

Miller, D. (1987) *Material Culture and Mass Consumption*. Oxford: Blackwell.

Pagnamenta, P. and Overy, R. (1984) *All Our Working Lives*. London: BBC Books.

Partington, A. (1987) 'The designer housewife in the 1950s'. In J. Attfield and P. Kirkham (eds), *A View from the Interior: Feminism, Women and Design*. London: The Women's Press, pp. 206–14.

Pilditch, J. (1956) 'What's in store?' *Sales Appeal*, July/August, pp. 60–2.

Radner, H. (1995) *Shopping Around: Feminine Culture and the Pursuit of Pleasure*. London: Routledge.

Ryan, R. (1957) 'Shopping in 1957'. In *Food in Britain*, a supplement published by *The Times*, 21 January.

Sales Appeal (1955) 'Find the link', September/October, pp. 26–32.

Sales Appeal (1959) 'Self-service: whom does it concern?', May/June, pp. 36–41.

Self-Service (1954) 'Come in ladies, and serve yourselves', July, 3(7), pp. 24–5.

Self Service Times (1959) 'Importance of short gondola in planning classification for self-service selling', February, p. 5.

Stores and Shops (1954) 'Self-service and semi-self-selection: their future prospects', May, p. 33.

Tarrant, M. (1964) 'Attitudes to supermarket shopping'. In *Shopping in Suburbia*. London: J. Walter Thompson Ltd, pp. 15–36.

Towsey, R. G. (1964) *Self Service Retailing*. London: Illiffe Books.

Williams, B. (1994) *The Best Butter in the World: A History of Sainsbury's*. London: Ebury Press.

9. Decisions in DIY: women, home improvements and advertising in post-war Britain

Jen Browne

Introduction

Do-it-yourself can be seen as part of the culture of post-war reconstruction, domesticity and then late 1950s consumerism; of people building a better world in the aftermath of World War II. Achieving the ideal home was an expression of faith in the future and the total belief in dominant ideologies that characterized the 1950s, based on technological control. An indication of the growing significance of DIY can be seen in the establishment of *The Practical Householder* and *Do-It-Yourself* magazines, first published in 1955 and 1957, respectively. F. J. Camm, the editor of *The Practical Householder*, wrote, 'The "Do-It-Yourself" movement has reached such proportions today that it can only be dealt with satisfactorily by a journal entirely devoted to it' (October, 1955, p. 18). The advice to the readers included painting, decorating, making pelmets, binding books, framing pictures, making lampshades, home carpentry and metalwork. In this chapter, I shall draw upon my analysis of these magazines, research in the Mass-Observation archive and oral history undertaken in Southampton, to argue that the decision-making power of women in the 1950s enabled them to create their own style of interior with do-it-yourself home improvements, reflecting both their identities and aspirations.

The social historian, John Benson, suggests that 'there can be no doubt that consumption offered women new ways of measuring, comparing and improving social status', going on to argue 'for in so far as consumption became more important as a means of defining social status, it tended to EMPOWER women who, as has been seen so often, exercised particular responsibility over household consumption' (1994, pp. 195–7). Much of 1950s advertising tapped into this aspect of consumption by being aspirational; examples can be seen in the do-it-yourself magazines of the time, which I shall discuss below, while arguing that homes were also created as a mark of achievement as well as being rationalized and comfortable environments. Certainly, the householders I interviewed were inordinately proud of their 'improved' homes, and of the things they had made themselves.

Since the time of industrialization, consumption decisions affecting the aesthetics of the home have largely been the domain of women, but as Benson observes, 'remarkably little attention has been paid to the history of working-class women consumers'. Within the wider context of sexual politics, feminine tastes and choices do play a part, as the design historian Penny Sparke (1996, p. 7) has pointed out, and this too is an area that has received little attention from academics. My particular focus, within the area of consumption, is on material culture. This, in the form of home improvements, is also a neglected area. Do-it-yourself tended to be a working-class/lower-middle-class activity in the 1950s so this chapter goes some way towards examining one area of working-class women's consumption and addressing these inadequacies. My interest in this particular area stems both from personal involvement in improving houses, and from vague memories of my father and his friends busily making home improvements when I was a small child in the late 1950s. The larger part of my remit is to disprove the notion of the 1950s as a time of mass consumption, and the process of the incorporation of the broad working class into consumerism, by analysing one of the ordinary practices of everyday life in 1950s Britain. This has been labelled an era of grey conformism by many writers (e.g. Featherstone, 1987, p. 55) with women assigned a central role.

I am suggesting that the 1950s in Britain did not mark the arrival of mass consumer culture; my research has shown that there were shortages of materials that made home improvers into creative make-do-and-menders. 'Make-do-and-Mend' was a slogan for the government's campaign to salvage all possible materials for the war effort. Launched by the Board of Trade, this initiative remained in effect both during and after the war, increasing domestic morale as well as encouraging practical recycling by getting people to save and to salvage materials, to literally make-do-and-mend. This was, as Marwick observes, 'In many respects . . . a return to the pursuits of pre-industrial society, to do-it-yourself and make-it-yourself, to dressmaking, to jam-making, and to the horticultural pursuits of the smallholder' (1976, p. 92).

Another area for debate is whether 1950s consumers followed design advice and the 'good design'[1] guidelines emanating from government agencies as well as private companies and media. Arguably, home improvements were atypical of popular culture, which is often perceived as a form of resistance to dominant ideologies of the period. For example, the British Council of Industrial Design (COID) adopted modernist ideologies in an effort to raise standards in design, spreading its ideals. They created an establishment canon of 'good design' and a consensus of values so modernism had a hegemonic hold throughout the 1950s. Having its roots in pre-1920s architectural practice, modernism was a stylistic and ideological movement in design with an emphasis on rationalization, standardization, objectivity, functionality and hygiene. To actively promote this, the COID began publishing the magazine *Design* in 1946. However, my qualitative study of 1950s home improvements in Southampton demonstrates that women exerted considerable power over consumption within this area. This chapter explores the nature of this power within the homes of the women interviewed.

Women and post-war homemaking

My argument about DIY rests upon the supposition that in post-war Britain women were a central force in the enterprise of reconstruction which, in many respects, centred upon the home, within which definitions of male labour and female domesticity, familiar in the nineteenth century, were re-established. A discussion of women's power in general, or a more specific engagement with the debates about the effect of wartime on women's power, is, however, beyond the scope of this chapter. It is worth pointing out that Daniel Miller has suggested that women's roles had not been re-appraised during the war, and indeed the British Restaurants and the nurseries, used by working women, were shut down as soon as the war ended (Miller, 1987). During World War II, women war-workers had been subject to propaganda about the importance of their job, and simultaneously mothering and homemaking, to the nation. A crucial tool in this government propaganda was the 1942 Beveridge Report (Beveridge, 1942), later enshrined in welfare policies. Both the Beveridge Report, and the consequent construction of the welfare state – the linchpin of post-war reconstruction – emphasized women's role as domestic workers, and more specifically mothers of children for whom the post-war nation was being reconstructed.

Consistent with a domesticated version of femininity, and Beveridge's 'equal but different' role for women, was the setting up of marriage guidance and family planning agencies, with the aim of establishing the new companionate marriage (Franklin, 1989). This emphasized togetherness and the concept of women as domestic managers which was also enshrined in women's magazines of the period. According to Peter Lewis, 'togetherness was the new wonder ingredient in marriage' and 'togetherness meant more than keeping each other company, it meant that a *man*'s place was also in the home' (1978, p. 46). The term 'togetherness' was actually imported from America; it was a slogan coined by *McCall's Magazine*'s editor and publisher to boost sales, encapsulating the idea that a man and his wife shared the same life in the 1950s and were family-orientated (Mayer, 1951, pp. 188–9). This emphasis on 'togetherness' was reflected on the covers of do-it-yourself magazines, although arguably, it was a myth that women were back in the home in the 1950s, peremptorily ejected from the paid labour market after World War II. Indeed, Miller has highlighted the difficult adjustments that the post-war emphasis on women in the home involved, and argues that men's solidarity was evoked 'in opposition to femininity, men were called upon to forget their class differences and pull together to defend, among other things, their families' (1987, p. 197).

Then, as now, a tension between roles for women, as mothers and workers, can be observed, and yet the 1950s saw the increased employment of married women. They were wives, mothers, and part-time workers in Britain, and in 1957 a third of married women were working again. They were being wooed back, as teachers and nurses, because of full employment. Many of them worked only partly for the money, and Lewis suggests 'it was often better-off women who sought jobs, to escape boredom' (1978, p. 64). In spite of this, the overwhelming advertising images of the 1950s are of women as wives, mothers and household drudges, representing femininity articulated through ideologies of consumption.

In examining images of women in printed advertisements of the 1950s from *Do-It-Yourself* and *The Practical Householder* magazines, togetherness was apparent in the sharing of 'our' drill in a Wolf Cub advertisement and this brand of power tools was described as 'the family favourite' (*The Practical Householder*, 1966, p. 149). The 'do-it-yourself couple' working together to create/improve their home was also a theme of advertising. One example of this was the Marley wall tile advertisement couple who proudly announced that they had tiled their bathroom over the weekend (*The Practical Householder*, November 1956, p. 928). The home was a project to be realized, in fact, a married lifetime's project. In some cases, the couples I interviewed had done the bulk of their improving in the early part of their married life and had never really stopped. Home improvements were also about their aspirations, how they saw themselves on the social scale. Crown wallpapers featured a couple in smart clothes, which at the time would have signified middle class, and they were described as wanting something different (*The Practical Householder*, July 1956, p. 614). This way of defining social status, though, was less important than occupation or income, as arguably class was more of an issue in the 1950s than it is now. Some home improvements could be seen as the aesthetic manifestations of feminine values and tastes. They were also a reflection of people wanting to be modern, of the present, up-to-date, and this meant future style. This style came from the utopian dimension of modernism embodied in government-backed design advice, from new materials, and from the new availability of materials on the do-it-yourself market; what could be called a collision of circumstances. I would suggest that women in working-class/lower-middle-class households were more active than just being selectors of products within this particular field of domestic consumption and they were certainly not passive consumers.

The mass consumer and the female consumer

Cultural critics often did look upon women as passive consumers, however. In the 1950s, Vance Packard, the American social critic concerned with new developments in the social sciences, expressed the view that through the techniques of mass persuasion via the unconscious, members of the mass market were potential victims of advertisers. He discussed how advertisements could influence purchasing decisions. When specifically discussing women, Packard considered merchandisers felt that typically females controlled about 80 per cent of family purchasing decisions among the 65 per cent who comprised the lower-middle and upper-middle strata of American society (1957, p. 100). The dust-jacket of the 1957 British edition of Packard's book read as follows:

> For better or worse, most American habits and tastes and institutions are eventually imported into Britain: American tobacco and films, American car-designs and hair styles, even American accents – and American advertising techniques, some of them what many people would term sinister.

The influence of the United States on British taste in the 1950s – Americanization – was feared by some cultural critics and seen as part of the new post-war mass culture. A notable critic was Richard Hoggart, who cited American television as intrinsically phoney, seeing the attempts of British teenage boys in milk bars to copy American film star mannerisms, clothes, hairstyles and facial expressions as depressing (1957, pp. 248–9). Americanization could be seen in do-it-yourself magazine advertising, where American kitchens were displayed as the dream kitchens that British women longed for and some products were labelled 'American-style'. For example, Super

New American-style wall paint for bedrooms and living-rooms

Special resin ingredient brings wall decorating right up to date

There is a new kind of paint for walls and ceilings on the market. It is as up to date as tomorrow's newspaper—different from any other kind of paint you've ever seen. It is called Super Siscolin and is a type not previously marketed here, though popular in America.

Super Siscolin contains a wonderful ingredient—a special new resin from America which, with the latest type of pigment, gives Super Siscolin astonishing one-coat properties.

Super Siscolin really does cover the boldest colour in one amazingly dense coat. Yet in the end it actually costs half as much to decorate with Super Siscolin as it does with other ready-mixed wall coverings. It costs only 25/6 per half gallon—enough for the average room.

Quicker, easier

Super Siscolin is so easy to use. It comes ready-mixed to exactly the right consistency. Open the tin and start painting. No guesswork. No bother. No mess with Super Siscolin. It is the easiest thing in the world to put on. A child can use it.

It is economical of both time and money, because you save a coat. It gives a fine matt finish with no trace of brush marks. It dries in an hour or so and leaves no painty smell. This means the room can be occupied the same day.

Super Siscolin is easy to keep clean, too! Just a light wipe and the wall or ceiling is bright as new.

Specially designed for bedrooms and living-rooms

Super Siscolin is made by Sissons, the makers of Siscomatte, the steamproof paint. Just as Siscomatte is specially prepared for kitchens and bathrooms, so Super Siscolin is designed specifically for bedrooms and living-rooms. There is a range of exciting colours, including a lovely lilac and other fashionable shades.

If you are thinking of decorating a bedroom or living-room, get Super Siscolin. You'll be delighted.

At most good paint shops. Or write to Sissons Brothers & Co. Ltd., Dept. S.K.1, Hull, giving address of your local dealer.

MADE BY
THE MAKERS
OF SISCOMATTE

One coat
SUPER SISCOLIN
New resin **wall paint**

Figure 9.1 Super Siscolin advertisement from *The Practical Householder*, May 1958. Reproduced with the kind permission of *The Practical Householder*.

Siscolin resin wall paint was advertised as 'New American-style wall paint for bedrooms and living-rooms' (see Figure 9.1). The advertisement read, 'It is called Super Siscolin and is a type not previously marketed here, though popular in America' (*The Practical Householder*, May 1958, p. 642). The built-in, co-ordinated kitchen containing gleaming appliances and labour-saving gadgets was the dream kitchen popular in 1950s America. 'If you want a beautiful AMERICAN STYLE KITCHEN' was the heading of an advertisement for *Homebrite* brand plastic-bonded hardboard and plywood, which fell somewhat short of the dream (*The Practical Householder*, February 1957, p. 175) (see Figure 9.2).

Female consumers in advertising

As far back as the 1920s, American advertisers had seen the mass consumer as female (Marchand, 1985, pp. 66–9). Mass is usually equated with passive but, on the contrary, I would argue that home improvements were a creative outlet for women who were forced to be home-based due to children, and a hobby for professional women. Jackson and Moores suggest 'practices of domestic consumption are shaped by dual forces of creativity and constraint' (1995, p. 5). This point is borne out by people whose answer to my questionnaire was that do-it-yourself was done 'from need'[2] although the decision-making involved in improving the home was a pleasurable task for the women involved, beyond just the purchasing decisions that women had long been credited with. Mr Brett, whom I interviewed, felt that improving their home was a hobby for him and his late wife who enjoyed planning improvements together. There were constraints on women's power as consumers, though, indicated in do-it-yourself advertisements by the contradictory, variable way that advertisers seemed to be subordinating women as well as liberating them, denying their power as consumers, as well as acknowledging it. Manufacturers, in their advertising, were forced to address customers *en masse* under the heading of 'lifestyle'. Sectioning of the population did not exist due to the limited range of consumer goods in the shops in post-war Britain. Some advertising images showed women in a limited number of dependent roles of housewife, mother, wife and domestic, marginalized as mainly passive consumers or users of do-it-yourself products, denying they had any power in the home, for example, a wife dreaming about having Tryka plastic tops in her kitchen (*The Practical Householder*, October 1956, p. 88).

The female DIY consumer was seen to be active in the softer areas of painting, decorating, tiling and applying plastic coverings while *Do-It-Yourself*

If you want a beautiful
AMERICAN STYLE KITCHEN-

Don't miss this
Special Offer
to all
practical householders!

modernise
your kitchen with—
Homebrite
REG. PAT'S APPLIED FOR

the easily cleaned stain
and heat resisting
PLASTIC
easy to work and
ALREADY BONDED
at your choice to ½in.,
⅜in. and ⅝in. plywood or
⅛in. hardboard.

at these amazing prices –

THICKNESS		SIZES (NOMINAL)			
		48" x 24"	32" x 24"	24" x 24"	48" x 16"
⅛" Homebrite HARDBOARD	...	28 –	18/8	14/–	—
½" PLYWOOD ...	...	39 6	26/3	19.9	—
⅜" PLYWOOD ...	...	44 8	29/9	22.4	—
⅝" PLYWOOD ...	...	49 6	—	24.9	33/–

Special quotations for other sizes up to 8' x 4' upon application.
N.B.—⅝" Homebrite Plywood, maximum size 4' x 4'.
All prices quoted are NET EX WORKS.

COLOURS
Six linen patterns, PINK, BLUE, BUFF, GREY, RED AND GREEN.
Two foam patterns, RED AND BLUE.

BERITE LTD., LAMMAS ROAD, LEA BRIDGE ROAD, LONDON, E.10.
Please send me FREE samples and colours of HOMEBRITE.
NAME...
ADDRESS ....
....
P.H.

Figure 9.2 Homebrite advertisement from *The Practical Householder*, February 1957. Reproduced with the kind permission of *The Practical Householder*.

'Skill does count, of course'

'. . . but this Brolac High Gloss goes on so easily and smoothly, Jane.'

'*Yes John, and the Browns' decorators chose Brolac for their outside years ago and it's still like new.*'

'What's that to do with us ?'

'*Nothing darling. I'm only just pointing out that Brolac can obviously take it.*'

'I see. Oh well, back to the grindstone.'

'*Don't overdo it darling, take a breather.*'

'Good heavens Jane, I've heaps of energy left.'

'*Oh darling, you mean you'll start the outside tomorrow ?*'

BRIGHTEN YOUR
HOME WITH BROLAC

COLOURCARDS FROM JOHN HALL & SONS
(BRISTOL & LONDON) LTD., HENGROVE, BRISTOL 4

Figure 9.3 Brolac advertisement from *The Practical Householder*, February 1958. Reproduced with the kind permission of *The Practical Householder*.

and *The Practical Householder* magazines actually addressed women readers both in articles and features and carried advertisements for vacuum cleaners and knitting machines as well as home improvement products. To some extent, advertisers acknowledged women's power by the way advertisements engaged with them. An advertisement for Fablon, a self-sticking flexible plastic covering, read, 'It's a Woman's World with Take-Life-Easy Fablon' (*The Practical Householder*, July 1960, p. 711). Women were rarely shown actually DIYing, though, which suggests the product manufacturers behind the advertising saw women's role as primarily designers and decision-makers. Alternatively, such advertising in the 1950s openly acknowledged women's power and, in some cases, her cunning use of it. The Murac PEP couple from *The Practical Householder* illustrate this very well. John and Jane appeared in several advertisements for Murac and Brolac paints in 1950s copies of *The Practical Householder*, representing the fashionable young couple of the time. In one advertisement Jane, shown painting with a roller, was described as 'fashion crazy and practical'. Her image was that of the American-influenced Beatnik look, the look that signified youth, comprising striped top and tapered trousers that ended above the ankle (*The Practical Householder*, January 1959, p. 169). In 1958 one showed John painting while Jane hung a painting; another showed John painting while Jane had a cup of tea, here filling the role of supporter/director and, by flattery, getting John to do the decorating work (*The Practical Householder*, February 1958, p. 252) (see Figure 9.3). The nature of Jane's power was that of the boss in the home. In a Formica advertisement for the same year, the wife decided what should be covered (*The Practical Householder*, March 1958, p. 162).

From social idealism to consumerism

According to Nigel Whiteley, '1951 signified the public moment when the balance shifted from social idealism to consumerism, from the old age to the new. The trend towards a consumerist society was an inexorable fact' (1987, p. 13). He suggests 1951 was a seminal moment in Britain's history, the year of the Festival of Britain, which embodied the social idealism in the Labour government's Utopian architecture and design ideas, a gesture of faith in a brighter future. It was also the year the Conservative Party returned to power. Design at the Festival was all about fun, fantasy and colour as controlled by the government's Council of Industrial Design. The Festival itself was entertainment, a demonstration of the country's achievements, and a morale booster for the nation. The bright, colourful, spacious, hygienic and fun style of living on show was labelled the 'contemporary style' and translated very well into do-it-yourself home improvements. The Homes and Gardens pavilion, in particular, addressed issues of homemaking. As Gavin and Lowe wrote of the Festival, 'women's *roles*, women's responsibilities – homemaking, home decoration, consumption; women were to be the centre of the newly designed households and neighbourhoods' (1986, p. 60). By 1955, television sets, refrigerators, washing machines, holidays abroad and other hints of the affluent society to come were within the reach of many workers in Britain's booming industries. Do-it-yourself versions of this 'contemporary style' appeared in *The Practical Householder* and *Do-It-Yourself* magazines, where readers were exhorted to modernize and thus improve their houses by making doors flush, panelling in stairs, building in cupboards to eliminate dust traps, rationalizing the tops of curtains with pelmets, tiling kitchens and bathrooms and using synthetic materials such as plastic laminates.

Home improvements in Southampton

In 1951, the same year that 'contemporary style' was launched at the Festival of Britain, two of my interviewees, Mr and Mrs Webb, bought their house in Southampton. They were one of the four couples from my oral history case study who are cited in this chapter. In common with all the interviewees, the Webbs' house was a modest turn-of-the-century brick-built dwelling which retained all its original features. It was in its original condition with a dresser in the dining room, an old ceramic sink and copper in the kitchen, and lead pipes. Mr Brett and his late wife Ethel had bought their house in 1942 when they got married, although it wasn't easy for them to do this. Apparently Mrs Brett had made up her mind and that was that. There was an old range in the house when they moved in and they were only able to have electricity supplied well after the war. Another couple, Mr and Mrs Bath, had moved into their 1911 semi-detached house just after the war, although they had started buying it in 1937–38. The last couple, Mr and Mrs Epps, got married and moved into their eight-room house in 1948 when it still had bells for summoning a maid, a coal boiler in the kitchen and open fires. For all of the couples I interviewed, improving these houses necessitated a certain amount of planning and decision-making, i.e. the consumption of design advice, of the images in magazines and ideas at exhibitions. This is where there is evidence of the power of the female consumer in the decision-making process. My own empirical investigations indicate that women's power in this area of home improvements was considerable.

Mrs Webb was, with her husband, a regular visitor to the Ideal Homes Exhibitions in the 1950s. She also studied colour, to some extent, in magazines and chose all the colours in the bathroom. She explained, for example, how a dark colour was chosen for the ceiling to bring it down and make the room cosier. In the 1950s they had red, yellow and blue paint in their bathroom, with black at either end. When I asked Mr Webb who chose the colour of the paint in the house, he said, 'Well, the wife.' When asked whether she had actually done much of the work in improving the house, Mrs Webb said, 'No, he's the expert. I just tell him what I want.' Mrs Webb was a full-time housewife and mother, and Mr Webb's attitude was that if he couldn't provide for his wife, then it wasn't worth getting married. Mrs Webb appeared happy with this view, expending much energy on designing and directing home improvements, while looking after their two young sons. Mr Webb was a painter and decorator in the 1950s and he worked on his own with Mrs Webb looking after his accounts. He had always been interested in woodwork and built a cupboard-cum-vegetable-rack-cum-shoe-rack in the kitchen and cupboards elsewhere in their home. The Webbs, along with some of my other interviewees, modernized their homes by boarding over their stairs and doors. The dust-collecting 'sculpture curly bits' of the stairs, as they called them, were taken off and the banisters were filled in. The newel post was streamlined, with the addition of oak, shaped and screwed in place by

Mr Webb, who also put oak straps on the edges of all their doors and hardboard on the sides (the old door panels were thought hard to clean because they collected dust) thus creating a rationalized and modernized interior.

All my interviewees were convinced that Formica was wonderful. Mr and Mrs Webb's front room fire surround was surfaced with Formica and they had also incorporated it in their built-in cupboard under the stairs as well as putting Formica on their kitchen walls. 'It lasts,' Mrs Webb explained. 'If you buy the cheaper stuff, now you have to replace it.' This laminated plastic was one of the most popular products advertised intensively in do-it-yourself magazines. These advertisements often instructed the reader on how to use the product for such things as resurfacing a kitchen table, with its wipe-clean surfaces, appealing to values of hygiene, conventionally linked to femininity. Being hygiene-conscious signalled being modern and Formica being heat-resistant, hard-wearing and inexpensive also had connotations of 'new technology' of the 'future'. Some of the claims made by the product were encapsulated in phrases in advertisements. These included 'clean at a wipe of a damp cloth' and 'heat- and stain-resisting' (*The Practical Householder*, March 1958, p. 355). Thus in the 1950s, this new decorative laminate was seen as a durable replacement for painted surfaces and such laminates superseded the enamel tops of kitchen tables of the 1940s.

Surprisingly, even colour became aligned to 'the rational programme of modernism' (Sparke, 1996, p. 181) as findings about psychology of colour had an influence. There is evidence that in the immediate post-war period amateur decorating to colour the home was undertaken by the housewife. In Mass-Observation's report, this was the case in 27 per cent of homes visited (Mass-Observation, 1948). Paint advertisements in 1950s do-it-yourself magazines addressed women as both decorators and designers. Mrs Webb had been the decision-maker where colour was concerned in her household, whilst Mr Brett's late wife had chosen the colours in their kitchen as well as doing most of the tiling. Mr Brett explained, 'My wife done most of the tiling. She took the size of the kitchen and she reckoned up how many tiles we'd need.' 'And how did you decide on the colour?' I asked. 'Oh, she decided on the colour,' Mr Brett said. 'The paint in the kitchen was the same colour as the tiles and it was all done in 1947.' Mrs Brett had also painted the kitchen stools to match. She liked bright colours and the pink and green paint used on much of the woodwork in the house was chosen by her. The late Mrs Brett had not been a mother or solely a housewife during the 1950s, having trained as a nurse before the war. Although Mrs Brett didn't worry about being modern and fashionable, they did cover the 'old-fashioned' doors in the downstairs back room with hardboard and put plastic handles on at the same time. 'It makes it tidy, boarding over,' Mr Brett pointed out.

The fitted kitchen is a further example of the modernization which became part of the aesthetics of modernism. Built-in furniture was another hygienic and space-saving feature of modern homes, seen in many magazine advertisements of the 1950s. My interviewees also favoured built-in units; several husbands had built kitchen cupboards for their wives. Mrs Epps, who had not been a housewife and mother in the 1950s, was a professional woman, married in 1948 when she was in her thirties. She continued to work as a teacher and did not have children. Mr Epps had constructed built-in cupboards for his wife, which ran along the entire length of the longest kitchen wall and consisted of floor cupboards with worktop across them, and wall cupboards. They were made of softwood and plywood bent into curved doors, and painted.

Mrs Bath, who had left her office job to become a full-time housewife and mother when the first of her three children arrived, also had fitted wooden floor cupboards built by her husband. He was a plumber and welder for a local boat-building firm. As well as these yellow floor cupboards, Mr Bath had also constructed built-in speakers in their front room. Mrs Bath explained it was her idea to have them in the corner of the room, 'I didn't want ugly speakers in here.' Instead, they formed an integral part of the room and made handy shelves. Mrs Bath described herself as a person who didn't change her mind so, when things were done, they were left. Hence the pelmets her husband made in the 1950s were still in place. She had decided that she wanted pelmets throughout the house and the late Mr Bath had designed and constructed them from hardboard and softwood, incorporating her idea for the large pelmet in the lounge to be constructed in three parts for easy cleaning.

Conclusion

After years of austerity, domestic interior design-related make-do-and-mend and self-help had become a way of life for the working and lower-middle classes in post-war Britain. This gradually grew into a do-it-yourself movement, a way that people could combat the poor housing conditions that were the legacy of war, and construct their own domestic version of Utopian modernism in contemporary 'good design' style. The growth of this movement led to companies tailoring their products to the skill level of the amateur and do-it-yourself becoming commercialized in the burgeoning British consumer society of the late 1950s. It has been demonstrated that women played a central role in post-war consumer culture, both by exercising choice over consumer products and by designing their home improvements. Do-it-yourself products were advertised heavily in do-it-yourself magazines where advertisers recognized women's decision-making power within the domestic sphere. The Homebrite kitchen and the American-style paint advertisements attempted to sell women the glamour that the magazine covers portrayed while getting their male partners to do the work involved in numerous surface treatments such as Fablon, Formica, tiles and paint.

My research suggests women's role in the 1950s was not that of the passive housewife and I have argued that women had more power within the realm of home improvements in post-war Britain than history often gives them credit for. For Mrs Webb, Mrs Brett, Mrs Bath and Mrs Epps, do-it-yourself homemaking was a process of negotiation between the discourses of commercial and official design advice within what they saw as the partnership of marriage. Do-it-yourself changes for family needs were also dictated by the original and often unsuitable infrastructure of the house as well as personal interests and identity. Consumption in this context represented a great deal of work, a home created by the owners' own labour where both functional and decorative changes were made. It was a balance between creativity and constraint, a means of expressing both how they saw themselves at the time and their aspirations for the future.

Notes

1. In 1950s Britain 'good design' embraced the notions of fitness for purpose linked with beauty, plus good workmanship which respected the material used, and finally simplicity and economy of means.
2. In 1994, 500 preliminary research letters were sent to households in Southampton occupied by the same family since the 1950s. From the 75 replies, 12 homes were identified where DIY home improvements had been carried out in the 1950s and were still extant. In my subsequent interviews, I attempted to pinpoint the sources of people's design ideas.

References

Benson, J. (1994) *The Rise of Consumer Society in Britain 1880–1980*. London: Longman.

Beveridge, W. (1942) *Report on Social Insurance and Allied Services*. Cmd. 6404. London: HMSO.

Browne, J. C. (1990) 'Representations of Women in DIY Advertisements and Other DIY Media 1950s–1989'. MA thesis, Middlesex University.

Browne, J. C. (1997a) 'The Active Consumer: Do-It-Yourself Home Improvements in Britain in the 1950s'. MPhil thesis, Southampton Institute.

Browne, J. C. (1997b) 'Consumption and craft: do-it-yourself home improvements in the 1950s'. Conference Papers from *Obscure Objects of Desire: Reviewing the Crafts in the Twentieth Century*, at the University of East Anglia. London: Crafts Council, p. 364.

Csikszentmihalyi, M. and Rochberg-Halton, E. (1981) *The Meaning of Things: Domestic Symbols and the Self*. Cambridge: Cambridge University Press.

Featherstone, M. (1987) 'Lifestyle and consumer culture', *Theory, Culture and Society*, 4(1), 55.

Franklin, A. (1989) 'Working class privatism: an historical case study of Bedminster, Bristol', *Society and Space*, 7(1), 96.

Gavin, O. and Lowe, A. (1986) 'Designing desire – planning, power and the Festival of Britain'. *Block* 11, 1985/6, 53–69, Middlesex University.

Hoggart, R. (1963) *The Uses of Literacy*. Harmondsworth: Pelican Books (first published by Chatto & Windus, 1957).

Jackson, S. and Moores, S. (eds) (1995) *The Politics of Domestic Consumption: Critical Readings*. London: Prentice-Hall.

Kenna, R. and Grandison, W. (1989) *Something Else: 50s Life and Style*. London: Richard Drew Publishing.

Lewis, J. (1992) *Women in Britain since 1945*. Oxford: Blackwell.

Lewis, P. (1978) *The 50s*. London: Book Club Associates.

Mackay, H. (ed.) (1997) *Consumption and Everyday Life*. London: Sage.

Marchand, R. (1985) *Advertising the American Dream: Making Way for Modernity 1920–4*. Berkeley: University of California Press.

Marwick, A. (1976) *The Home Front*. London: Thames & Hudson.

Mass-Observation (1948) 'Paint, colour and the housewife'. Mass-Observation Archive, Sussex University.

Mayer, M. (1961) *Madison Avenue USA*. Harmondsworth: Penguin (first published by Bodley Head, 1961).

Packard, V, (1957) *The Hidden Persuaders*. London: Longmans.

Sparke, P. (1996) *As Long As It's Pink: The Sexual Politics of Taste*. London: Pandora.

Whiteley, N. (1987) *Pop Design: Modernism to Mod*. London: The Design Council.

10. 'As seen on TV': design and domestic economy

Alison J. Clarke

Introduction

Throughout the 1970s a range of advertisements for 'problem-solving' and 'lifestyle-enhancing' gifts and gadgets pervaded British television. Popularizing the phrase 'As seen on TV' these moulded plastic items, which originated in North America, appealed to the intricacies of everyday domestic economy and household labour. Typical of the genre was the trademarked Ronco Buttoneer, a hand-held punch gun used to insert plastic tags, which promised to replace the laborious 'old-fashioned way' of sewing (using 'needle and thread') with a new miracle invention (Popeil, 1995, p. 86). Manufactured by an American company associated with the production of plastic 'T' tags for labelling in the retail industry, the smaller miniaturized version had initially failed to sell in any sizeable amount as a domestic product. However, re-released as a labour-saving device, marketed under the slogan 'As seen on TV', the 'new automatic button fastener that attaches any kind of button' became a best-seller; for 'the problem with buttons', the accompanying sales slogan reiterated to an empathetic television audience, 'is they always fall off'. Like its numerous counterparts the Buttoneer was advertised in saturation campaigns preceding gift-giving events such as Mother's Day and Christmas, thus increasing sales by an estimated 100 per cent (*ibid.*, p. 87).

From the mid-1950s onwards 'As seen on TV' products embodied the gendered workings and politics of everyday American households; so acute was their materialization of recognized domestic 'problems' that the devices were easily transposed to 1970s British culture. Although the products were not exclusively geared towards domestic labour (events such as Father's Day provided an ideal focus for promotion of the gadgets such as the Portable

Smokeless Ashtray and the automatic Pocket Fisherman), their integral relation to household provisioning and social relations framed women as the arbiters of domestic consumption. Women and the specifics of their daily chores were at the forefront of the product's advertising rhetoric. 'Everyone likes coleslaw,' espoused the voice-over for a Chop-O-Matic vegetable slicer, 'everyone, that is except Mother. The reason she doesn't like it is because she's the one who has to make it on that old grater, and, oh, the scrapes on her poor knuckles' (Popeil, 1995, p. 51). As well as overtly addressing women as would-be consumers, the advertisements acknowledged women's tacit knowledge as the historical matriarchs of the domestic sphere, referring, for example, to grandma's kitchen wisdom. Furthermore, as this chapter explores, such gadgets constituted the perfect gift and were purchased by friends, relatives and children as recognizably normative expressions of modernity and usefulness. While this suggests a broad consumer base, it is important to note that numerous studies of industrial societies premise women as the primary force (directly or otherwise) behind gift acquisition (see Cheal, 1988).

In class terms 'As seen on TV' consumers were conceptualized as belonging to working or lower-middle groups, although the 'miraculous' nature of the gadgets (as direct sales leaders acknowledged) was intended to cross class and ethnic boundaries equated with the domestication and status of television itself.[1] Although by the early 1960s 'As seen on TV' advertisements in America prompted direct response through tele-sales (with telephone order price reductions and other incentives), the majority of purchases were made through affiliation with 'reputable' High Street outlets. By 1968, F.W. Woolworth Company accounted for almost a quarter of retail sales for the leading TV direct-sales company, the Popeil Brothers (Clarence, 1989). 'As seen on TV' gadgets reveal the normative and socializing aspects of mass consumption for they quite literally became part of the family. 'You grew up with me and my products,' declared Ronco's instigator. 'Everybody has their own favorites, whether it's the Pocket Fisherman, Mr. Microphone, or Chop-O-Matic' (Popeil, 1995).

Initially introduced with the domestication of television in 1950s North America, 'As seen on TV' products have subsequently been popularly derided as objects of 'bad taste' and consumer naïveté; flimsy, plastic testaments to the alienation of the late capitalist consumer society. Indeed, once removed from their elaborate packaging, such products rarely fulfilled the miraculous or labour-saving claims espoused by their enthusiastic hard-sell advertisers, yet they continued to sell in their millions (Bush, 1989).

The conflation of television viewing, mass consumption, alienation and moral decline has been a consistent theme in discussions of the post-war domestication of television. When, in 1958, manufacturers of the new

'Sylouette' television announced that, unlike their competitors, they had managed to engineer a 'Slim Look' television model that fitted with ease into a bookcase, social critic Vance Packard commented sardonically that there 'hardly seemed to be a crying need, since most television-set owners did not own bookcases' (Packard, 1960, p. 124).

As well as associating television viewers with the demise of literacy and cultural standards, popular critiques of post-war consumption, such as Packard's *The Waste Makers*, defined the rise of the feckless and uneducated consumer as a specifically gendered character. The American housewife, Packard argued, had turned her home from a place of rational provisioning to a mere showcase used to display 'fashion lines for the kitchen' and promote 'keeping-up-with-the-Jones rivalry'. Indicative of this perceived transition towards wanton materialism and conspicuous consumption was the increase of 'easy-does-it automatic appliances'. The use of bogus technological innovations merely 'flatter[ed] the housewife's ego' and eased the guilt generated by her newly found leisure time (*ibid.*).

At first glance, 'As seen on TV' items such as the Inside-the-Shell Egg-Scrambler, the Whip-O-Matic, the Hav-A Maid and the Miracle Broom seem to exemplify the elaborate but essentially useless gadgetry described in Packard's critique of mass consumption and built-in obsolescence (see Figures 10.1 and 10.2). Certainly, these products blatantly exploited television's newly acquired status (thriving on the implicit sociality encapsulated in the phrase 'As seen on TV') and, borrowing the stylistic trappings of modernist avant-garde design, optimized passing trends and fashions. But, ultimately the significance of these 'kitchen wizards' resided in their pertinence to the realities and intricacies of women's everyday labour, household provisioning and social relations.

This chapter traces the history of 'As seen on TV' products and the origins of tele-shopping as a specific form of acquisition defined by women's work as consumers in the late twentieth century. It begins with a discussion of the domestication of television and its relation to the everyday routines of women's work as perceived by the early television corporations of 1950s America. Television is considered, as a number of cultural historians have argued, as an arena of sociality (epitomized by the term 'the electronic hearth') and in this study so too are its objects of mass consumption, namely 'As seen on TV' gadgets.[2] Although devised as mass-produced commodities, intended to accrue maximum profit through minimal capital outlay and broad consumer appeal, 'As seen on TV' products were proffered as gifts of modernity. Adapted over several decades as a form of material culture easily identifiable with televisual culture, the artefacts were contrived in response to the expanding roles of the twentieth-century female consumer and the

Ronco™

Figure 10.1 The Ronco 'Inside-the-Shell Egg-Scrambler' designed to blend eggs inside the shell automatically in 5 seconds – 'clean, safe and time-saving' – proved an international success due to the world-wide expansion of direct-sales television advertising in the early 1980s.

Figure 10.2 The 'Miracle Broom', made from brown and beige moulded plastic, was a staple 'As seen on TV' gadget which became a best-selling Ronco product of the 1970s using the sales slogan 'cordless electric'.

growing conflation of work and leisure. While in the 1950s labour-saving 'slice and dice' contraptions prevailed, by the 1970s mug-making kits, macramé devices and rhinestone- and stud-setters appealed to the contemporary notion of consumption as a means of leisure and self-provisioning.

The origins of 'armchair shopping'

In 1950, Television Department Stores Inc. introduced 'armchair shopping' to the modern American housewife's home. The channel promoted itself as an information service, providing especially selected merchandise for on-screen demonstration where women coached in 'discriminating buying!' by the 'shopping counsel of . . . buyer specialists' could place purchase orders by catalogue or telephone. In this way television allowed women to shop from the comfort of their own home, thus eradicating the tedium of old-fashioned and laborious shopping trips. They would be spared the hazards of 'crowded buses and subways' and 'catching cold in the snow and slush of winter weather' (Allen Du Mont Collection).

Despite the immense post-war success of television within the home, the earliest retail experiments in television distribution deemed the medium inappropriate as a domestic technology. Television broadcasters fully intended to institutionalize the medium as a *public* form of consumption, whereby each set acted as a miniature and portable type of cinema screen ideal for specialized advertising tasks. Corporations, such as Du Mont, who described television as 'the best show window in the world', enthusiastically explored the retailing potential of the medium. A demonstration of 'intra-store' television, in the Bloomingdales' exhibit at the New York World's Fair in 1939, promoted collective 'tele-sites' where annexed areas used public on-screen product demonstration to replace individual, personal sales services.

By the late 1940s, General Electric, capturing the novelty and modernity of television, promoted 'Intra-Tel systems' with the promise that it would 'increase store traffic on all floors', 'give customers a more lasting impression of the qualities of the products presented', and 'create the desire to buy' (Allen Du Mont Collection). These early television systems courted the shopper's gaze using the orthodox vocabulary of department store display and the conflation of information and entertainment. While drawing on the popular theories of consumer psychology, advertisers of in-store television promoted a crucial relation between *seeing* and *buying*. Directly combining advertising copy and sales demonstration, television offered a unique and three-dimensional consumption 'space'. As one promotional plea read, 'Surveys show that impressions made through life-like presentations on the television screen leave lasting impressions greater than printed illustrations' (*ibid.*).

While public use of television had minimal impact, during the period 1948 to 1955, over two-thirds of American households acquired a television set for their homes (Spiegel, 1992, p. 1). Notably television viewers remained a distinctly gendered group: in 1954 an NBC survey calculated that the audience consisted of 52 per cent adult women, 26 per cent adult men, and 22 per cent children (*ibid.*, p. 81). Prime time programming and 'armchair shopping' channels directly addressed the female consumer and quickly adapted to domestic consumption. The everyday routines of the household economy were reflected in the showing of soap operas, household tips, and variety shows which dealt with the issues of everyday social relations and domesticity. In this context television acted as a surrogate companion in the complex world of modern, post-war consumption.

The 'electronic neighbourhood'

In *Make Room for TV*, a study of television and family life in the immediate post-war era, Lynn Spiegel argues that with the increased suburbanization of post-1945 America, television and its products provided 'an imaginary social life, one that was shared not in the neighborhood networks of bridge clubs and mahjong gatherings, but on the national networks of CBS, NBC, and ABC' (Spiegel, 1992, p. 132). The duality of television's appeal to the public and private domain placed it in a unique position which created a visible intersection between institutional and corporate concerns and private and domestic lives. In this context, women's work became pivotal rather than incidental to larger issues of policy-making and social debate. On a practical level, as television expanded into the domestic sphere, the significance of women's work and patterns of everyday routines led, rather than followed, the planning and structuring of programmes and advertisements. Dr Tom Coffin, manager of NBC research, optimistically described the average daytime viewer as a 'modern active woman' with a kitchen 'full of labor saving devices' (*ibid.*, p. 82). 'Mrs Day Time Consumer', it was hoped for commercial expediency's sake, would integrate television advertising into her housework schedule as a helpful, informative boon to her role in provisioning the household.

Unfortunately, 'Mrs Day Time Consumer' did not prove as predictable and malleable as desired. Daytime programming consequently proved unpopular with major networks due to its unstable profile, as Spiegel notes, 'even while the aggregate size of the daytime audience rose in the early fifties, sponsors and broadcasters were uncertain about the extent to which housewives actually paid attention to the programs and advertisements' (*ibid.*, p. 77). Large corporations used peak viewing times, sophisticated role models and dramatic settings to sell their products but had little evidence of their effectiveness.

In stark contrast, amateur network advertisers inverted formal advertising wisdom and sequestered inexpensive daytime television slots to transmit live product demonstrations. In the mid-1950s the 'know-how' and dynamism of street market trading were transposed to the television screen in the form of low-budget, intensely verbalized and fast-paced commercials. Where the mainstream 'armchair shopping' channels failed, the tenacity of working-class street traders succeeded. The relentless rhetoric and emotional investment of the traditional street pitchmen created the demonstrations of 'As seen on TV' gadgets which addressed the 'problems' of everyday contemporary housework and household provisioning with uncanny perception.

The earliest electronic direct marketing began with radio broadcasting in the 1920s, which, like its successor, television, relied on the significance of women's work within the home for the foundation of its advertising strategies. The alliance between an institutionally male-dominated technology and the feminized domestic sphere initially proved problematic; 'some advertisers resisted using the home – seen as both a woman's workplace and as set apart from the harsh economic realities of the marketplace – as a site of consumption' (Smulyan, 1994). Street pitchmen, however, keenly took up radio selling for the promotion of commodities, as diverse as health remedies and baby chicks, to localized audiences. Television merely opened up a visual dimension for established live, on-air direct-sales demonstrations.

For many critics the intrusion of television, and its commerce, into the sanctity of the American home proved contentious; they prophesied increased juvenile crime, the demise of marital relationships and the breakdown of moral values. Protagonists, on the other hand, viewed the medium as the ideal means through which to *reinstate* sociality, family and domestic values. Women's magazines, for example, suggested ways in which the television set could successful blend with the interior decor and enhance the home as a place of leisure. The term 'electronic hearth' exemplified the new sociality associated with the medium and object (Tichi, 1991). From the 1950s onwards, selected broadcast stations made a literal reference to this notion by featuring burning Yule logs on their screens over Christmas Eve. Similarly, advertisers represented the television set as the ideal family gift or the focus (replacing the symbolism of the piano) at family gatherings. The direct sales marketers of 'As seen on TV' items posited *their* products at the nub of familial relations, and prided themselves on a democracy opened up through televisual consumption. Certainly, the coining of the phrase 'As seen on TV' signalled a vital ontological shift created by television which demanded new forms of knowledge, perceptual skills and cognitive practices to accompany the mass introduction of television (Spiegel, 1992, p. 38).

It is in this context that 'As seen on TV' items developed as accessible material adjuncts in the celebration of modernity and the 'television age'. The objects' 'universal' appeal to function, novelty and the enhancement of everyday lifestyle ensured they acted as gifts to the inhabitants of the new 'electronic neighbourhood'. But most importantly, they countered the potentially alienating aspects of this new technology through their studied and acute comprehension of domestic economy which traversed class, age, ethnic and gender boundaries. And, as one marketer noted, 'What better way to sell products for the home than through television, the product that had become the focal point [in the 1950s] of most American living rooms?'[3]

The sociality of consumption

The household, in the post-war period, became the focus for the development of a new sociology of leisure which connected media-influenced patterns of leisure-time activity and consumption and, more significantly, the relation of mass consumption practices to the formation of the American 'character' in general. In 1954, David Potter wrote *People of Plenty: Economic Abundance and the American Character*, a thesis later expanded by Philip Gleason in *American Identity and Americanization*, which emphasized a national identity dependent on a belief in the democratic ideals of the Constitution, accessed through the notion of the American standard of living rather than direct political activity. Post-war American citizenship focused on consumption as a vital aspect of the nation's productivity drive.[4]

Cultural historians, from Daniel Boorstin to Roland Marchand, have developed this theme of mass consumption, advertising and identity as crucial tenets of American history. Historian Andrew Heinze has argued that, as early as the nineteenth century, mainstream American consumer capitalism acted as a vital means of cultural assimilation: 'If there is one single factor that unifies the Americans it is the emphasis on consumption itself, the belief that individuals should expect an increasingly rich choice of products' (1990). More specifically, in his historical analysis of American Jewish identity, he maintains that material culture took on a crucial role in bridging class and ethnic identities for new and otherwise alienated immigrants: 'Consumer goods had more than practical and social functions . . . they served as the most accessible tools with which Jewish newcomers could forge an American Jewish identity' (Heinze, 1990).

In a similar sense, television acted as the locus for the socialization of the diverse post-war consumer (Boorstin, 1973, p. 393). A large percentage of the American population was economically excluded from the suburban lifestyles depicted in a plethora of sitcoms ranging from *I Love Lucy* to *Ozzie and Harriet* (Haralovitch, 1989). Many were culturally disenfranchised by television advertising's predominantly white, middle-class images of affluence. Yet belonging to this newly defined cultural space proved integral to social survival and to an association with the benefits of modernity. 'As seen on TV' wares socialized the new television consumer in the merits and knowledges of modernity; their value resided in their 'televised' status rather than their functional prowess.

This marketing phenomenon originated from the barrows of Eastern European Jewish street peddlers. Product demonstrations which had abounded on the street corners of large cities such as New York and Chicago from the mid-nineteenth century onwards combined showmanship, wit, stamina and verbal finesse in aesthetic presentations which sold novelties and luxuries to a population precluded from the spectacle of formal retail outlets.[1] The interactive process – the dynamic between salesperson, product and consumer – led to a highly tuned and tacit understanding of the process of sale and acquisition. In the 1930s small direct-sales businesses, such as the Popeil Brothers, began to buy space in stores such as Sears and Roebuck. They employed teams of personal demonstrators to sell household gadgets in a highly personalized and theatrical, performance-led style which sharply contrasted with the formality of the department store and its reliance on the *depersonalization* of sales exchanges. In her study of American direct-sales organizations, Nicole Biggart (1990) argues that the revival and growth of personalized forms of selling coincided with the increasing alienation of formal market processes. Makers of specialist items, she suggests, preferred personal demonstration of their wares in order to differentiate them from competition and emphasize their unique characteristics:

> A number of manufacturers did not want their products to have to compete with the cornucopia of goods in the big emporiums. They preferred to rely on salesmen whose financial success depended on selling their products and only theirs. In addition some believed that a sincere personal appeal or knowledgeable demonstration would show the goods to better advantage. (Biggart, 1990)

Ultimately, the peddling skills of family businesses like the Popeil Brothers, a staple symbol of the Jewish diaspora for centuries, were transplanted to the television screen, in the form of 'As seen on TV' advertisements. Contrary to the increasingly impersonal nature of commodity exchange, direct sales imbued goods with a status more akin to imparted possessions than commodities. Immigrant peddlers selling goods door-to-door, or from town to rurality, had traditionally carried with them specialized knowledge, coupled with personal and demonstrable interaction with the objects. These forms of knowledge, transferable through the elision of social relations and commodities, linked otherwise distanced cultural domains and involved women as pro-active rather than passive consumers.

Accounts of direct salespeople in the twentieth century reveal that they served as far more than dealers in commodities. In some respects, their sales acted more as gifts to their buyers: gifts of modernity. For they introduced urban manners and ideas to rural areas and imbued manufacturers' goods with cultural meanings. 'The travelling salesman was the exotic representative of slick city style, with his fancy suits, polished manners and speech' recounts Biggart of the early twentieth-century direct seller (1990). In this sense, by the 1950s, according to a contemporary study, 'the travelling salesman [had become] an instructor, a guide, and a handbook of city life and manners to all those anxious in the nuances of modern social relations' (Reis, 1958, p. 23; cited in Biggart, 1990).

In post-1945 America, direct sales concerns thrived as women, and other groups disenfranchised from the formal workplace, keenly took up part-time employment. Direct selling became an increasingly respectable community-based activity promoting consensus and sociality. The growth in household consumption led to the popularization of schemes such as the 'hostess party', used by Stanley Home Products and Tupperware Home Parties Inc., which elaborated door-to-door selling and home demonstration into charismatic social networks (Clarke, 1997).

The promotion of non-formal sales skills and the union of economic and everyday life provided the underpinnings of direct-sales activity. Direct-sales practices which sought to maximize social relations were ideal for generating sociality in new suburban areas. Yet many of the sales techniques proved anathema to prevailing capitalist, market economist theories. Whereas bureaucratic organizations sought to minimize non-work social relations in the cause of efficacy, direct sales optimized and courted them; through direct sales social relations and goods were effectively inseparable. Similarly, television info-mercials (as a newly formulated mode of direct sales) blessed 'As seen on TV' products with a historically specific aura of inalienability; they acted as celebratory gifts rather than the functional commodities they espoused themselves to be.

In *Gifts and Commodities* James Carrier discusses this tension between possession and commodity. He traces gift giving as the act of exchange which, incorporating the donor's identity, transforms the impersonal, alienable object. He casts North American advertising, not in terms of public status values and lifestyles, but in terms of how the notion of possession is invoked. The catalogue is identified as a prime example of this notion:

> Shopping in a catalogue is anonymous: there are no humans there to make one feel comfortable or feel obliged to buy. Thus, for many shoppers the careful and polished symbolism of the catalogue may be more attractive than the more haphazard cheeriness of the live clerk. (Carrier, 1995, p. 128)

Television also offered an anonymous form of purchase and interaction but unlike 'the careful and polished symbolism of the catalogue' or the 'haphazard cheeriness of the live clerk', its products symbolized possession through the social identity of the 'As seen on TV' brand. These goods conjured up the social relations, service and information of the traditional direct salesmen and the ontological significance of the new domesticated media. Like the perfect gift, they transcended the mere 'material expression and economic worth' of imparted goods (Cheal, 1988). Like the peddlers and travelling salesmen of the previous century, television acted as a surrogate social network. Its public and private status mimicked the social relations integral to direct sales and provided a normative and consensual forum.

'Here's why women love Veg-O-Matic'[5]

By the mid-1970s the two most prominent companies in the 'As seen on TV' product field, Ronco Incorporated (derived from the Popeil Brothers) and K-Tel International, had expanded distribution to a world-wide tele-visual market. Best-selling products, such as the Kitchen Magician, the Smokeless Ashtray and the Miracle Broom, embodied a sophisticated understanding of the 'moral economy' of the household[6] (Cheal, 1988). Product descriptions outlined and reiterated the inter-relation of social and functional uses. A commodity-specific language developed to substantiate the specificity and effectiveness of the product's use-value (examples include Mince-O-Matic, Seal-a-Meal, Power Picker-Upper, E-Z Wash, etc.). Despite their promotion as technological innovations, the majority of designs demanded the simplest and least expensive engineering and manufacturing requirements. They condensed the maximum popular cultural appeal into the minimum capital outlay. This notion was extended to the popularization of the K-Tel compilation album which omitted the tedium of listening to separate singles or the less familiar tracks of long-playing records.

Typical practical items included the Inside-Outside Window Washer ('washes the outside same time you wash the inside'), which consisted of two handled units with a magnet inside each, to be situated either side of a window-pane. This contraption solved the window-cleaning problems encountered by numerous high-rise apartment dwellers, saved the costs of professional window-cleaning and prevented familial arguments over delegation of the chore. Similarly, the Bagel Cutter, a plastic tube which holds a bagel in place while it is sliced (retail price $20 including bagel knife), was advertised as helping prevent accidents in the home (Popeil, 1994). The popular Trim-Comb Family Barber Set allowed the parents of large families to reduce the costs of haircuts and included a supply of blades, a styling handbook and a sturdy case, retailing in the mid-1970s at $2.99. The equivalent cost, so the copy emphasized, of a single trip to the barber's shop. The rationale behind the purchase of numerous televisual products was their appeal to an ethos of good housekeeping: short-term expenditure to achieve long-term savings and the subtle negotiations of thriftiness.

'As seen on TV' products also transcended basic houseware designs in their celebration of the potential artistry of contemporary living in the form of Ice-Cream Making Machines, Ornamental Ice Moulds and Food Glamourizers. The conspicuous transition from housework to 'homemaking', from the mundane to the leisurely, emphasized the post-war notion of the home as a place of 'creativity'. Products which did not rely on 'revolutionary' problem-solving features used the images and language of transformation. The Rhinestone and Stud-Setter ('it changes everyday clothing into exciting fashions') offered 'mom' the opportunity to partake in mainstream fashion by creating 'decorative handbags, hats and patterns on pillows'.

Items such as the Hand-Held Portable Sewing Machine offered women the promise of modernity in the transformation of arduous labour into leisurely self-provisioning. Most significantly, the sales pitch recognizes the product as a potential gift:

> Here is one of the most useful, time-saving items to come along in years; the New Ronstin cam-action hem stitcher and miracle button-sewer. Developed for mothers who are just plain tired of shortening pants or skirts the old fashioned way . . . you can hem, baste or blind stitch with ease – you can have pleasure experimenting with zig-zag stitching and many other tasks like an expert – comes gift wrapped with guarantee![7]

Numerous products exported to a European market in the 1970s made self-conscious reference to the fashionable modernity of Americanization; the Burger-Matic made authentic beef patties and the Glass Froster (which coated glasses in a chemical soon after banned by governmental policy) imitated the chilled glasses of advertisements getting 'parties off to the right start'. Similarly, the Crêpe Kit and Swiss-style Yoghurt Maker offered American and British audiences the sophistication of a Continental lifestyle.

Redundant commodities and normative gifts

Popularly derided as the lowest common denominator of consumer culture, at first glance these gadgets, comprised of low-grade plastic moulded parts, pronounce themselves as the fodder of the least discerning consumer. Despite the intensive promotion of these products as labour-saving devices, ingenious contraptions and facilitators of burgeoning creativity, in fact, they rarely fulfilled basic functional expectations. Removed from their elaborately illustrative packaging the paucity of their materials and construction frequently rendered the objects next to useless: a mere simulacrum of their use-value exalted through tele-visual demonstration.[8] They might be judged as the desperate manifestations of an expanding post-war market economy; the symptom of a naïve, duped and uninitiated television audience described in Packard's contemporary social critiques.

Yet despite their status as 'gizmos' and 'novelties' the products sold as consistently as those of any 'respectable' appliance manufacturer over a two-decade period. By 1978, the Miracle Broom had become a best-seller while the enduring Veg-O-Matic (a variation of the Chop-O-Matic still advertised in North America, West Germany, Australia, New Zealand and Canada) has sold over 15 million units since its inception in the 1950s (Palmeri, 1993). Through the 1980s, items such as the Food Dehydrator, Ginsu knives and Spray-On Hair (for the balding gentleman) continued the 'As seen on TV' tradition, the precursor of contemporary dedicated home-shopping channels (QVC) and scripted celebrity info-mercials.

To many consumers 'As seen on TV' gadgets held resonance as accessible manifestations of technological ingenuity and modern design; the advertisements offered an invitation to share the fruits of a democratized consumer culture. As such, they constituted ideal contemporary gift objects. Direct-sales companies, through tacit market research, acknowledged the significance of television products as gifts although they had not originally intended the items as such. Crucially, 'As seen on TV' products also appealed to the nuances of familial relations and kinship gifting and the complexities of women's work as consumers in the late twentieth century. The Ronco and K-Tel companies ran saturation advertising campaigns over Christmas and Easter holidays while the Ronco Inc. 'Year-Round Gift Center' offered point-of-sale displays in reputable high street shops. Weddings, Valentine's Day, graduations, birthdays, holidays, anniversaries – the giving of 'As seen on TV' products enhanced and expanded a range of traditional rituals and celebrations. Under the promotional slogan 'Gifts To Make Your Life Run Smoother,' one advertisement posed a series of rhetorical questions to be answered by a selection of ideal gift types; 'Ssratchy [sic] records? They need Record Vacuum'; 'Fuzzy Teeth? They need Mr Dentist!'; 'Indoor Smog? Help smokers and non-smokers get along with the Smokeless Electric Ashtray'.

These gimmicky gift objects apparently substantiate classic theories of the demise of social and moral relations in industrial capitalist society. Adorno, lamenting the demise of authentic social relations in 1944, writes:

We are forgetting how to give presents. Violation of the exchange principle has something nonsensical and implausible about it. Today even the private giving of presents has degenerated to a social function exercised with rational bad grace, careful adherence to the prescribed budget, reciprocal appraisal of the other and the least possible effort . . . The decay of giving is mirrored in the distressing invention of gift-articles, based on the assumption that one does not know what to give because one really does not want to. (Adorno, 1978)

Yet emphasis on the degeneracy of the commodity form and our over-simplistic assumptions regarding commodity exchange, as more recent analysis of consumption argues, merely reaffirms the relation between inauthentic social relations and mass consumption (see Miller, 1987, 1993). Numerous examples in anthropological literature cite the reduction of commodity to gift. Yet moving beyond this general point of analysis of material culture allows for an examination of the specificity and range of objects used to resolve the contradictions in cultural transformation at a given time. In this case, it is only by understanding the historical role of television, the changing domestic economy and women's labour that we can understand why functionally useless objects best served the useful role of gifting at a particular stage in the development of North American and European society.

'As seen on TV' products excelled as symbolic gifts while masquerading as fully operational gadgets. During a period of increasing technological advancement they embraced sociality and enhanced traditional practices (self-provisioning, festivals, anniversaries, etc.) and social relations. Ultimately, they served as 'collective gifts' of modernity to humanity; normative rather than personal expressions which served to create community and 'homeyness' in television's newly formed consumption space.

In this context, the limitations of economic models and theories of consumption which cast the household as a realm of trivialized and privatized activities and interests are exposed (Jackson and Moores, 1995). The historical exploration of these everyday 'As seen on TV' items highlights the 'work' of consumption as a gendered issue, rather than incidental manifestation of productive institutions and 'real' economic and social worlds, and highlights the socialization of women as newly skilled televisual consumers in the late twentieth century.

Notes

1. For a discussion of the 'cross-cultural' commercial advantages of direct sales through television and the consciously 'universal' appeal of 'As seen on TV' products, see Witek (1981).

2. The author would like to acknowledge the invaluable help of Paul Neale, collector of 'As seen on TV' products, in allowing access to his private collection of objects.

3. Witek (1981) examines the key historical figures and theories behind post-war direct television selling and its impact on contemporary home-shopping channel marketing techniques.

4. For a comprehensive bibliography regarding the impact of television during this period see Lukow (1984).

5. The lengthy, fast-paced television pitch for the Popeils' most popular item began, 'Here's why women love Veg-O-Matic. It slices a potato in one stroke' (cited in Clarence, 1989, p. 71).

6. Cheal refers to practices 'weakly institutionalised' in social theory; such as love and the nurturing and provisioning relations between mother and child. He also highlights that 'the gendered value of giving has often been overlooked in theories of the political economy of gift transactions' (1988, p. 7). In this sense 'As seen on TV' products positively excelled in what he describes as 'the ritual construction of small social worlds' (*ibid.*, p. 16). As a thoroughly domesticated medium, television, it is argued, as information, technology and object forms an integral part of the moral economy of the household.

7. Pitch from American television demonstration of a portable hand-held sewing machine, Ronco Incorporated *c.* 1972 from author's collection of edited advertisements.

8. In fact the Federal Complaint Commission prosecuted the Popeil Brothers in October 1971 regarding consistent false product claims concerning the Veg-O-Matic and Hi-temp frozen food and slicer knife, neither of which cut all the vegetables suggested by the commercials (see Clarence, 1989).

References

Adorno, T. (1978) *Minima Moralia: Reflections on Damaged Life*. London: Verso.

Allen B. Du Mont Collection, General Electric advertisement pamphlet 'Intra-Tel Systems Will Produce Greater Sales Volume', no. 18 (Archives Center, National Museum of American History, Smithsonian Institution, Washington, DC).

Biggart, W. N. (1990) *Charismatic Capitalism: Direct Selling Organizations in America*. London: Chicago University Press.

Boorstin, D. J. (1973) *The Americans: The Democratic Experience*. New York: Vintage Books.

Bush, A. (1989) 'Sliced, diced and pureed', *Advertising Age*, 16(60), part 41.

Carrier, J. G. (1995) *Gifts and Commodities: Exchange and Western Capitalism since 1700*. London: Routledge.

Cheal, D. J. (1988) *The Gift Economy*. London: Routledge.

Clarence, T. (1989) 'It chops, it slices, it dices: television marketing and the rise and fall of the Popeil family business', *Journal of Popular Film and Television*, 17, part 2, 67–73.

Clarke, A. J. (1997) 'Tupperware: suburbia, sociality and mass consumption'. In R. Silverstone (ed.), *Visions of Suburbia*. London: Routledge.

Haralovitch, M. B. (1989) 'Sitcom and suburbs: positioning the 1950s homemaker', *Quarterly Review of Film and Video*, 11(1), 71.

Heinze, A. R. (1990) *Adapting to Abundance: Jewish Immigrants, Mass Consumption and the Search for an American Identity*. New York: Columbia University Press.

Jackson, S. and Moores, S. (eds) (1995) *The Politics of Domestic Consumption: Critical Readings*. London: Prentice-Hall.

Lukow, G. A. (1984) 'The archaeology of television: a bibliography of the transformation of American economy, consumption, leisure, advertising and marketing 1920–1960', *Quarterly Review of Film Studies*, 9 (Summer).

Miller, D. (1987) *Mass Consumption and Material Culture*. Oxford: Blackwell.

Miller, D. (1993) *Unwrapping Christmas*. Oxford: Clarendon Press.

Miller, D. (ed.) (1995) *Acknowledging Consumption*. London: Routledge.

Packard, V. (1960) *The Waste Makers*. London: Longmans.

Palmeri, C. (1993) 'Vego-Matic does Europe', *Forbes*, 151, 15 March.

Popeil, R. (1995) *The Salesman of the Century*. New York: Delacorte Press.

Reis, R. E. (1958) 'The American Salesman: A Study of a Direct Sales Organization'. Unpublished PhD dissertation, University of Illinois.

Silverstone, R., Hirsch, E. and Morley, D. (1994) 'Information and communication technologies and the moral economy of the household'. In R. Silverstone and E. Hirsch (eds), *Consuming Technologies: Media and Information in Domestic Space*. London: Routledge.

Spiegel, L. (1992) *Make Room for TV: Television and the Family in Post-war America*. London and Chicago: Chicago University Press.

Witek, J. (1981) *Response Television: Combat Advertising of the 1980s*. Chicago: Crain Books.

11. Advertising difference: women, Western Europe and 'consumer-citizenship'

Anne M. Cronin

Through two case studies – a 1992 Martell advertisement (Figure 11.1) and a 1990 Smirnoff advertisement (Figure 11.2) – this chapter investigates the relation of the abstraction of the available viewing positions with the paradoxical *embodiment* of national signifiers through the (white, European, classed) sign of 'Woman'. The British advertisement for Martell cognac represents *'The Art of Good Breeding'* with the classed body of a white woman carrying the signification of bourgeois French identity. A cheetah lying next to her signifies the 'exoticism' and danger of a European mythologized image of Africa. The 'Europeanness' of the French signifiers in the context of a British advertisement is abstracted as a 'universal', yet it functions to frame the available viewing positions through 'differences' and their relation to social privilege. In analysing these adverts, I will address a series of questions; how does viewing an advertisement articulate with national and 'European' identities? How are consumerism and citizenship linked? And what happens when signifiers of such identities become disrupted through ironic, self-conscious displays of difference as a 'consumer resource'?

The emergence of 'consumer-citizenship' shifts the terms in which belonging and difference can be understood. In the context of transformations in the constitution of national and 'European' identities, I approach consumerism in a broad sense, examining how the advertising industry's targeting of markets of consumers inter-relates with the ways in which women and other overlapping subordinated groups are positioned through citizenship status. (This informs the reformulation of material rights, for example, differential access to welfare.) Indeed, in the terms of consumer-citizenship, the category 'woman' is positioned through a series of paradoxes; the terms of citizenship legislation are based on an exclusively white, classed,

Figure 11.1 Martell cognac advertisement, 1992. Reproduced with the kind permission of Seagram United Kingdom Limited.

heterosexual male model of the individual, thus excluding women, yet 'the nation' within Europe is often visually represented through a female figure. For instance, in Figure 11.1, the Martell cognac advertisement uses the sign 'Woman' as representative of the 'Frenchness' of the cognac, simultaneously demarcating the idea of French nationhood and defining the category 'Woman' as white, and middle/upper class. Yet, at the same time, consumerism, and popular culture more generally, are represented as feminized and denigrated domains in which women are licensed with a (limited) power to act (Radner, 1995). In the following sections, I explore these paradoxes through the ways in which two advertisements differentially position viewers and enable certain meanings to articulate belonging and difference. I would argue that the ways in which advertisers produce rhetoric about specific target markets and consequently use certain forms of address in advertisements draw on a particular, exclusionary model of 'the generic individual' and the citizen. This in turn relates to redefinition of 'European culture' as an *explicit* resource for identity production.

Nation, citizen and 'consumer-citizenship'

'Consumer-citizenship' links conventional ideas of consumerism and citizenship in new ways, actively transforming the meanings of the two terms in the links between political affiliation and consumerist aesthetic self-expression. Citizenship is based on a range of nationally specific legal criteria which define citizenship 'rights' and 'obligations'. Yet these criteria are not rigidly defined, but are informed by more diffuse notions of legitimate 'belonging' and 'identity', often framed in terms of 'cultural similarity' or 'difference' (Soysal, 1996; Stolcke, 1995). These ideas of identity and difference are being challenged by contemporary transformations in ideas of 'nation' and belonging, within and beyond Europe, in for instance the end of the Cold War, the dissolution of the USSR, the war in the former Yugoslavia, and the development of economic networks such as the World Bank, and forms of union like the EU. Conventional bilateral exchanges between bounded nation-states are being displaced by *flows* (of finance, trade, emigrants, tourists, media images and information) making certain national and regional boundaries more fluid and open to redefinition (Appadurai, 1993). The terms of who counts as a legitimate national and 'European' citizen with rights of movement, residence and employment are in a process of reformulation. Image networks produced through the media become an arena through which these ideas of boundary, belonging and citizenship rights are visualized and contested (Murdoch, 1992). For example, images of 'nation', as in Figure 11.1, form a visual dialogue of identity and difference between Britain and France, and simultaneously between 'Europe' and Africa mediated by the essentialized sign of 'Woman' as white and classed.

Yet the status and rights of 'the citizen' were never equally available to all within the conventional borders of nation-states in Western Europe. A number of feminist theorists have argued that the political category of 'the individual' which informs that of 'the citizen' has been based on an exclusively white, male, classed, heterosexual model (Diprose, 1994; Fraser, 1989; Pateman, 1988; Yeatman, 1994; Young, 1990). The ideal of 'the citizen' is 'neutral' in that it ostensibly refers to a generic, disembodied, unsexed, 'non-racialized' person, yet in fact, it functions to define this norm as white, classed, heterosexual and male. Paradoxically, this defines the male as both the disembodied, neutral 'citizen', and also as an embodied, male individual. Ironically, then, certain formulations of the sign 'Woman' represent 'nation-ness' (McClintock, 1995; Yuval-Davis and Anthias, 1989) as in the Martell advertisement, and yet women are marginalized in terms of access to national citizenship. This model of 'the citizen' brackets out 'differences' from this norm and subordinates the overlapping categories of women, racialized groups, lesbians and gays, children, and sections of the working class to this norm. In effect, women can only be addressed in legislation around citizenship and accorded (limited) access to *rights through their relation to men* and the (heterosexual, nuclear, Western) family, that is, in their roles as wives, daughters, mothers, widows and so on (McClintock, 1995; Pateman, 1988).

In contrast to conventional discourses of citizenship which posit certain circumscribed rights and obligations to the state, consumerism has generally been seen as an area of individual choice and self-expression not fully subordinated to state control. For instance, legal criteria of citizenship materially determine rights of immigration, work and residence, whereas consumerism is often considered an arena for pleasure and the exercise of the rights of 'choice' and of 'free exchange' of commodities and finance. But definitions of 'the consumer' in contemporary discourses have broadened to include a range of identities and roles which encompass more than the purchase and consumption of specific goods and services. Yiannis Gabriel and Tim Lang (1995) map out the ubiquitous presence of 'consumerist' rhetoric in public and private life.

The concept of the consumer sits at the centre of numerous current debates. Policy-makers, marketers, politicians, environmentalists, lobbyists and journalists rarely lose the consumer from their sights. The supermarket has become a metaphor for our age; choice, its consumerist mantra . . . Our rights and powers derive from our standing as consumers, our political choices are votes for those promising us the best deal as consumers, our enjoyment of life is almost synonymous with the quantities (and to a lesser extent qualities) of what we consume . . . Consumption is not just a means of fulfilling needs but permeates our social relations, perceptions and images. (Gabriel and Lang, 1995, p. 1)

This consumerist emphasis is not merely confined to political and popular rhetoric, but has material effects through its articulation and implementation through social policy. In the context of the USA, Nancy Fraser (1989) demonstrates how this focus on the social and political standing of 'the consumer' has material consequences for those such as women, blacks, and the working classes who fall short of the ideals of consumerist identities. Deemed 'different' from the white, middle-class, male norm of 'the individual', they are addressed as 'special cases'. Fraser argues that white men are represented as 'economically active' citizens through their engagement in paid work and the contribution of taxes, and therefore qualify as 'social citizens' and consumers. They are therefore positioned by welfare discourses as 'rights-bearers' who are 'entitled' as consumers to welfare should they become unemployed. Yet women are considered economically inactive in what is seen as a 'natural' relation to the household and unpaid work, such as childcare. They are not seen as contributing to the state, and are positioned as 'beneficiaries of government largesse' or 'clients of public charity' rather than rights-bearers. They are dependent recipients of welfare, rather than active consumers of services to which they have a right (Fraser, 1989). In this sense, women do not have *automatic* access to citizenship rights in the same way as white, Western men.

In the British context of the contestation of the definitions of belonging and rights, 'consumer-citizenship' has emerged as a discourse through the *Citizen's Charter* (HMSO, 1991). This charter was produced in the context of a Thatcherite imperative for the privatization of public services where, in 'the rhetoric of a share-owning democracy, the concept of the citizen was itself being privatized' (Gabriel and Lang, 1995, p. 179). In the terms of the *Citizen's Charter*, 'citizens' are redefined as taxpayers and consumers of these privatized services, as well as of goods and images (Miller, 1993; Walsh, 1994). This is a displacement of political agency from the voting citizen onto the consuming individual, and this reworking of the terms of political engagement opens the terms of belonging and identity to redefinition. Yet in what terms do women have access to this process of redefinition?

In the context of shifts in ideas of 'nation' and transformations in the terms of consumer-citizenship, access to images as a source of definitions of identities is increasingly produced as a *right* of citizenship (Miller, 1993; Murdoch, 1992). In terms of advertising images, this rhetoric should be seen as producing images of national and 'racial' difference as a *resource* for 'the consuming individual', to which the (white, male) individual has *rights of access* and from which subordinated groups are marginalized. This is an ironic shift as consumerism has often been regarded as a feminine domain (Lury, 1996; Radner, 1995) in which women are considered by manufacturers and advertisers as 'the prototypical consumer' and are licensed with a (limited) power to act, through consuming goods and images (*ibid.*). For instance, women's magazines have been seen as a 'woman's space' through which women can address specifically female pleasures (Hermes, 1995; McCracken, 1993). Yet, the images which are available as resources to women form part of a discourse of racialized and classed national and European identities which marginalizes women and racialized groups through the terms of citizenship. In these images, an essentialized formulation of 'Woman' is used as a visual currency for the confirmation and rearticulation of white, middle-class, male identities. Yet women cannot access the authorization to mobilize this currency as they in fact constitute the very terms of the currency. The following section explores how these processes of the rearticulation of identity occur through advertising images and how they operate in conjunction with, and work to redefine, citizenship rights.

Imagining belonging: images of difference

Images link 'the material' (of citizenship rights) and 'the abstract' (of rhetoric of 'belonging' and identity), through the interaction of *situated* viewing perspectives and the interpretation and contestation of meaning. Vision is situated both through a contextual location and activity, for instance, reading a magazine as leisure, and through a matrix of identity including gender, 'race', class, nationality, age, sexuality and ability. As Donna Haraway argues, the operation of vision and meaning 'requires a semiotic-material technology linking meanings to bodies' (1991, p. 192). In advertising and other visual forms, women's bodies are often used as the bearers or the currency of this dialogue which links meanings to specific bodies (Williamson, 1978), for as I discussed earlier, male subjects are positioned as disembodied and neutral.

This movement between vision, meaning and particular bodies can be traced in the Martell cognac advertisement (Figure 11.1). Here, a particular white, classed female body comes to represent the 'Frenchness' of Martell cognac, and the viewer's interpretation and consumption of the image are reliant upon their own positioning. For example, a heterosexual male viewer is offered the image of the woman as a sexual object of visual consumption with associations of high-class 'taste'. In these terms, an advertisement positions the viewer as consumer in three inter-related ways: as consumer of the image and its situated meanings; as potential consumer of the product or service on offer; and as part of a target market of consumers which can be presented by advertising agencies to their clients as a lucrative market segment. Agencies do not merely rely on market research data to target groups which are 'already out there', but actively attempt to generate markets based on certain characteristics they identify as gaining popularity at particular times, for example, 'Yuppies', or the 'New Man'. Agencies then present this ideal target market to clients, arguing that their agencies can best identify and tap into the tastes and habits of particular groups (Mattelart, 1991; Schudson, 1993). This is a way in which agencies attempt to link certain meanings to certain groups,[1] and do so by drawing on images of difference and identity such as gender, class and racialized nationality and actively reformulating them. In these terms, the 'differences' of 'race', gender and so on should not be seen as 'natural' categories, but actively contested definitions which continually shift.

In a larger piece of research, I have analysed how advertising agencies have shifted the terms in which they address viewers through advertisements from the conventional use of naturalized signs, for example 'Woman' as nation, as in the Martell advertisement, to more ironic and self-consciously 'artificial' terms of address. Advertising agencies consistently attempt to target female consumers using a 'literal' form of address which mobilizes a naturalized relation of images of white, middle-class femininity to the agencies' broad category of 'women'. In contrast, some contemporary advertising targets male consumers through a reflexive and often ironic form of address, as I discuss in later sections, which makes available a flexible, mobile positioning in relation to images of difference and shifting ideas of 'nation'.[2] This can be related to the way in which certain magazines in which advertisements are placed target a male readership through innovative, ironic techniques (Cronin, 1997; Mort, 1996), while female-targeted magazines tend to repeat established formulae and forms of address. The magazines reflexively 'sell' an image of their readership to advertising agencies who buy advertising space and, in turn, sell this image of target markets to producers of goods, their potential clients. This image of target groups is based more on a creative pastiche of various styles drawn from market research data than on the existence of 'real' groups in society (Mattelart, 1991; Schudson, 1993). Through this reflexive circulation of images of the target groups, the innovative male target groups are produced as active, flexible and creative consumers of goods and images, whereas female target groups are produced as passive consumers, aligned to conventional associations of femininity as domestic, narcissistic and frivolous. The production of images which address these groups and allow for certain interpretations is based on the imagined categories of social groups produced by the media industries, and on the limited availability of privileged perspectives of 'the individual'. Despite the dubious status of this targeting, the demarcation of groups and the presentation of available interpretive positions actively influence the ways in which viewers relate to representations of group identity and can have material effects through the ways in which belonging is then defined (Nava, 1992).

In the Martell advertisement, a conventional approach is taken to the presentation of difference contrasted with the Smirnoff advertisement (Figure 11.2) which demonstrates a more flexible form of address, which I will examine in the next section. In Figure 11.1, the viewer is positioned as consumer of the image, a potential consumer of the product, and the target market for manufacturers by drawing on images of sexual, ethnic, national, 'European' and class differences. The setting functions to place the image within a tradition of European 'art' and 'culture'. A gold border frames a sepia-tinted photographic image of an elegant white woman, a cheetah and antique furniture in a stylish 'period setting'. Several elements of the image work together to evoke ideas of traditional European ideals of 'art', refinement and culture which are offered to the viewer for consumption. The period furniture and the sepia-tint, drawing on ideas of photographs from the past, locate the image in a historical tradition of European art and culture. At the same time, the modern dress of the female figure functions to link these historical associations of 'culture' to the present day. The lines which flank the image, *'The Art of Good Breeding'* and *'Cognac. L'Art de Martell'*, indicate that 'the art' of refinement and distinction associated with French chic can be achieved through the appreciation and consumption of both the images and product of Martell cognac.

Drawing on traditional ideas of 'Woman' as nation, the elegant female figure here embodies classic French bourgeois ideals of sophistication, class and artistic refinement. The image of the woman is presented as an object of art to be appreciated by male viewers who can exercise their connoisseurship of ideal femininity, antiques, and fine cognac which are offered to them as collectors' items on display. The body of the white, middle-class woman functions as the embodiment of French identity, as the bearer of national signifiers, and as a sign for male viewers which, in their engagement with the image through visual consumption, aligns ideals of (white, male) citizenship and consumerist rights of access to images.

The 'Europeanness' is doubly signified through 'Frenchness' and through visual references to European colonialism in Africa. For a British audience, Frenchness can represent the 'high culture' of Europe in a way which other nations within Europe cannot, for example, Turkey.[3] The rhetoric of European high culture and refined connoisseurship is seen as a *Western* European characteristic, yet is presented as the essence of a unified Europe. In such an evidently 'European' context, the cheetah staring back at the viewer seems strangely out of place, yet in fact makes visible a link by presenting a visual reference to Africa and the colonial era historically associated with the antique furniture. This temporal link is made explicit by the text *'since 1715'* at the bottom right of the frame, referring to the date the business was established. The presence of the cheetah functions to link Europe geographically to Africa and to link contemporary consumption to a history of European colonialism,[4] in which animals were brought back from Africa (alive or as furs) as exotic trophies from 'wild' and 'savage' lands. The 'savages' that the colonizers encountered and exploited were seen as 'wild', 'uncivilized' and 'irrational', and indeed, animal-like. Their supposed wildness provided a foil against which (male, upper- and middle-class) Europeans could produce an image of themselves as civilized, rational, democratic and cultured, and therefore, innately superior (McClintock, 1995; Parekh, 1995; Pratt, 1992).

Categories of 'Woman' and colonial ideas of 'race' are inextricably linked through the historical process of the construction of the idea of the exclusively white, male, middle-class 'individual'. In the Martell advertisement, the meanings of 'race' and femininity are woven together and generate ideals of class and European 'civilization' which are offered to (white, male) viewers for consumption. The caption *'The Art of Good Breeding'* has its reference in class refinement, but also in the 'purity' of 'European stock', in which women, represented by ideal white femininity and reproductive capacity, were seen as the guardians of racial boundaries (McClintock, 1995; Yuval-Davis and Anthias, 1989). The references to European colonial history are not necessarily offered in terms of an explicit interpretation, but the residue of those associations is present and available for consumption; the inscrutable gaze of the cheetah and the associations of African 'exoticism' are used to lend the image of the woman mystery, and unknowable yet fascinating sexuality, and so reproduce the ideal of timeless, 'natural', white, European femininity. Ideas of 'race' mediated through Africanness, femininity, class and European culture operate together and cannot be adequately understood in isolation from each other. The mutual operation

Figure 11.2 Smirnoff vodka advertisement, 1990, reproduced from a double-page spread. Reproduced with the kind permission of International Distillers & Vintners Ltd.

of differences produces a 'norm' of femininity and European identity which is *white*, but this whiteness is not seen as 'race'; it is an unrecognized standard against which black 'others' are seen as different, and as bearers of 'race'. Simultaneously, the image of 'Woman' linked to nationhood and democratic traditions functions as representative of European 'civilization' and 'culture'.

These associations are, in effect, *branded* by the bottle of Martell cognac which is transposed across the framed image. Its intermediate status between the framed image and the white border functions to link the image with its associations to the titles *'The Art of Good Breeding'* and *'Cognac. L'Art de Martell'*. The implications are not only that the 'art' of a refined lifestyle can be achieved through the consumption of Martell cognac: the interpretation and appreciation of the images are themselves a refined cultural 'art' which confers status. In this way, a consumerist engagement with images draws on the historically constituted rights of 'the individual' to consume images of difference, and the consumer-citizen can 're-state' *his* status in that moment of visual consumption.

Yet, as I have argued, not all viewers have equal access to this privileged position; it is white, middle-class, male viewers who are *authorized* through their 'neutral', 'disembodied' status to interpret 'civilized' culture and national and European identities through images of 'Woman' as object/body. The (white) male body is the neutral mass, or body, of national (and 'Western European') citizens that is represented through the particular white female body as 'nation'. The white, male body is abstracted and comes to signify 'the citizens' and their rights, whereas women are tied to the body and cannot attain this abstraction. In this sense, 'self-abstraction from male bodies confirms masculinity. Self-abstraction from female bodies denies femininity' (Warner, 1993, p. 240). This accessing of the rights of citizenship through the abstraction from the body forms the key to 'consumer-citizenship'. Through this abstraction, the 'differences' of 'race', gender, class and nationality are ejected from the 'neutral' individual and citizen, and are presented as *resources* for the consumer-citizen to confirm *his* identity.

In the next section, I explore how this logic of abstraction is being taken to new limits by dispensing with an explicit dialogue using images of 'Woman as nation', and instead mobilizing an implicit masculine 'neutral' perspective. This does not make for a more egalitarian arena of visual consumption, but rather redefines the terms in which difference is visible and rights are articulated.

Disembodied perspectives

In Figure 11.2, a Smirnoff vodka advertisement, ideas of nation are represented with no explicit reference to sexual difference, and yet I would argue, sexual, racial and national difference are structural to the operation of the advertisement's meaning. The image elicits ideas of the history of the 'Wild West' through the use of a grainy, sepia photograph of an imagined North American Indian settlement. The image is entirely sepia-coloured except for the black border and the red and yellow Smirnoff label which cuts across the foot of the frame.

In contrast to the Martell advertisement, ideas of 'nation' and difference here do not refer to naturalized relations between the sign 'Woman' and 'nation', nor explicitly to traditions of European high culture. Instead, national difference is constructed as self-consciously 'artificial' through an ironic, anachronistic use of the satellite dish, television and vodka bottle visible in the entrance to a teepee. This hi-tech teepee is contrasted with the others through the slogan 'One step ahead'. The ironic commentary relates not only to a humorous idea of upwardly mobile American Indians, but also to the ironic interpretation of images of difference made available to viewers. This ironic viewing response is *a sign of cultural status in itself,* above and beyond the purchase and consumption of the goods being advertised: the act of viewing and interpreting the images is the (self-) expression of the rights to the abstracted viewpoint. These rights of the European construction of the category of 'the individual' were constituted in and through colonial histories of mastery and the production of ideals of 'civilized' European culture, yet this context is only obliquely referenced through the North American Indian images. The privileged white, middle-class viewer can access these rights of 'the individual' and so abstract the visual signifiers from their conventional geographical, historical and political contexts in order to rearticulate them in an ironic interpretive move. 'Differences' become a resource or a kind of 'consumer menu' for this fluid image-play which actively re-states those rights to abstraction and social privilege. Female, black, working-class viewers can, of course, engage in ironic responses but, crucially, cannot access the social status involved in this interpretation as the exclusionary constitution of the categories of 'individual' and 'citizen' forecloses these possibilities.

Conclusion

Consumerism may offer women ways of acting through consuming images and goods (Radner, 1995), yet, paradoxically, this form of agency is overlaid by the powerful rhetoric and structures of 'consumer-citizenship', which work to define identity and belonging and function to marginalize women. Women are not 'powerless' in terms of their consumption of images and goods, yet their exclusion from the status of 'the individual' and 'consumer-citizen' means that their interpretations and identity formations cannot hold the same authorization and social influence as those of white, middle-class men. For these men, images of sexual, racial and class difference from the (white, male, middle-class) norm function as cultural resources for forging identities. This can take the form of traditional ideas and images of naturalized identities such as 'Woman' as nation, or a more fluid, ironic image-play detaching and re-attaching elements of images to produce new definitions of national and European identities. This ironic stance is produced through, and made possible by, the development of the category of 'the individual'. In effect, what these privileged individuals are consuming is their own hierarchical status represented by their capacities for an ironic, detached, 'universal' view.

Access to 'culture' as a resource for producing and reinforcing identities is increasingly being defined through the discourses of the *Citizen's Charter* in Britain as a *consumer right* and an intrinsic way in which the ideal individual relates to the national and European community (Gabriel and Lang, 1995; Miller, 1993). Indeed, at the European summit held in June 1997, one of the draft proposals of the European Union Treaty of Amsterdam is the affirmation of European citizens' access to media images as a social, political and cultural *right* (Palmer, 1997, p. 10). These new ways of imagining belonging, identity and (consumer) rights of citizenship may have material consequences for those who are seen to fall short of the ideal of the 'consumer-citizen' as in Nancy Fraser's (1989) account of who are thought 'not to belong'. In inter- and intra-national terms, ideas of exclusive national and 'European' cultural identity, and 'legitimate' belonging mediated through images, may become legally implemented in tighter immigration controls excluding certain groups, and limiting the rights of those defined as 'ethnic minorities' within the nation and European Community (Soysal, 1996; Stolcke, 1995). 'Consumer-citizenship' may be an emergent rhetoric of defining belonging, but it is one based on *new forms* of exclusion and subordination which actively redefine categories of 'race', gender and national/European belonging.

Acknowledgements

I would like to thank Celia Lury, Ruth McElroy and Beverley Skeggs for their helpful comments on earlier drafts of this chapter.

Notes

1. This discursive production of certain target markets does not always translate into increased sales of the product, which suggests that the generation of meaning is a highly contested affair (see Lury and Warde, 1997; Schudson, 1993).
2. For a more detailed analysis of this form of address in relation to temporality and status see Cronin (1997).
3. See Morley and Robins (1995) in relation to the production of 'Europe' in the image of 'Western' Europe.
4. See McClintock (1995) for a detailed discussion of European colonialism and the commodity form.

References

Appadurai, A. (1993) 'Disjuncture and difference in the global cultural economy'. In B. Robbins (ed.), *The Phantom Public Sphere*. Minneapolis: University of Minnesota Press.

Cronin, A. M. (1997) 'Temporalities of the visual and spaces of knowledge: branding "the third dimension" in advertising', *Space and Culture: The Journal*, 1(1), 28–38.

Diprose, R. (1994) *The Bodies of Women: Ethics, Embodiment and Sexual Difference*. London: Routledge.

Fraser, N. (1989) *Unruly Practices: Power, Discourse and Gender in Contemporary Social Theory*. Cambridge: Polity Press.

Gabriel, Y. and Lang, T. (1995) *The Unmanageable Consumer: Contemporary Consumption and Its Fragmentation*. London: Sage.

Haraway, D. (1991) *Simians, Cyborgs and Women: The Reinvention of Nature*. London: Free Association Books.

Hermes, J. (1995) *Reading Women's Magazines: An Analysis of Everyday Media Use*. Cambridge: Polity Press.

HM Government (1991) *The Citizen's Charter: Raising the Standard*. White Paper, July, Cmnd 1599, London: HMSO.

Lury, C. (1996) *Consumer Culture*. Cambridge: Polity Press.

Lury, C. and Warde, A. (1997) 'Investments in the imaginary consumer: conjectures regarding power, knowledge and advertising'. In M. Nava, A. Blake, I. MacRury and B. Richards (eds), *Buy This Book: Studies in Advertising and Consumption*. London: Routledge.

Mattelart, A. (1991) *Advertising International: The Privatisation of Public Space* (trans. M. Channan). London: Routledge.

McClintock, A. (1995) *Imperial Leather: Race, Gender and Sexuality in the Colonial Context*. London: Routledge.

McCracken, E. (1993) *Decoding Women's Magazines*. Basingstoke: Macmillan.

Miller, T. (1993) *The Well-tempered Self: Citizenship, Culture and the Postmodern Subject*. Baltimore: Johns Hopkins University Press.

Morley, D. and Robins, K. (1995) *Spaces of Identity: Global Media, Electronic Landscapes and Cultural Boundaries*. London: Routledge.

Mort, F. (1996) *Cultures of Consumption: Masculinities and Social Spaces in Late Twentieth-Century Britain*. London: Routledge.

Murdoch, G. (1992) 'Citizens, consumers and public culture'. In M. Skovmand and K. Schrøder (eds), *Reappraising Transnational Media*. London: Routledge.

Nava, M. (1992) *Changing Cultures: Feminism, Youth and Consumerism*. London: Sage.

Palmer, J. (1997) 'A charter of rights for citizens of EU', *Guardian*, 18 June, p. 10.

Parekh, B. (1995) 'Liberalism and colonialism: a critique of Locke and Mill'. In J. N. Pieterse and B. Parekh (eds), *The Decolonization of Imagination: Culture, Knowledge and Power*. London: Zed Books.

Pateman, C. (1988) *The Sexual Contract*. Oxford: Blackwell.

Pratt, M. L. (1992) *Imperial Eyes: Travel Writing and Transculturation*. London: Routledge.

Radner, H. (1995) *Shopping Around: Feminine Culture and the Pursuit of Pleasure*. London: Routledge.

Schudson, M. (1993) *Advertising, the Uneasy Persuasion: Its Dubious Impact on American Society*. London: Routledge.

Soysal, Y. N. (1996) 'Changing citizenship in Europe: remarks on postnational membership and the national state'. In D. Cesarani and M. Fulbrook (eds), *Citizenship, Nationality and Migration in Europe*. London: Routledge.

Stolcke, V. (1995) 'Talking culture; new boundaries, new rhetorics of exclusion in Europe', *Current Anthropology*, 36(1), February, 1–24.

Walsh, K. (1994) 'Citizens, charters and contracts'. In R. Keat, N. Whiteley and N. Abercrombie (eds), *The Authority of the Consumer*. London: Routledge.

Warner, M. (1993) 'The mass public and the mass subject'. In B. Robbins (ed.), *The Phantom Public Sphere*. Minneapolis: University of Minnesota Press.

Williamson, J. (1978) *Decoding Advertisements: Ideology and Meaning in Advertising*. London: Marion Boyars.

Yeatman, A. (1994) *Postmodern Revisionings of the Political*. London: Routledge.

Young, I. M. (1990) *Justice and the Politics of Difference*. Princeton, NJ: Princeton University Press.

Yuval-Davis, N. and Anthias, F. (eds) (1989) *Woman-Nation-State*. Basingstoke: Macmillan.

12. Strange bedfellows: feminism in advertising

Mary M. Talbot

My interest in feminism in advertising is part of a broader interest in responses to feminism, in the form of representations in the media (elsewhere I have looked at, for example, lip-service to feminism on Page Three of the *Sun* newspaper[1] (Talbot, 1997)). It is an interest that has been rekindled recently by reading Susan Faludi's *Backlash* (1992): a sense of needing to know the opposition. We need to keep track of feminism's transformations and mutations. I think it is particularly important to be sensitive to perceptions of feminism outside the academic world, to be aware of how it is being represented or, more to the point, misrepresented to the world at large. With these concerns in mind, the present chapter investigates articulations of liberal feminism, 'power feminism' and 'post-feminism', and considers the articulation of 'rights' issues in relation to consumption. As a preliminary, it briefly considers feminist hostility towards advertising and the impact, in general terms, of feminism on advertising practice.

Feminist hostility towards advertising

On the face of it, feminism and advertising seem an unlikely combination. Feminists have been among the fiercest critics of advertising practices. Prominent among them in the 1970s and 1980s were scholars in the Birmingham Centre for Contemporary Cultural Studies; for example, the 'images of women' criticism of Butcher *et al.* (1974) and Winship (1981). Judith Williamson's semiological analyses of advertisements were unequivocally hostile (Williamson, 1978). Mica Nava has a good deal to say about the intensity of invective heaped on advertising by cultural critics generally

(Nava, 1997). As she observes, advertisers have been demonized, singled out for moral and political condemnation, sometimes to the extent that advertising seems to be held to blame for 'the spread of capitalism and the rise of commodity culture' (*ibid.*, p. 37).

Nevertheless, it is not difficult to understand why feminists have had nothing but bad things to say about advertising. Over the decades, advertisements have perpetuated sexist stereotypes. They have located women squarely in the domestic sphere of the home (where they have some authority, as Jen Browne demonstrates, this volume). The stereotypes are all too familiar. We are used to seeing advertising for cleaning products representing woman-as-cheerful-domestic-skivvy. Such stereotypes have a long history. The domestication of women is endemic in adverts (it is, of course, classed, hence realized rather differently in magazines at the top end of the market like *Vogue* and *Queen*). Occupational stereotyping outside the domestic sphere has also been a common feature of advertising over the decades, with secretarial work, nursing and the glamour model being favoured as women's occupations. In the 1950s and 1960s, women workers in adverts had even fewer opportunities than their real-world sisters. Moreover, advertisements, along with the fashion and manufacturing industries, have contributed to tying up femininity with patterns of consumption – to the extent that femininity is, to a considerable degree, defined *as* a pattern of consumption: a phenomenon I have investigated, and been very negative about, in a lipstick advertorial[2] in *Jackie* magazine (Talbot, 1992, 1995). It has to be said that advertisers are not known for being staunch supporters of feminism.

Feminism's impact on advertising

Unlike feminism, of course, the advertising industry has no stake in subverting conventional forms of femininity. Why should it? From the advertisers' perspective it would be anathema, given the vast array of commodities that femininity generates. However, advertisers do have to be in step with the popular; they have to be aware of contemporary issues, to use contemporary language, and so on. Since the impact of the Women's Liberation Movement in the 1970s, advertisers have had to take feminism on board. Feminism acquired some institutional power. Once it did, it could no longer be ignored or simply rejected as another form of marginal, left-wing politics. Advertisers cannot afford to be seen as in any way oppressive or, worse, old-fashioned.

But adverts are omnivorous. They can absorb anything – feminism, environmentalism, you name it – transforming it into a means of stimulating consumption (with particular ironies and contradictions in the case of green issues). From the 1970s onwards, we begin to see a feminist discourse in advertisements. A discourse, roughly speaking, is a social construction of reality: a body of historically constituted knowledge and practices that is articulated discursively. It has to be said that feminist knowledge and practice are very patchily applied in advertising strategies, though. For instance, it has taken advertisers a long time to realize that the traditional market-research categories of 'housewife' and 'head of household' are becoming redundant (Bate, 1993). These categories no longer fit in with women's perception of themselves or their relationships. They certainly do not fit in with reality.

So advertising has managed to absorb feminism. Some varieties of feminism have proved more congenial to adverts than others, however. Predictably, the magazine variety of liberal feminism, which Winship describes in *Inside Women's Magazines*, has been particularly digestible. It has been widely incorporated into advertising practice. This does not, of course, prevent advertisers from appropriating the vocabulary of more revolutionary feminist political discourses. Advertisers have long been inclined to talk about 'freedom' offered by 'revolutionary' products. It is hardly surprising, then, that in advertising for sanitary towels and tampons, claims to offer women 'liberation' sometimes took on a pseudo-revolutionary ring in the 1970s. Similar products in wartime Britain had equally spurious references to the war effort.[3] The lifting of vocabulary from diverse discourses is an issue I will return to later.

Liberal feminism in advertisements

Liberal feminism is one of the main streams of feminist political thought and certainly the oldest. It was first fully articulated in 1789 by Mary Wollstonecraft in *A Vindication of the Rights of Women* (1985). Its best-known exponent in the twentieth century is Betty Friedan, author of *The Feminine Mystique* (1963) and founder of the National Organization for Women in 1966. The concerns of contemporary liberal feminism are freedom for women as individuals, equality of opportunity for women and men, the individual's right to fulfilment free from the strictures of sex-role stereotyping. In 1970s advertising, there was a broadening of scope in the way women were represented, presumably in direct response to the increasing numbers of women joining the workforce. Alongside the weary old stereotypes in advertising, we also began to see positive images of working women.

But what is more interesting, I think, is that women were being offered equal opportunities as consumers. In 1970s advertising aimed at women, a notion of 'women's rights' was sometimes incorporated into the appeal the advertisement was making. Moreover, women were increasingly targeted as consumers in their own right outside the domestic domain, notably as drinkers and smokers.[4] Women's rights, in advertising terms, means equal opportunities as consumers: whatever men can buy, women should be able to buy too. We now see women targeted as buyers of mortgages and insurance (traditionally the domain of men). In this case, the market has opened up because of legal changes. Since this is a direct result of the impact of feminist discourses on legal institutions, it probably represents the biggest 'genuine' response to feminism in advertisements that we are likely to see. The rest, in one way or another, is just a matter of style consumption, as I go on to demonstrate.

An example of this general trend is an advertisement for Virginia Slims, the cigarette that's also a fashion accessory. The product is American; the advert I am referring to appeared in the British edition of *Cosmopolitan* (March 1977, p. 11). Visually, it presents a contrast between the bad old days and the liberated 1970s. A sepia photograph depicts a woman, in what seems to be 1920s clothing, 'slaving over a hot stove'. Beneath it, a colour photograph displays a smiling 1970s woman, dressed in what appear to be lurex lounging pyjamas and holding a cigarette. The accompanying text reads as follows:

Women are at their best slaving over a hot stove.

We've come a long, long way.

VIRGINIA SLIMS

Virginia blend. Longer & slimmer than the fat cigarettes men smoke.

At last, a cigarette we can call our own.

It presents a rather strange notion of progress, that would hardly hold up to scrutiny. Of course, the ad is not claiming that the product is responsible for bringing about social changes. But the product is presented as though it were one of the achievements of the Women's Liberation Movement. There are two appeals to sisterhood, to *us women*: 'We've come a long, long way' and 'At last, a cigarette we can call our own'. Here we have feminism being offered as a pattern of consumption; or, if you prefer marketing discourse, as a 'lifestyle accessory'. Through ads like these, the freedom to consume is passed off as real autonomy. Seen through the distorting lens of advertising, self-determination for women – part of the project of feminism – is deflected on to identity-construction through consumption, self-expression through shopping.

In the decade of Reagan and Thatcher, gone are all signs of feminist solidarity, implicit in appeals to *us women*. According to Susan Douglas, advertisers began to reinterpret women's liberation as women's self-centredness (Douglas, 1995). Competitive individualism was unleashed. The personal as political reverted to the wholly personal. In the 1980s, cosmetics companies in particular, in their biggest advertising boost since the 1950s, urged women to exert their constitutional right to indulge themselves:

> Women's liberation metamorphosed into female narcissism unchained as political concepts and goals like liberation and equality were collapsed into distinctly personal, private desires . . . These ads were geared to the woman who had made it in a man's world, or who hoped she would, and the message was Reward yourself, you deserve it. There was enormous emphasis on luxury, and on separating oneself from the less enlightened, less privileged herd. The ability to spend time and money on one's appearance was a sign of personal success and of breaking away from the old roles and rules that had held women down in the past. Break free from those conventions, the ads urged, and get truly liberated: put yourself first. (*ibid.*, p. 246)

Cosmetics advertising and the glamour that surrounds it present potential consumers with dominant standards of feminine appearance. Liberation through self-indulgence – the 'narcissism as liberation campaign', as Douglas calls it (*ibid.*, p. 250) – required conformity to these standards. Feminist insights into women's relation with their appearance have identified oppressive patriarchal standards as a major source of feelings of inadequacy and discontent (e.g. Coward, 1984). The issue here is women's self-esteem being dependent on male approval. Cosmetics advertising offering self-indulgence as liberation was, and is, vigorously anti-feminist. It seems to me that the 'narcissism as liberation campaign' was a major step backward and constituted a serious undermining of feminist discourse.

In the 1990s, equal-rights issues in advertisements are only likely to be articulated in parodies. In Ikea advertising on British television we have seen images of women marching around with placards, seemingly demanding their rights but chanting the slogan: 'Chuck out the chintz!' This is evidently a command to throw out all our girlie Laura Ashley furnishings; Ikea are makers of relatively cheap, self-assembly furniture, sold in flat-packs. The television advertisement I am referring to is just another bit of 1970s retro. The filming, which has a look of newsreel footage, certainly presents it as ancient history. It has irritated at least one journalist. Suzanne Moore, writing for the *Independent*, is puzzled by the use of 1970s feminism to sell furniture. 'If the problem with feminism was that it couldn't sell itself to "ordinary women",' she muses, 'how come it is being used to sell them wardrobes?' (Moore, 1996). She deflects her irritation on to the inconvenience of Ikea's self-assembly products:

> Perhaps the difference is that feminism still makes a lot of people uncomfortable by pointing out what is wrong with men. Ikea is the only institution that I can think of that makes us realise that there is something right with them. They are the only ones who can put those damn flat-packs together. (*ibid.*)

Recently there have been some adverts doing this – pointing out what is wrong with men – to sell women commodities. Insurance companies offer reduced rates of car insurance for women, acknowledging that it is men who are statistically far more likely to drive recklessly. As an advertising strategy, this is a fairly new recognition of women as special category of car insurance consumer. It does seem to be an application of feminist knowledge and practice (naming the oppressor, perhaps? Certainly pointing the finger.) I have noticed quite a few versions of this tactic recently, especially on local radio. As far as I know, only car insurance brokers are using it. Other advertising pointing out men's shortcomings is British Telecom's 'It's good to talk' campaign, which has drawn implicitly on feminist research on male and female 'interactional styles' to establish women as superior consumers of telephone units (Talbot, forthcoming, 1999a).

Liberal feminism in the market-place, then, has both provided a justification for self-indulgence ('Go on, spoil yourself!' as the cream cake ads used to say) and transformed a politics into a lifestyle accessory. My next topic is actually a continuation of this notion of commodified feminism, of feminism as a lifestyle accessory. I now go on to advertising for the ultimate empowering commodities for women: namely firearms. Yes, firearms.

Refusing to be a victim: 'power feminism'[5]

Male violence against women has always been a key concern of feminism. Physical violence, or the threat of it, is an obvious and crude way of wielding power. In patriarchial societies, it is used to dominate and control women. Second-wave feminism has exposed the massive scale of violence against women, generating, in particular, a growing awareness and concern about domestic violence (e.g. Dobash and Dobash, 1980).[6] The constant identification of women as victims is, to put it mildly, depressing. Indeed, victim status can be damaging, as research on female sexuality has found: 'If women increasingly view themselves entirely as victims through the lens of the oppressor and allow themselves to be viewed that way by others, they become enfeebled and miserable' (Vance, 1992, p. 7). Among those feminists who have spoken out for the need to refuse victim status is Andrea Dworkin. She stresses that it must be non-violent:

> The refusal to be a victim does not originate in any act of resistance as male-derived as killing. The refusal of which I speak is a revolutionary refusal to be a victim, any time, any place, for friend or foe . . . so that male aggression can find no dead flesh on which to feast. (1976, pp. 71–2)

Viewing violence as 'male-derived', she is emphatic about the non-violent nature of this resistance.

The personal empowerment given by firearms can hardly be what Dworkin had in mind. In the United States, the recreational use of firearms by women is on the increase, as is gun ownership in general.[7] Of course, the gun-toting woman is not entirely new, either in fact or in fiction. Just think of Annie Oakley. While the fiction-producing industries overwhelmingly represent women as victims, there are some outstanding exceptions. *Thelma and Louise* are two women victims fighting back. In the *Alien* films, the protagonist is a potential victim who fights back. Ripley is a powerful woman who handles guns with confidence and considerable proficiency (Vasquez too in *Aliens*). These characters have put a whole new inflection on the theme of female self-reliance, a theme that took a rather nasty turn in Helen Zahavi's revenge novel, *Dirty Weekend* (1991).

According to Naomi Wolf, 12 million women bought a handgun in the 1980s (1993, p. 216). She presents this as a big increase in firearms-ownership among women and sees it as a manifestation of 'the unlabeled power feminism of women in the American mainstream' (*ibid.*, p. 217). Firearms are big business in the United States. Why not for women too? There is now a range of small-frame handguns designed for women (e.g. the Beretta Tomcat reviewed in *Women & Guns*, March 1997). A whole range of products are available for women carrying guns: handbags with concealed gun pockets and steel-reinforced straps, outer clothing designed to conceal a

Figure 12.1 Advertisement in *American Rifleman*, 1996, showing the use of women for modelling firearms. Reproduced with the kind permission of Dillon Precision Products Inc.

weapon, and so on. *Women & Guns* is a monthly magazine catering specifically for women who are gun users; it is owned by the Second Amendment Foundation. Women are now favoured for modelling firearms in catalogues. A catalogue called *The Blue Press* is advertised with the help of a smiling, feminine machine-gunner (see Figure 12.1). The *American Rifleman*, in which these ads appear, is the official magazine of the National Rifle Association (NRA) of America.[8]

The gun lobby in the United States often makes the association between gun ownership and good citizenship. Like their male counterparts, American women are now addressed as responsible gun-carrying citizens. An association of police officers and members of the law-abiding public known as the Law Enforcement Alliance of America exists. The text of an advertisement for it reads as follows:

Helpless Victim or Responsible Citizen?
LEAA Defends your Freedom to Choose . . .
NOT To Be a Victim!

(American Rifleman)

The text accompanies two cartoon-like drawings, rather like 'spot the difference' pictures. Both of them depict a woman with two children being approached by two thugs. In one the family is cowering in fear, menaced by the thugs. In the other the mother is drawing a gun from her bag; it is the villains who look fearful. Put this way, being a victim is something you bring on yourself, a consequence of irresponsibly not carrying a weapon.

The NRA itself addresses women. As a political force it is hardly known for its feminist activism, but a current campaign promotes women's right to choose to 'Refuse to Be a Victim'.[9] One can only speculate about the connection between the name of this campaign and Dworkin's pleas for 'refusal to be a victim' back in the 1970s. Weapons were clearly *not* what she had in mind, however. The 'Refuse to Be a Victim' campaign is part of a massive public-relations exercise after the Brady Bill.[10] When the Bill went through, in 1992, the NRA's public image had never been worse. At the centre of the campaign are seminars where women develop their own 'personal safety plan'. The NRA also offers an advice sheet providing '42 Strategies for Personal Safety'. While great emphasis is placed on lack of pressurization to buy firearms, Number 42 of these strategies involves *thinking about* buying a gun. Gun ownership by individuals is presented as a constitutional right (in fact, this claim is contested):

Firearms, A Personal Choice

42. Make an informed choice about firearm ownership. Firearm ownership is a deeply personal and profound decision. NRA does not promote
firearm ownership. We only advocate your constitutional right to choose
whether to lawfully own a gun. For women who do choose to exercise
that right, NRA offers information on the pros and cons of ownership,
types of firearms, legal issues, and education and training for responsible
use and safe storage of firearms with children in the home.

The NRA has co-opted the discourse of reproductive rights, using phrases
familiar from pro-choice rhetoric. Compare it with the following, part of a
full-page advertisement placed in the *New York Times* in 1989 by the pro-choice
organization, NARAL:

ON JULY 3, AMERICANS LOST A FUNDAMENTAL LIBERTY.

Now it's up to you to win back your right to choose.

The Supreme Court's ruling . . . has given politicians the power to intrude
on the most personal decision an American can make – whether or not
to have an abortion. (quoted in Cameron, 1992, p. 119)

Both speak of 'the right to choose'. Deciding whether to have an abortion is
'the most personal decision an American can make'; similarly deciding
whether to go out and buy a weapon is 'a deeply personal and profound
decision'. The service the NRA is offering might almost be a parody of other
campaigns. In fact, it is not only pro-choice discourse which has been
appropriated; their 'personal safety plan' recommendations also mimic safety
plans for preventing battering produced by the crime prevention divisions of
police departments, by shelters, crisis counsellors, etc.

So the NRA promotional material articulates a feminism based on 'personal
choice', 'freedom', 'rights' and, not least – picking up on weariness with victim
status – 'refusing to be a victim'. It is clearly liberal feminist and is very useful
for arms manufacturers. Women have not been good at buying firearms; at
least, not good enough. The NRA's campaign is helping to open up a whole
new market, by setting up the NRA as a defender of women. However, given
that the NRA is committed to opposing attempts to legislate or restrict in order
to protect women from men with guns, this pose is hypocritical. US figures
relating to domestic violence are phenomenal, yet the NRA opposes a new
federal gun law, passed in 1996, dictating that any person convicted of domestic

violence cannot own a gun. Instead, it presents guns as empowering commodities, preying on women's legitimate fears to tap into a new potential market. According to the NRA, legislation is not empowering but repressive. Power resides in a simple commodity: a handgun.

'Post-feminism'

The gushing enthusiasm of 1970s advertising was part of the enthusiasm in the media more generally. Suddenly women had 'made it' – such was the media-constructed myth. In the 1980s, according to various cultural critics, feminism – in particular, feminist anger – became 'uncool', not stylish (Faludi, 1992, p. 95). The media decided that feminism was dead and the 'press soon struck up a dirge' (*ibid.*, p. 101). 'Post-feminism' only makes sense in this context.

The advertising industry itself is still a male enclave, but it knows about feminism. This might explain 'post-feminism', for which I think a better name would be anti-feminism, at its most extreme in advertisements ridiculing feminism's more radical forms. Some Guinness advertising on British television, for example, gives a chilling black and white panoramic view of empty maternity wards, followed by a bizarre scene with a fish riding a bicycle. The visual reference is, of course, to that well-known challenge to conventional wisdom in graffiti: 'a woman needs a man like a fish needs a bicycle'.

There is a 'post-feminist' view of feminism as historically distant in a recent advertisement for the crispbread, Ryvita. It appeared at the peak of VE-Day anniversary celebrations in Britain, in the *Radio Times* and various glossies (as it happens, I took the ad from *Marie Claire*). I will focus on discourses. It contains a very peculiar mixture, including several political discourses. The slogan in the headline is more or less contemporary Tory discourse: 'Another back to basics campaign. Conservative it's not.' The other slogan ('Enjoy the liberation') and the brand-name logo (incorporating a Victory 'V') are in the discourse of a wartime political arena, now historically distant (there are also self-referential elements involved here, especially to two old Ryvita campaigns involving 'The Battle of the Bulge' and 'The Inch War'). The text reads as follows:

Sisters. For too long you've held back. Now's your chance to stand up for what you want. You want crispy bacon, fried tomatoes and a free-range egg. You demand real food values. Ryvita, with the basic ingredients of rye, water, a pinch of salt and oatbran gives you that freedom. You've got the fibre. Now dig in for victory.

In the body of text, the final imperative sentence 'Now dig in for victory' is playing with the British wartime slogan 'Dig for victory' (exorting citizens to take a spade to their cherished flowerbeds and lawns and grow vegetables instead). It also contains a feminist discourse: 'Sisters', 'stand up for what you want', 'you demand', 'freedom'. There is also, of course, a discourse of nutrition. Presumably it is the slimming or healthy-eating campaign that's not conservative. What the 'sisters' are supposed to be standing up for is the basic human right to eat a full English breakfast. Much of the forcing together of these discourses is achieved with heavy-handed use of that device advertisers love: the polysemic pun ('campaign', 'conservative', 'liberation', 'freedom').

Does the Ryvita advert make sense? Well, there are lot of meanings in it, but they don't appear to fit together. It is as though they slide off one another. It presents a parody of feminist activism, with women's struggle for emancipation reduced to a problem of healthy eating being boring. Women's liberation is reduced to a dietary issue, rather than a social one. It is sidetracked away from the personal-as-political and back to the really personal-personal. Women have never had it so good, because they can have anything they want: crispbread, fried egg, bacon . . .

Advertising needs continuous variety. It draws upon diverse discourses, including feminism. But the feminist discourse has to be interpreted in its surrounding context and in the process it is undermined. The incompatible elements in the advert don't make it unreadable; they just make it interesting.

Conclusion: feminism in advertising?

Well, yes, after a fashion. Clearly, liberal feminism – based on issues of individuals' rights – poses no problem for advertising. Manufacturers can only stand to gain from equal consumer rights and equal consumer opportunities. And sexist stereotypes are easy enough to change, when market researchers finally realize that they are ineffective. Moreover, the definition of femininity in terms of consumption has intensified in recent years. Feminism itself can be presented to us as a pattern of consumption: whether of liberatory Ikea flat-pack furniture or of empowering machine guns. In being rewritten as a pattern of consumption, the project of feminism appears to have undergone a radical shift: from changing the world to changing the furniture, maybe. Worst of all, perhaps, feminist politics can be utilized in the superficial 'post-feminist' way we saw in the Ryvita ad, rendering it meaningless, or at least, only meaningful as a historical moment, part of 1970s retro. This constructs feminism as a period style. It is a thing of the past, which is why we are now, supposedly, in a state of post-feminism.

I opened with the need to be aware of perceptions of feminism. In looking at recent representations of feminism in advertisements and other media texts, I find myself feeling almost nostalgic for the bad old days when you knew how things stood. I have a distinct suspicion that the objectives of feminism are being buried under an endless stream of 'post-feminist' advertising. You knew where you were with those old sexist stereotypes.

Notes

1. The *Sun* is a British national tabloid. 'Page Three' has been the customary location of nude pin-ups for the past 30 years or so.
2. An advertorial is a conventional combination of advertising and editorial material: a genre hybrid which has been common in magazines since the 1930s.
3. As Alia Al-Khalidi has demonstrated (this volume), many apparently new advertising appeals for menstrual products in fact have a long history and are not new at all.
4. This is not to say they never were before. There was an attempt in the 1950s, for instance, to market a new product as a woman's cigarette. It was called Marlboro. The campaign failed miserably, so they relaunched with the now familiar, macho, image.
5. For fuller discussion of this topic, see Talbot (forthcoming, 1999b).
6. In Britain, violence against women in the home was identified as a problem as early as the 1870s, during the first wave of feminism. An influential pamphlet, *Wife Torture*, produced by Frances Power Cobb, led to the Matrimonial Causes Act in 1878 (Tuttle, 1987, p. 31).
7. In the United States, women's traditionally low participation in outdoor pursuits, including the recreational use of firearms, has been identified as a problem. To counter this perceived problem, 'Becoming An Outdoors-Woman Workshops' have been set up to encourage women to participate (see: http://gf.state.wy.us/html/education/bowpage.htm). A major sponsor is the National Rifle Association of America.
8. The National Rifle Association of America (NRA) is a powerful political force in the United States. It was set up in 1871 to 'protect the 2nd Amendment' of the Constitution ('A well regulated militia, being necessary to the security of a free State, the right of the people to keep and bear Arms, shall not be infringed'). Until recently the NRA has been highly successful in blocking attempts to set up gun-control laws. Arms manufacturers are its biggest supporters; they are also its richest ones. Four members of its board of directors are Congressmen.

9. The NRA has a high profile on the Internet. Their 'Refuse to Be a Victim' campaign material is readily available at: http://www.nra.org/rtbav/rtbvhome.html
10. The Brady Bill is an attempt at gun control instigated by the Clinton administration. It was a major blow to the gun lobby, which is no longer perceived as invincible.

References

Bate, S. (1993) 'Women on the verge of a serious shakedown/ off with the head of the household', *Marketing Week*, 19 February, pp. 37–41.

Browne, J. (1999) 'Decisions in DIY: women, home improvements and advertising in post-war Britain'. Chapter 9 in this volume.

Butcher, H., Coward, R., Evaristi, M., Garber, J., Harrison, R. and Winship, J. (1974) *Images of Women in the Media*. London: Centre for Contemporary Cultural Studies: Women's Series Occasional Paper No. 31.

Cameron, D. (1992) *Feminism and Linguistic Theory* (2nd edn). London: Macmillan.

Coward, R. (1984) *Female Desire*. London: Paladin.

Dobash, R. J. and Dobash, R. P. (1980) *Violence against Women: A Case against the Patriarchy*. New York: Free Press.

Douglas, S. J. (1995) *Where the Girls Are: Growing up Female with the Mass Media*. Harmondsworth: Penguin.

Dworkin, A. (1976) *Our Blood: Prophecies and Discourses on Sexual Politics*. New York: Harper & Row.

Faludi, S. (1992) *Backlash: The Undeclared War against Women*. London: Vintage.

Friedan, B. (1982) *The Feminine Mystique*. Harmondsworth: Penguin (first published 1963).

Moore, S. (1996) 'When Ikea sells women's lib, it's time to move on', *Independent*, 24 September.

Nava, M. (1997) 'Framing advertising: cultural analysis and the incrimination of visual texts'. In M. Nava, A. Blake, I. MacRury and B. Richards (eds), *Buy This Book: Studies in Advertising and Consumption*. London: Routledge, pp. 34–50.

Talbot, M. M. (1992) 'The construction of gender in a teenage magazine'. In N. L. Fairclough (ed.), *Critical Language Awareness*. London: Longman, pp. 174–99.

Talbot, M. M. (1995) 'A synthetic sisterhood: false friends in a teenage magazine'. In K. Hall and M. Bucholtz (eds), *Gender Articulated: Language and the Socially Constructed Self*. London: Routledge, pp. 143–65.

Talbot, M. M. (1997) '"Randy fish boss branded a stinker": coherence and the construction of masculinities in a British tabloid newspaper'. In S. Johnson and U. Meinhof (eds), *Language and Masculinity*. Oxford: Blackwell, pp. 173–87.

Talbot, M. M. (forthcoming 1999a) '"It's good to talk"? The undermining of feminism in a British Telecom advertisement', *Journal of Sociolinguistics*.

Talbot, M. M. (forthcoming 1999b) 'Choosing to refuse to be a victim: "Power feminism" and the intertextuality of victimhood and choice'. In *Proceedings of the 5th Berkeley Women and Language Conference*. Berkeley: University of California.

Tuttle, L. (1987) *Encyclopedia of Feminism*. London: Arrow Books.

Vance, C. (ed.) (1992) *Pleasure and Danger: Exploring Female Sexuality*. London: Pandora.

Williamson, J. (1978) *Decoding Advertisements: Ideology and Meaning in Advertising*. London: Marion Boyars.

Winship, J. (1981) *Woman Becomes an 'Individual': Femininity and Consumption in Women's Magazines 1954–69*. London: Centre for Contemporary Cultural Studies: Women's Series Occasional Paper No. 65.

Winship, J. (1987) *Inside Women's Magazines*. London: Pandora.

Wolf, N. (1993) *Fire with Fire: The New Female Power and How to Use It*. New York: Fawcett Columbine.

Wollstonecraft, M. (1985) *A Vindication of the Rights of Women*. Harmondsworth: Penguin.

Zahavi, H. (1991) *Dirty Weekend*. London: Macmillan.

13. 'Thanks for stopping by': gender and virtual intimacy in American shop-by-television discourse

Mary Bucholtz

Introduction

As a cursory inspection of any shopping mall in American suburbia can confirm, consumer culture has reinvented space as spectacle. It would be premature, however, to declare that the image has superseded the word as the organizing principle of mass culture, for many forms of consumer culture rest on a solidly linguistic foundation. Nowhere is the enduring power of language more evident than in the shopping channel, a peculiarly American and highly gendered form of mass consumption that was made possible in the past decade through widespread access to cable television programming. I focus here on QVC ('Quality Value Convenience'), the channel that holds the greatest market share.

The shopping channel is, in essence, a 24-hour commercial for a vast array of products. Although the network lacks programmes in the traditional sense, it presents a variety of shows that cater to particular consumer needs and desires, each of which addresses an element of the larger social matrix in which the consumer locates herself, and each of which mediates between the consumer and the social world by interpreting every aspect of daily life as a commercial event. This unremitting call to consumption is by no means new, but the singleness of the network's purpose is. Whereas commercials on traditional network television are constructed in relation to a programme which ostensibly provides the primary reason for viewing, on the shopping channel the commercials have moved from the margin of the television landscape to its centre, and thus the very fact that they are advertisements is obscured.

The format of the channel likewise distracts attention from the profit motive. Professional hosts, stationed on sets designed to mimic the decor of a typical

Middle American home, describe and display a constant parade of merchandise with ceaseless good cheer. Supplementing hosts' regular sales pitch is a more conversational discourse style that invites viewers to imagine themselves as part of a friendly community. Hosts face the camera full front and seemingly address the audience members – overwhelmingly white, lower-middle-class women in suburban areas – directly and individually, a characteristic of the mass media more generally that Norman Fairclough (1989) has termed *synthetic personalization*. They may also engage in conversation with other network employees, such as fellow hosts, camera crew members, and others on the set.

This effect is not avoided, however, for artificiality is a central value of the shopping channel. An aesthetic of fakeness pervades the network, which celebrates the faux (and hence affordable) over the genuine (and hence unattainable, and even undesirable, for most lower-middle-class-identified viewers): shoppers use fake money – credit cards – to buy imitation merchandise from hosts who impersonate an upper-middle-class ideal. The promise of membership in this class, implicit in every sales pitch, is equally spurious. More important, so is the promise of membership in the shopping-channel community itself, although it is precisely this promise that keeps shoppers coming back for more. Through on-the-air telephone conversations with hosts, which are permitted only to those who first make a purchase, callers tap into a fictive community founded on the shared value of mass consumption. Yet the shopping channel that is the centre of this community is no place, a literal utopia. Using the methods of discourse analysis, the close examination of moment-by-moment interaction, I will demonstrate that it is this powerful sense of shared location, community, and intimacy, far more than the opportunity to buy goods over the telephone at discounted prices, that draws women to the shopping channel. As numerous other contributions to this volume show, the images of domesticity and promises of support and friendship deployed by the shopping channel are time-honoured tactics among the purveyors of consumer culture for enlisting women's participation in consumption.

The shopping channel and the linguistic market-place

I have argued elsewhere that the on-air telephone conversations of the shopping channel offer a place for women to take up positions of discursive authority that are then destabilized and commodified as authentic testimonials by the capitalist imperative of the network (Bucholtz, 1999). Much more obviously, however, the linguistic strategies of the host are also commodified by the network. Pierre Bourdieu (1977) has suggested that the social power of language can be understood via the metaphor of the linguistic market-place, in which speakers' linguistic practices may be seen as symbolic capital through which they accrue profit. In the linguistic economy of the shopping channel, the host's language use is symbolic capital that is invested in and produces a sense of community around consumption. The linguistic labour of the host reconfigures the economic exchange into one in which language and the sense of community it constructs replace material commodity as the symbolic object of consumption. At the same time, however, the shopping channel supports a literal economy in which the host's labour is invested in the promotion of material commodities. Both economies, it is important to note, yield financial profits for the corporation, but the linguistic economy yields a symbolic profit as well. The construction of this fictive community ensures that viewers will mark their community loyalty through repeated transactions with the network, thereby producing continued profits. In such a system Bourdieu's metaphor takes on a literal sense: symbolic capital becomes inextricably linked to corporate capital in the shopping-channel economy.

Mary Talbot's (1992, 1995) research on the rhetoric of sisterhood in a teen magazine reveals a similar process at work in print media. Talbot demonstrates that the discourse of a feature article on lipstick locates teenage girls within a 'text population' of real and ideal readers whose subject positions are assigned by the text itself. As a one-way medium, advertisements necessarily offer only the most attenuated form of community. Talbot points out that although readers may easily enrol in such communities on the basis of consumption practices alone,

> being a certain kind of consumer does not in itself form relationships; consumption communities cannot exist in the same way as real communities based on locality, kinship, or work relations. They can provide a sense of belonging, of group membership – no more. (1995, p. 147)

The shopping channel, however, provides not only membership but relationship by means of the interaction between host and shopper. The telephone conversation is itself the network's pre-eminent commodity: only a tiny fraction of viewers can acquire it, and its rarity makes it desirable. In the hopes of talking on the air with a favourite host, viewers will watch for hours on end and dial in regularly. Here the linguistic exchange comes to displace the economic exchange as the source of pleasure. But it is only by purchasing products offered by the shopping channel that viewers may fully enter the shopping channel's world. Consumers quite literally buy into the notion of community. Thus, in the newly configured transaction, linguistic exchange does not mediate economic exchange; instead, economic exchange mediates linguistic exchange.

Nevertheless, the relationship remains artificial, even in the relatively two-way medium of interactive television. Fairclough (1989, p. 217) notes that synthetic personalization may occur in both one-way and two-way interactions, for the phenomenon 'may be a matter of constructing fictitious individual persons, for instance as the addresser and addressee of an advertisement, or of manipulating the subject positions of, or the relationships between, actual individual persons (in the direction of equality, solidarity, intimacy, or whatever) as in interviews' – or, I would add, as in the discourse of the shopping channel. In the following pages, I trace the discursive moves by which this repositioning is achieved.

Manufacturing loyal customers

Like the magazine Talbot examined, the shopping channel sets itself up as a trustworthy source of information about consumer goods. Yet the proliferation of such pseudo-information on the network, as in other media, obscures the network's inadequacy as a consumer guide: all products are promoted at the same fever pitch and no item is ever criticized. Not surprisingly, then, callers buy readily and almost as readily return their purchases for refunds. By encouraging shopper loyalty, the network ensures that more transactions will be permanent.

One way the network enforces repeat purchases is by promoting an ideology of opposition against 'the stores'. Callers are so well versed in this oppositional discourse that any mention of 'the stores' by hosts triggers a testimonial of the superiority of QVC over traditional retail establishments (transcriptions have been simplified; a key to the transcription conventions is provided at the end of the chapter):

H = *host*, C = *caller*

(1)
H   Have you been (pause) had a chance to go into the stores and see any of the other Corning pieces and how they're priced?
C   We have a Corning outlet near where I live
H   Really.
C   and the prices are
                                         outrageous.

I mean QVC justs beats them (pause) by a mile.
H Well great great.
That's a great price.
Because (pause) indi<u>vid</u>ually those Corning pieces Dorothy and
I'm- you I'm sure <u>you</u> know living by an an <u>out</u>let, that individually
the pieces can be <u>very</u> expensive.
C   Yes.
                                    <u>Very</u>.

Many callers volunteer such comparisons without any prompting from the
host, and in fact, this oppositional consciousness is so acute that callers may
apologize for their disloyalty to QVC when they are forced actually to shop
in a store. Television itself is also positioned against the shopping channel.

(2)
C I- I saw them I've seen them advertised at on <u>TV</u>
H Mhm
C You know just on com<u>mer</u>cials,
H Right.
C But I can't remember that price that they had,
but I <u>know</u> it was nothing like the price that (pause) that that I'm
getting to- tonight on the air <u>here</u>,
so.
I jumped on that when I saw it come up.
H Good for you.

Callers here testify to the distinctiveness of the shopping channel's offerings
and the significant savings it provides, yet the national-brand products that
constitute the bulk of the network's merchandise can be found in any shopping
mall for comparable prices. The appeal of the network is not economic, then,
but emotional. As suggested by hosts' reactions in (1) and (2) above, being a
price-savvy shopper earns one praise in the shopping-channel world. Equally
praiseworthy is generosity; gift giving is encouraged, even in the absence of
a holiday or other special occasion, but in the worldview of the shopping
channel, just as important as giving merchandise to others is keeping it for
oneself, and this pattern seems to predominate among QVC's customers.

(3)
H now is that—
is the double burner <i.e., exerciser> for you or is it for
someone else?

C   Mainly for me.
H   Excellent.

Self-indulgence is praised as an act of well-developed self-esteem. Any occasion can be an excuse to buy. Shoppers are urged to give themselves gifts for Christmas and their birthdays and to reward their every action and mood with commodities. Even buying for another can warrant buying for oneself, as (4) illustrates. The caller has just told the host about a gift that she bought from the shopping channel.

> (4)
> H   Now I hope you'll be able to stick around because we got some nice gold.
> Since you did such a nice thing for someone else you might be able to treat yourself tonight.

Such exemplary shoppers are offered up as models for other viewers to emulate. In (5), the host commends the caller's shopping behaviour to the wider audience:

> (5)
> 1   C   Yeah my birthday's Saturday so I'm shopping for myself.
> 2   [<laughter>]
> 3   H   [Oh good] <hand clap>
> 4   Well, happy birthday to you [Sue]
> 5   C   [Thank] you.
> 6   H   Welc-
> 7   C   Thanks.
> 8   H   Congratulations.
> 9   That's
>   wonderful.
> 10 C   Thanks.
> 11 H   And uh certainly (pause) treat yourself as much as you want.
> 12   Okay?
> 13 C   Okay.
> 14 H   All right.
> 15   Take care.
> 16   Have a good day.
> 17 C   Bye bye.
> 18 H   Mm bye bye now.
> 19   (pause)
> 20   <to camera> A lot of people do like to treat themselves

21   whenever their birthday rolls around they say, (pause)
22   Good heavens I'm going to go out and just buy myself
23   something that I can uh (pause) en<u>joy</u>,
24   something that will make me feel good.

Thus the network presents constant consumption of its merchandise as
normal and healthy. In order to maintain this practice, however, women must
also maintain the practice of constant viewing. Callers regularly assure hosts
of their faithfulness, and hosts rally callers with a few well-chosen words
of encouragement, such as *Hang in there* or *Thanks for staying up*. Viewing and
buying form a symbiotic relationship: viewing enables shopping, and with
the appropriate purchases viewing can become even more pleasant.

      (6)
      <discussing an exercise machine>
H   The nice thing about this is,
      you can put it in front of your TV,
      <u>watch</u> QVC,
      and a half an hour will go by like <snaps fingers> <u>that</u>. You know?
C: (I have to do it.)
      If I don't have to jump off to call QVC and order something,
      [that'd be fine.]
H   [<laughter>]
      Well you'll just have to have your cordless <u>phone</u> standing <u>by</u>,
      so you can keep on pumping.

But because many of the same products are repeatedly offered for sale,
viewers are not motivated to tune in simply to seize a one-time chance at a
great bargain. Far more rare are the opportunities to get on the air – or even
to hear one's friend or neighbour phoning in:

      (7)
C: Can you say hello to my friend Lori?
H   Oh I would love to!
      <u>What</u> is her name?
C   <u>Lori</u>.
H   Lori?
C   She and I are QVCites.
H   Uh huh.
      And is she there with you now (pause) Janet?
C   No,

but I know she's home [watching]
H   [<laughter>]
We already know where Lori is [then huh?]
C   [<laughter>]
H   Well you have to tell her hello,
     and if she just happened to step away tell her <inbreath>
     <creaky voice> that's what she gets for not watching every minute
     of the day!
     <laughter>

The host's joking manner does not entirely invalidate her message: when you're not watching, you're missing out not just on commodities, but on community. As this exchange indicates, QVC is the link that binds viewer to viewer in a nationwide community of consumers. Within such relationships of mediated intimacy, social links are forged through talk.

The social network: QVC and community

Technological advances have often been used to promote solidarity across space and social groups (Anderson, 1991; Rheingold, 1993). What makes the shopping-channel community different from these other forms of mediated communication is the centrality of the interactive relationship between viewer and network. The discourse of the hosts, especially in television conversations with viewers, projects a community of shared opinions, experiences, and lives.

In order to promote a sense of common values, telehosts take care to maintain harmony and good will in their on-the-air conversations with callers. In Example (8), the host hastily deflects a potential conflict when a caller expresses disagreement with her:

(8)
1   H   <u>Tell</u> me,
2   <u>What</u> do people <u>say</u> about those earrings?
3   [Do they like]   them on you?
4   C   [Oh they <u>love</u> them].
5   Really.
6   H   Mhm.
7   C   My granddaughter almost took them [a]way from me.
8   H   [I-]
9   You got to watch out for those <creaky voice>
10   granddaughters.

11   C   Yeah [<laughter>]
12   H   [And those <u>daug</u>]hters.
13   C   Right.
14   H   <laughter> They both are culprits in that regard.
15   C   <u>She's</u> kind of sweet [though.]
16   H   [Oh] that's great.
17   Oh yeah.
18   It's kind of like,
19   you think,
20   <dental click> Oh she <u>took</u> my <u>ear</u>rings.
21   And then you break out in a smile,
22   right?
23   [<laughter>]
24   C   [yeah.]
25   H   <inbreath> Good.

Although the host's playful tone (marked by her creaky voice quality in line 10) initially elicits laughter from the caller, her continuation of the topic in lines 12 and 14 finally leads the caller to object mildly (line 15), using contrastive stress and the contrastive marker *though*. The host quickly emphasizes her agreement with the caller's position, narrating a hypothetical scene and soliciting the caller's approval (line 22). Her intake of breath and evaluative marker (*Good*, line 25) signal that the caller's hesitant agreement has brought them both back onto solid – and solidarity – ground. The host's narrative here does double duty: not only does it resolve the conflict but it also displays an idealized interaction between family members, in which mothers and grandmothers exhibit attitudes of patient fondness toward their wayward progeny.

Just as important as a sense of common values is a feeling of shared space and experience. The topics that hosts introduce in telephone interaction are crucial in bringing about this effect. At various points the host may more or less seamlessly slip out of product description and into a more intimate discourse, a discourse of community. These shifts are only apparent disjunctures, however, since the host usually incorporates them back into the larger linguistic project of commodity promotion. Such disjunctures are most obviously seen in the telephone conversations, but they are supported by other on-camera interactions as well.

Conversations that foster intimacy may draw on the shared experience of popular culture, as when a host asks a caller, *Remember that plot on General Hospital?* Hosts may use similar tactics in interaction with other network employees, evoking a sense of shared culture and community that envelops the viewers as well.

(9)

1 **H** \<to model\> Have you um had a chance uh Laura to (pause) uh
2   listen to the radio at all today?
3 **M** \<low volume, off microphone\> Uh no.
4 **H** Did you (pause) hear about what happened to <u>uh</u> <u>Ea</u>gle one oh
    six?
5 **M** \<low volume\> No.
6 **H** It's \<breathy voice\> <u>gone</u>. (pause)
7   \<inbreath\> \<to camera\> Philadelphia just got-
8   just this weekend in fact,
9   its <u>first</u> jazz radio station.
10   Non (pause) public.
11   First com<u>mer</u>cial jazz radio station.
12   And that's exciting.
13   This kind of necklace reminds me of something you might <u>wear</u>
14   to like a jazz concert,
15   because we have a jazz <u>ra</u>dio station now,
16   there's gonna be lots <u>more</u> of them.

The introduction of topics unrelated to consumption, particularly in the telephone conversations, creates a feeling of expanded time, in contrast to the manufactured urgency generated by the timer in the corner of the television screen, counting down to zero to imply that each offer is for a limited time only (in fact, most products are regularly available for sale). The message is that the imperative to purchase must be fulfilled quickly, so that the shopper can enjoy at leisure the community feeling that is the fringe benefit of consumption. Indeed, this example shows that the topic of consumption is never far away; any subject can be linked to the buying process.

In (9) the host recognizes and tries to bridge the physical distance between himself and the network's viewers by turning to the overhearing audience in line 7 and explaining his conversation to them. But just as often, the hosts minimize this distance by broaching topics of shared experience, such as the weather:

(10)

1 **H** Did you all get much snow there in West Virginia?
2 **C** Oh we've got um (pause) we got about three <u>foot</u> of snow and
3   [um   ]
4 **H** [Whoo!]
5 **C** we've got drifts up to six<u>teen</u> feet. [So   ]
6 **H**   [Wow.]

7	C	It-
8		We're snowed <u>in</u> for a couple of days. [<laughter>]
9	H	[That's-] so are <u>we</u>
10		I tell [you.]
11	C	[I'm] sticking by the TV. <laughter>
12	H	I was I was <u>glad</u> to come in today.
13		I was bouncing off the walls a little earlier so <laughter>
14	C	Yeah
15		we went out and <u>tried</u> to to take a walk earlier but we
16		didn't get too far. <laughter>
17	H	I can imagine with three feet of snow
18		[goodness.]
19	C	[Yeah.]
20	H	Well (pause) g- try to stay warm and thanks for stopping by.
21	C	Thank <u>you</u>.
22	H	You have a good night Dorothy.
23	C	You too.

The host's query about the weather is, in context, especially useful for forging a sense of community, since it is prompted by a large snowstorm that swept the eastern states. He thus taps into a pre-existing notion of community around the crisis. The sense of shared space created in this fashion, moreover, is exaggerated by the host's use of the expression *thanks for stopping by* (line 20). The expression *to stop by* is part of the register of the guest/host relationship and presupposes that the guest is visiting the host's home, a shared physical location. The idea of 'stopping by' suggests that the shopping channel is tied to place, and that that place is welcoming and friendly, designed and appointed like a private home, from the evidence of the various sets that are used for merchandise display. It is remarkable that language can construct the illusion of domestic hospitality so readily in the absence of any shared location. This linguistic power is even more noteworthy when juxtaposed with the failed attempts to build a community of consumption within other capitalist institutions, most obviously the shopping mall. The strategy of the shopping mall has been to heighten the sense of community as shared place by reproducing the material trappings of community in the form of the historic village shopping district, but this bid to unify consumers through nostalgia has failed (Crawford, 1992), perhaps partly because it emphasizes physical over interactive aspects of community. The privileged status of language in producing a sense of community becomes apparent by contrast.

Equally important, however, is the difference between the public 'town square' replicated in malls and megastores and the private, domestic sets displayed on the shopping channel. Although the shopping channel is public on a scale far greater than that of any shopping mall, the intimacy of its setting licenses exchanges of equal intimacy, which bind viewers more closely to the network and its products. Thus topics seemingly outside the economic exchange may come to be associated with it, and the reverse is also true: discussions of consumption can take on other meanings, especially intimacy. This phenomenon is most evident in the narratives of self-disclosure that are crafted by hosts and viewers alike. In one of the few academic treatments of teleshopping, Mimi White (1992) argues that the discourse of the shopping channel is therapeutic in that it offers viewers an opportunity to confess their personal habits of consumption to a recognized expert, the network host. White's discussion is both incisive and wide-ranging, but I differ with her on this point. Confessional discourse necessarily invites either absolution or punishment, yet the teleshopping host's role is not to judge the actions reported by the caller but to applaud them. Further, Robin Tolmach Lakoff (1990) has suggested that therapeutic change is enacted through the covert adversarial component of the therapeutic process. But both this adversarial stance and the goal of change are absent in the shopping channel. What is present, in abundance, is self-revelatory discourse. Self-disclosure is not, however, synonymous with confession; confession is only one of the many uses to which self-disclosure may be put. More commonly, the revelation of self is utilized as a technique for creating intimacy.

In the narratives of the shopping channel, self-revelation is most often associated with consumption. These are modelled by the host both in conversations with viewers and in presentations of merchandise. The host uses several methods to prime callers to provide self-disclosing testimonials about commodities, including hypothetical scenarios about how consumers might use a given item; unsolicited narratives of her or his own experience with a product; and invitations to viewers to share their consumption experiences. Hosts use the hypothetical scenario primarily during their descriptions of merchandise. These suggestions translate into future narratives that a buyer could share in call-in testimonials to the network. Lines 13–14 in example (9) above illustrate the use of the hypothetical scenario: *This kind of necklace reminds me of something you might _wear_ to like a jazz concert.* Such scenarios not only present ideas for how the viewer might best put some item to use, but also evoke the ideologies of the consumption community. The hypothetical world of the consumer that is sketched by the host is one in which women have office careers, work out at health clubs, buy gifts for their professional husbands, have children, entertain frequently, decorate their houses attractively, and stock them with up-to-date electronic equipment (see also Clarke, this volume).

The host may go a step further, however, and report her or his own use of a commodity. This type of narrative shows up both in telephone conversations and in product presentation and is frequent in banter between the host and other network employees. But self-revelatory discourse does not serve merely as a model for callers. In telephone interaction, hosts' self-disclosures follow rather than precede those of teleshoppers, an indication that hosts disclose their personal experiences not simply to elicit caller narratives but to show support when a caller volunteers a testimonial. For example, in (11), the host follows up the caller's account of why she has purchased home exercise equipment (1–11) with a similar story of her own (13–20):

(11)
1   C   I you know even though I have a club <u>mem</u>bership,
2   H   Mhm.
3   C   I still I
4   like sometimes (I like doing I xxx)
5   one thing a body can never get on the <u>ones</u> that they have
6   at the <u>club</u>.
7   H   Right [(xx)]
8   C   [So if] I was at home (it's gonna) I'll be able to
9   utilize <u>this</u> at home,
10   better than I would trying to get on one of them
11   at the club.
12 H   That's a good point to make.
13   Whenever I go to my health club?
14   I always have to sign up and wait in line to use
15   my [stuff]
16 C   [you got] a waiting list and a line to wait and <u>uh</u>.
17   Can <u>nev</u>er get on it,
18   so
19 H   And who needs <u>that</u>,
20   you know?

The parallel narratives of caller and host contribute to the creation of a sense of community, of shared experience. Moreover, the readiness of the host to demonstrate membership in the caller's world is matched by the caller's eagerness to exhibit her proficiency in the world of the shopping channel.

This fact is seen in the testimonials provided by callers in response to queries from the host or occasioned by spontaneous enthusiasm for the product under discussion (see Bucholtz, 1999).

Likewise, callers and hosts are quick to point to their shared tribulations, such as the problems of body size and shape: one caller confides, 'See, I have big hips. My hips are big but my top is nothing', and a host laments his 'hazardous waist'. Lexical items also contribute to this aura of intimacy, for example in expressions of well-wishing like *Take care, Good luck, Stay warm,* and *I hope the snow starts to melt for you.* Such expressions may additionally make reference to the viewer's purchases, such as *Bon appétit on your new dinnerware set,* or, to the purchaser of exercise equipment, *I hope you get in tip-top shape.*

Callers and hosts enter each other's worlds in other ways as well. In particular, when conversation moves away from commodities, it often turns towards the topic of family and home life.

    (12)
<dog barking in background>
C   [Sh- oh I'd better go]
H   [Oh there's the <u>pu</u>ppy,]
      [What's] <u>his</u> name?
C   [Huh?]
      I have three puppies. <dog barking>
H   Oh, three of them. <laughter>
C   <hands clapping in background>
      Yep. <laughter>
H   They sound like they're pretty excited.
C   Kiko,
      Mischief,
      and Chocolate.
H   Oh my goodness.
      That sounds cute.

As Example (12) illustrates, hosts seize such opportunities whenever they present themselves. Although the caller tries to end the conversation when her dog starts barking, the host's questions and comments keep the caller talking and revealing details about her pets. This show of interest on the part of the host, like most of the discourse on the shopping channel, is formulaic despite its improvised appearance: hence in Example (5) above, the host slips in her response to the news of the caller's approaching birthday, launching into a welcoming routine and then quickly correcting herself (line 6).

Likewise, the *What's your X's name?* routine is a frequently used device for manufacturing intimacy:

> (13)
> C   You all are great I tell you,
> H   <low volume> Well thank you.
>   What's your husband's name?
> C   Uh (pause) Michael.
> H   <mock shout> Hi Michael how you doing?
> C   <laughter> He says hi.
> H   <laughter> Okay.
>   Well I'm glad both of you stopped by to say hello.

The host is able to call upon this strategy because the caller has made reference to her husband earlier in the call – not explicitly, but with the pronoun *we*, which most callers use to invoke their marital relationship (see also Example 10, lines 15 and 16: *We went out and tried to to take a walk earlier but we didn't get too far*). And the very act of using a pronoun rather than a full noun phrase like *my husband and I* reveals the caller's own orientation towards an intimate, private discourse in which heterosexual union is taken for granted – a discourse that she (correctly) assumes the shopping channel shares.

   In fact, husbands have a special cachet on the shopping channel. Men are in the minority among both hosts and viewers, but husbands are a constant topic of intimate conversation. Thus the breathless excitement of one viewer, who called in to say she had encountered the host's husband by chance, becomes understandable. This near-brush with near-fame brings the host more firmly into the viewer's world, making the fictive community of the shopping channel almost real, as suggested by the way the caller sums up her story:

> (14)
> C   I almost felt like I knew him because I- I watch you so much.
> H   And and I tell you our little secrets which you won't tell.
>   <laughter>
> C   Absolutely. <laughter>

The host's response brings together the issues of community, intimacy, and artificiality that lie at the heart of the shopping channel. Playfully aligning herself in an intimate friendship with an utter stranger, the host immediately calls attention to the artifice of this relationship by humorously invoking a friend's obligation to keep one's secrets. Yet by reminding viewers that they are part of a wider audience that shares in the day-to-day life of hosts, even superficially, the host manages to leave the illusion of community stronger than before. The greatest pleasure that the shopping channel offers, ultimately, is not faux diamonds but faux friendships with the network hosts.

Conclusion

The shopping channel both replicates and improves upon viewers' own communities. The network offers an image of the home as refuge, made self-sufficient through regular purchasing of consumer goods. The isolation of the suburban home is thus reinforced by the shopping channel's ideology, although the network also counters this sense of isolation by providing viewers with a set of appealing friends who are always ready with advice and support. Many women stay up and watch late into the night after the rest of their household has gone to bed, finding fellowship on the television screen and the phone line.

But besides providing the comfort of community, the shopping channel does make life easier for many women in other ways. Shopping by television is convenient for women whose homes are far from retail areas and for those with small children or with ailments that keep them tied to their homes. The relatively low prices of QVC's merchandise can ease the costs of holiday gift giving, and the 24-hour broadcasts make it possible for women who work the night shift to get their shopping done.

These real benefits of teleshopping, however, are eclipsed by the artificiality of the shopping-channel world. The language of loyalty, intimacy, and community that pervades the network recasts the corporate world of the shopping channel as a folksy, cosy place. Thus, in the economic system of the shopping channel, commodity fetishism is displaced by community fetishism. Language transmutes the public experience of transaction in the market-place into a private experience of pleasure in the home: callers are situated at home and make frequent references to their domestic environment, and the image of domesticity is reflected back at viewers through the setting and language of the shopping channel. At the same time, however, the private world of women's lives is displayed publicly in telephone conversations between host and caller. The blending of public and private has gendered consequences, for the illusion of community that the shopping channel fosters through the linguistic practices of its pro-gramme hosts makes women willing subjects for market research and corporate monitoring. The language of the shopping channel, then, is a particularly crucial site for understanding how the slippage in late-capitalist America between the economic market-place and Bourdieu's market-place of linguistic exchange shapes the lives of women as consumers and viewers.

Transcription conventions

.	falling intonation
,	fall-rise intonation
?	rising intonation
—	self-interruption; break in the intonation unit
-	self-interruption; break in the word, sound abruptly cut off
underline	emphatic stress
(pause)	pause of 0.5 seconds or less
( )	uncertain transcription; each x marks one syllable
< >	transcriber comment; vocal quality or nonvocal noise
[ ]	overlap beginning and end

Line breaks correspond to intonation units.
Spatial arrangement reflects sequential organization of talk.

References

Anderson, B. (1991) *Imagined Communities*. New York: Verso.

Bourdieu, P. (1977) 'The economics of linguistic exchanges', *Social Science Information Bulletin*, 16(6), 645–68.

Bucholtz, M. (1999) 'Purchasing power: the gender and class imaginary on the shopping channel'. In M. Bucholtz, A. C. Liang and L. Sutton (eds), *Reinventing Identities: The Gendered Self in Discourse*. Oxford: Oxford University Press.

Clarke, A. (2000) '"As seen on TV": design and domestic economy'. Chapter 10, this volume.

Crawford, M. (1992) 'The world in a shopping mall'. In M. Sorkin (ed.), *Variations on a Theme Park*. New York: Noonday, pp. 3–30.

Fairclough, N. (1989) *Language and Power*. London: Longman.

Lakoff, R. T. (1990) *Talking Power*. New York: Basic Books.

Rheingold, H. (1993) *The Virtual Community*. Reading, MA: Addison-Wesley.

Talbot, M. (1992) 'The construction of gender in a teenage magazine'. In N. Fairclough (ed.), *Critical Language Awareness*. London: Longman, pp. 174–99.

Talbot, M. (1995) 'A synthetic sisterhood: false friends in a teenage magazine'. In K. Hall and M. Bucholtz (eds), *Gender Articulated*. New York: Routledge, pp. 143–65.

White, M. (1992) *Tele-Advising: Therapeutic Discourse in American Television*. Chapel Hill: University of North Carolina Press.

14. A self off the shelf? Consuming women's empowerment

Deborah Cameron

Academic interest in women as consumers has often focused on their relationship to popular cultural commodities produced by the publishing industry, such as romantic fiction and teenage magazines. Studying these specifically textual commodities gives insight into 'the cultural consumption and transmission of ideas about gender, selfhood and interaction with others' (Simonds, 1992, p. 2).

Currently, a key locus where women (and men, though arguably in a different way – see below) engage with ideas about gender, selfhood and interaction with others is through consuming the textual genre of popular self-help, a genre which takes gender, selfhood and interaction with others as its overt subject-matter. The growth in this genre's popularity and salience is one of the publishing industry's major recent (and continuing) success stories. The self-help formula has also proved well adapted to media other than print, providing a popular format for radio phone-ins and TV talk-shows of the 'confessional' type, as well as the inspiration for quasi-educational 'products' like seminars and training courses.

In sum, there is an awful lot of self-help around, it exists in an ever-increasing diversity of forms, and women (especially middle-class professional women) are probably the most important market for most of them. As with other cultural commodities consumed by large numbers of women, arguments rage about the meaning and effect of consuming self-help; does this practice offer women a means to empowerment and self-realization, or does it merely console them for their powerlessness while reinforcing, at a deeper level, the beliefs and attitudes responsible for that powerlessness?

In this chapter I will consider these questions by discussing women's consumption of books and other products (e.g. audio and videotapes, seminars and training courses) which purport to be about 'empowerment'; in other words, they deal directly and specifically with the question of power. I began studying this phenomenon out of an interest in language and gender; specifically, my interest was in the tradition of linguistic advice that I have called 'verbal hygiene for women' (Cameron, 1995). Advice to women on how to use language in order to construct and display a particular kind of feminine subjectivity is not new: it can be traced back to the conduct books of medieval and early modern Europe (Jones, 1987). Recently, however, for a variety of reasons, questions of gender, language and communication have become increasingly salient in the culture, producing a striking upsurge in the popularity of this kind of advice.[1] It is notable that two of the most successful advice books published this decade have belonged to the verbal hygiene subgenre: Deborah Tannen's *You Just Don't Understand* (1990) and John Gray's *Men Are from Mars, Women Are from Venus* (1992).

These books are, at least superficially, very different from the verbal hygiene of pre-feminist eras. The female recipients of present-day verbal hygiene advice are explicitly or implicitly addressed as members of a historically disempowered group which now seeks 'empowerment'. What they are presumed to need, therefore, is not – as it usually was in the past – guidance on the forms of language behaviour thought appropriate to their (subordinate) social position. Rather, it is the knowledge and skills required to transcend that positioning, and/or to deal with the kind of gender trouble that arises from it.

My concern in this discussion is to place this new, 'empowerment'-oriented verbal hygiene in context and to raise the question of what makes it a popular commodity. While I am certainly critical of it, and will not be trying for a 'redemptive reading' in which women's consumption of advice literature becomes a subversive activity, I will follow other analysts in rejecting the idea that consumers are merely dupes. Some of the texts mentioned below have been cited as evidence of the anti-feminist 'backlash', which is discussed at times as if it were a conscious conspiracy. Even if it were, I see no reason to suppose that, on its own, it would work: women are plainly active interpreters of the products on offer to them, and my own findings, as well as those of other researchers, suggest those products are often read 'against the grain'. I do think, however, that any understanding of why particular strategies of consumption and interpretation become relevant to large numbers of women in particular times and places requires us to consider the cultural/political context those women inhabit. And whether or not one believes in an external backlash against it, it is clear feminism itself has changed.

Changing feminisms: from CR to self-help

There is a possible historical account of recent feminism which goes something
like this. Once upon a time, in the 1970s, both academic feminists and
movement activists – who were sometimes, indeed, the same individuals –
grounded their thinking in an undifferentiated and unproblematic category
of 'women's experience'. In practices like consciousness-raising (CR), in
support groups and discussion groups of all kinds, they (we) went poking
through the rubbish heap of patriarchal conditioning and oppression in search
of authentic female selves. In the 1980s, this procedure was questioned: on
one hand, in 'high' theory, where fashionable post-structuralism and later
postmodernism encouraged feminists to reject the myth of the unified self
with its authentic experience; and, on the other hand, in the move towards
an ever-more fragmented identity politics, where authenticity was still all,
but selves were increasingly narrowly defined and differences among women
insisted upon.

As history, I think this account can be questioned (see Cameron, 1993).
As psychology, however (using the term in its everyday, loose sense), it has
more resonance. Arguably, there has been a loss of old certainties about the
(unified) female self and of confidence in appeals to women's (undifferentiated) experience. It has been claimed – and again, I think there is some
truth in this – that as a consequence, feminism has lost the quality of being
a 'broad church', disseminating ideas that were capable of commanding
relatively wide interest and allegiance among fairly 'mainstream' women.[2]
But what the counter-culture now declines to offer, popular culture provides.
Or as a friend remarked: 'The self didn't die, it just moved to a different
shelf in the feminist bookstore.'[3] That shelf bears the label 'self-help'.

Some of the most successful mass-market non-fiction books of recent years
fall into the category of women's self-help. 'Classic' titles like *Women Who
Love Too Much* (Norwood, 1985) and *The Cinderella Complex* (Dowling, 1981),
as well as the more recent works on communication problems cited above
(Tannen, 1990; Gray, 1992), are likely to be familiar to anyone who regularly
reads women's magazines, visits libraries or bookshops. Such titles do not
only sell in volume, they also sell steadily: the most successful can stay on
best-seller lists for several years.

The main theme of all these books (despite the equal opportunities
disclaimers you find in some of them[4]) is the female self and the problems
thereof, as encountered, primarily, in male–female relationships (especially
heterosexual ones). The formula for writing a book in this genre is to define
a problem or syndrome (e.g. 'loving too much' for Norwood, 'male–female
misunderstanding' for Tannen), illustrate it copiously with anecdotes about

various archetypal characters, and offer advice on how to cope with it. The preferred advice borrows from a model associated with many forms of therapy: it stresses acceptance, understanding and tolerance rather than change, whether personal or social. Thus, for instance, the answer to male–female misunderstanding as proposed by Tannen is not for either sex to alter their behaviour, nor is it to try to change the institutions within which misunderstanding is occurring (the heterosexual couple, the family, the workplace, etc.). It is for both sexes to understand and be tolerant of gender difference.

As this brief account implies, the self-help genre has both continuities with and differences from feminist political discourse. The focus on personal experience, personal relationships (especially male–female ones) and, most particularly, on that which is problematic, troublesome and liable to make women unhappy, is reminiscent of many feminist discussions. One might say that this is precisely the kind of mainstream women's concern that feminism in its later high-theoretical mode has more or less ceased to talk about. On the other hand, the quasi-therapeutic emphasis on tolerance rather than action for change is, historically speaking, rather unfeminist. The members of 1970s CR groups, say, did not air their troubles only for the sake of airing them. They were talking in order to formulate analyses which were meant to lead on to both personal and collective action. The slogan was 'the personal is political', meaning that what were taken for personal problems in fact had their roots in a larger political system. In self-help, personal problems become personal once again. It is important that they be depicted as shared troubles, suffered by all women to a greater or lesser extent, but it is also important that the solutions offered should posit neither thorough-going collectivism (the point is to help oneself, by oneself) nor serious disruption of the existing social order.

These may seem like sweeping statements; the evidence for them comes partly from surveying the content of the texts, and partly from those reception studies that have been undertaken by social researchers. The latter have found, intriguingly, that regular and committed consumers of self-help literature *apparently do not read it for the purpose of getting help and advice.* That is to say, the ostensible *raison d'être* of the entire genre – to solve problems, to change lives, to help people help themselves – seems virtually irrelevant to the reading pleasure.

The sociologist Wendy Simonds (1992) carried out in-depth interviews with 30 women who consumed self-help books in a quantity and with a dedication reminiscent of the romance readers famously studied by Janice Radway (1987). She found that their main interest was in recognizing themselves, having their problems labelled and their perceptions validated by an 'expert'. They were not much interested in the strategies an author offered for solving or coping with the problem, whatever it might be. The benefit they identified was 'understanding' or 'reassurance'; and they identified this specifically as a source of empowerment because it made them more confident in their own judgements of what to do. Thus Simonds quotes 'Carol', an informant who told her:

> [Reading self-help] has given me a lot of the ideas I've always had [sic] . . .
> But it's given me the reassurance that I was pretty much on target with
> my thoughts and that I was heading in the right direction, and it's just
> given me the confirmation to go with my feelings and be more self-
> confident. (1992: 1)

So impressed was Simonds with the apparent gulf between what authors seemed to be saying ('you can change this') and what readers seemed to be hearing ('this is how things are') that she gave her book the subtitle *Reading Between the Lines*.

Paul Lichterman, similarly, interviewed self-help readers of both sexes (Lichterman, 1992). He was struck by the failure of informants to recall, just a few weeks after reading, the details of the advice offered in books they claimed to have found inspirational. Like Simonds he concluded that there was very little investment on the part of readers in actual change. Rather, he suggested that they were seeking 'a new language for personal life' (*ibid.*, p. 443).

This is an interesting observation, since the term 'empowerment', much used in the literature and other practices associated with self-help, is itself part of a new language, or rather discourse, through which, increasingly, members of Western cultures are encouraged to understand not only our personal lives but social and political processes too: the language/discourse of therapy. Therapeutic language is not new in itself, of course, but what is a relatively recent development is its appropriation and diffusion across a much larger set of contexts than just therapy, and thus its increased salience in everyday as well as expert discourse. This is the process the critical linguist Norman Fairclough (1992) calls discourse 'technologization': a linguistic practice that was once associated with a very particular social setting and purpose (in this case, clinical) comes to be seen as a context-free tool which may be applied to any situation (thus, for instance, counselling techniques are now commonly used in such entirely non-therapeutic speech events as the job interview).

As Jenny Rankine has noted, the transfer of therapeutic discourse to new contexts or domains has had consequences for the way we understand and talk about social or power relations; these consequences may well be felt by feminists in particular, since the feminist concept of politics always did relate it to the domain of 'personal life' which is therapy's special concern. Rankine observes that:

> The meaning of political concepts like 'power', 'rights', 'freedom' and 'choice' have all been changed . . . by the gradual predominance of therapeutic meanings. In self-help groups, rituals and counselling, power has become talked of as an individual's personal possession. (Rankine, 1996, p. 13)

The therapeutic way of talking about power, as something an individual has, or else lacks, by virtue of the choices she makes and the way in which she conducts herself, is more conducive to the commodification of power than alternative ways of understanding it. It goes along with the idea that 'empowerment' – the process whereby power is acquired and possessed – can be an object of individual consumption. (In linguists' terms, empowerment is a 'nominalization', a noun or noun phrase produced by compressing a whole sentence ('X gives power to Y') and then reifying the process by deleting the agents involved.)

Paul Lichterman clearly believes that this concept of power is illusory, a way of talking rather than a material condition, and in many cases adopted at a fairly superficial level. His article is titled 'Self-help reading as a thin culture'; 'I name this culture "thin"', he comments, 'because it does not support a deep commitment from readers' (1992, p. 427). This remark is in one way surprising, since he seems to be documenting a significant commitment, as measured by the facts of consumption (how many books, how often, with what degree of enthusiasm). Perhaps what he means is that consumption is itself 'thin', compared to other practices focusing on the self. If so, I am sympathetic to this point of view. I would argue, in fact, that the 'thinness' of current gender-related self-help culture lies in its separation from any collective supports (such as were provided by active social movements like the early Women's Liberation Movement) that might enable consumers actually to 'live' the new understanding of the world they claim to get from books. Without alternative communities to provide reinforcement for alternative (that is, oppositional or non-mainstream) analyses, practices and values, understanding, and the associated sense of 'empowerment', stay contained within the boundaries of a private and solitary activity, namely reading.

Reading pleasures: recognition and reassurance

While researching *Verbal Hygiene* (Cameron, 1995) I carried out interviews with 16 women who had undertaken various forms of communication training (mainly assertiveness training, in fact). In many cases they were also readers of self-help texts about gender and communication, and in particular of Deborah Tannen's best-selling *You Just Don't Understand*, which was then at the height of its popularity. I will come to their talk about this specific text presently, but overall the conclusion I drew from the interviews was that the appeal of self-help texts and practices lies in the picture they present, not of what *might be* but of what *is*. 'Empowerment' is identified with *understanding* how things are. This, furthermore, is mostly a matter of confirming existing understandings of the world: like Simonds's informant Carol, my own informants often felt that the material they read and the input they received on training courses just recapitulated 'a lot of the ideas I've always had', though perhaps more explicitly and in more elegant language.

To the extent readers are looking for guidance on anything, it is whether their own experiences of male–female relations, and their own ways of dealing with problems in those relations, are *normal*. Self-help functions as a kind of normalizing discourse; it is taken to describe the state of 'normal' male–female relations, and this offers consumers a norm against which to judge themselves.

The most significant norm embodied in self-help is the idea that men and women are (and should be) irreducibly different from one another. This, of course, is an idea that feminism (in both liberal–humanist and postmodernist guises) has called into question. The women I interviewed were certainly not anti-feminists who longed for the return of traditional sex roles – on the contrary – but they nevertheless found any radical questioning of funda-mental sexual difference threatening. They were far from Conservative-with-a-capital-C in their views on gender, but in important respects they were small-c conservatives. What self-help held out to them was the possibility that we could get rid of certain persistent gender troubles without actually getting rid of gender in the forms we know it.

Wendy Simonds's informants told her on a number of occasions that the pleasure of self-help reading lies not in discovery but in recognition. I found exactly the same thing when discussing Deborah Tannen's *You Just Don't Understand* with interviewees (the categorization of this title as 'self-help' is mine, and not one the author would accept; my criteria for classifying it as I do are (a) that it fits the generic formula in almost every respect, and (b) – admittedly a *post hoc* generalization – it is invariably read as a self-help book, and was frequently sold as such in bookshops). Tannen's book has an argument which is made very clearly, repeatedly and at length. It is that because of pervasive separation in the formative years of childhood and adolescence, men and women have different goals, and thus norms, when they engage in conversation; that unawareness of this leads to systematic misunderstanding when they talk to one another; and that since neither way of talking is 'better' than the other, the solution to the problem of misunderstanding is for each sex to be more aware and more tolerant of the other's difference. This thesis is illustrated with numerous vignettes of men and women misunderstanding one another. But women who talked to me about the book never mentioned either its overarching argument about how and why men and women were so different, or Tannen's proffered solution to the problem of male–female misunderstanding. Even when I prompted them, many could not reproduce Tannen's argument, although most could reproduce her 'tolerance' prescription. Unprompted, they concentrated entirely on the vignettes, and in particular on whether they 'recognized' the behaviour attributed to men and women in them. For those women who liked the book (the majority), the main reason they gave was that the anecdotes matched their own experience. For the minority who disliked it, the main reason they gave was that the anecdotes *didn't* match their experience. One woman in the latter category commented, tellingly, that she had had a negative reaction after reading only a few pages, because 'it made me feel as if I wasn't really a woman'. This woman could not identify with the actions and feelings attributed to the women in Tannen's vignettes, and she took this as a kind of slight. This is not surprising if one of the questions with which women tend to approach texts in this genre is 'am I normal?' They do not expect, or want, the answer 'no'.

The only other reason anyone gave for not liking *You Just Don't Understand* was that it portrayed men in a stereotypical and very unfavourable light. That is not Tannen's stated intention – on the contrary, her message is that male and female speech styles are 'equally valid' – but it is not an entirely unreasonable interpretation, since the men in many vignettes do come over as insensitive, boorish or just interpersonally useless. While no one who did like the book explicitly said that they relished this portrayal of men, many did specifically cite the *accuracy* of the portrayal as a source of pleasure. In other words, it is at least possible to read *You Just Don't Understand* as a celebration of women's superiority in a domain that is (by Tannen's own account) important to women, namely forging intimate connections with others. For the readers I interviewed, the book's overt message that gender differences and the failure to be tolerant of them cause women serious problems in their day-to-day lives seemed to be undercut by two other messages: 'it's normal to have these problems with men' and 'the fact that you have them is a sign of your superior sensitivity'.

These discussions of *You Just Don't Understand* threw light, in retrospect, on a response I had puzzled over when I was trying to locate women to be interviewed about assertiveness training. Many women whom I approached told me they were unsuitable informants because even if they had experienced AT, they had not needed it: they were 'too assertive already'. This (ironically) was often said not assertively but apologetically; which could be interpreted as signalling some ambivalence, or anxiety, about whether one is a 'normal' woman if one does not require empowerment.

Feminism in a new age: different but equal?

It emerged from my interviews that many informants preferred the 'different but equal' brand of self-help represented by *You Just Don't Understand* as compared to the classic forms of 'empowering' feminist verbal hygiene such as assertiveness training. The latter, though still current, flourished most visibly in the 'heroic' period of feminist activism, and it seems that many women (not all of them young, incidentally) now regard it as 'old-fashioned', belonging to the 1970s and early 1980s. One former trainee described the enterprise of AT by saying 'I suppose it's the verbal equivalent of power dressing.'

As an image of feminism, 'power dressing' has more to do with representations in popular cultural sources like *Cosmopolitan* and *Working Woman* magazines than with the dress codes of, say, Greenham Common women. (I found it fascinating that feminism is often remembered in terms of such commodified representations, even sometimes by women who were directly involved in 'real' feminist groups.) But what my informant was trying to convey with the 'power dressing' analogy was a perception many others shared with her, of AT as something that focuses directly on power as most people common-sensically understand it: getting ahead at work, being listened to when you complain about goods and services, adopting a demeanour that conveys to other people that you are confident, competent and not to be trifled with. 'Power dressing' conveys the message using culturally coded garments (tailored jackets with shoulder pads, for instance); 'assertiveness' conveys it through the use of particular linguistic strategies, like repeating yourself until such time as you are 'heard' and performing even the most face-threatening speech acts on record and directly, without hedging ('just say no' – meaning (a) say no rather than yes, maybe or nothing and (b) say no without further elaboration – is classic AT-speak). Like power dressing, assertiveness was viewed by a number of informants as a stage women had to go through (being 'strident' about our demands, in certain respects aping men), but this version of 'empowerment' is, thankfully, no longer necessary or desirable for women in the 1990s.

As a matter of fact, the history of AT is more complicated than my informant's comment might suggest, and her description of it as 'the verbal equivalent of power-dressing', while probably reflecting the emphasis of the particular course she was involved in, did not match the perceptions of all other informants. Historically, AT does not belong with the 'how to get ahead' species of advice and training, even if it is commonly offered on management and 'leadership' courses. Its roots have nothing to do with feminism either. AT was developed as a behaviour therapy in the late 1940s, and its purpose was to help rehabilitate patients in psychiatric hospitals, many of whom understandably lacked the communication skills needed to function in normal life because they were psychotic or severely depressed. Some, in addition, had been hospitalized because of antisocial or deviant behaviour (including male homosexual activity) which, it was thought, would diminish if they were taught techniques for expressing feelings verbally and resisting peer pressure to 'act out'.

The story of how a behaviour modification technique targeting 'deviants' and people with severe psychiatric illness came to be regarded as a feminist technology of empowerment is a fascinating one (though too long to tell in detail here), and it is partly a story of commodification: the repackaging of therapeutic 'products' for mass consumption. In this process of commodification, it is typical for the goals, methods and ideological underpinnings of an originally well-defined activity to become vague, blurred and mixed with imports from elsewhere, to suit the preferences of various potential customers. This leads to considerable variation: in market terms, diversification. Some forms of AT on offer today are of the 'how to get ahead', verbal power-dressing type, but many others have more affinity with various kinds of therapy, stressing that AT is about 'clear, honest and direct communication' (a quote from one leading provider's mission statement) – which may or may not make trainees more 'successful', but which will surely make them better-adjusted individuals.

Whether it is embodied in some form of AT or in the newer, 'male–female misunderstanding' type of self-help literature, this quasi-therapeutic view of 'empowerment' as a process whereby the individual gains understanding of her/his behaviour and its effect on others seems to be perceived by many women as more in tune with the temper of our times than more directive advice on how to talk, dress or behave. (A number of my informants alluded to that 1980s icon Margaret Thatcher – who was, of course, 'made over' both linguistically and sartorially – and expressed relief that women now have more and better choices about their self-presentation.) Analogously, feminism itself for many women is now viewed as a politics of individual choice (to work for wages or not, get married or not, etc.) rather than a politics of collective action.

Postscript (May 1997)

I have been saying, in essence, that times change; we, and our pleasures, change with them. Self-help/advice literature might seem to be a genre whose very existence testifies to *displeasure*: on the face of things it is all about the aspects of our lives and selves that prevent us being truly happy, fulfilled or 'empowered'. Yet studies of its consumers have suggested that this is an over-simple account of the genre's meaning. It offers pleasure to many consumers by *recognizing* that which is problematic in their experience, by *reassuring* them that they are not alone or abnormal in finding life difficult in particular ways, and by offering them *understanding* of their condition.

Does this amount to 'empowerment'? While I cannot deny the value of reflection and understanding – I'm an academic, after all! – I belong to the generation of feminists who believed that understanding was empowering only if it led to change. On the other hand, I am well aware that, largely because of the changes this generation of feminists was able to effect, women today stand in a quite different place, and it is idle to dream of going back.

One of the differences between now and then is, undoubtedly, the commodification of feminism itself, and of its principal goal (rendered in today's discourse as 'women's empowerment'). One could argue that market diversification, and particularly the advent of less overtly prescriptive forms of self-help, give women consumers more autonomy as well as more pleasure: it allows them more space in which to negotiate their own relationship to various kinds of femininity and power. On the other hand, this 'autonomy' may be deceptive; if it is accurate to say that the main pleasures on offer to self-help readers are recognition and reassurance, then arguably what women are being encouraged to do is take comfort from fairly traditional ideas about femininity and gender difference and rather unthreatening ideas of power or empowerment.

Since I conducted the research discussed here, there has been a burgeoning of discourse – both expert and popular – suggesting that where language is concerned, women's strength lies in their difference; indeed, the world would be a better place if men were in certain respects more like them. British Telecom based an entire advertising campaign on this idea (see Talbot, forthcoming, for discussion), and more significantly it was a prominent theme when, on 1 May 1997, the British electorate returned a record number of women – 119 – to Parliament. We were told over and over again that, in the words of the *Observer* newspaper (4 May 1997), 'Westminster will be less of a bear garden.' As women's influence is felt in the legislative process and in its discourse, gladiatorial debate will be replaced by more constructive and co-operative ways of working, conflict by consensus politics.

To me this sounds uncomfortably like the mission with which women have been entrusted since time immemorial: to civilize men. That is also an important part of the hidden agenda in the new literature of 'women's empowerment', which says we empower ourselves by being ourselves, embracing our difference and insisting it is respected by the culture too. Clearly, this idea has a long and not dishonourable history in feminism, from the nineteenth-century suffrage movement to the farther fringes of post-structuralist theory. Essentialist though it may be, I cannot criticize it as inherently antithetical to the feminist project. But still I wonder why it now occupies the central ground in mainstream understandings and representations of that project. Is it what feminists want, or is it just the gendered version of Paul Lichterman's 'thin culture', easier than alternative visions of feminism to sell?

Notes

1. One of these reasons is the long-term shift in attitudes and expectations (especially women's) brought about by post-1968 feminism; but there are others. It is a characteristic of contemporary society that all kinds of social and economic problems, from youth unemployment to marital breakdown, are presented discursively as partly if not wholly problems of communication. Economic developments (e.g. the move from manufacturing to service work and 'knowledge work', aided by electronic technology) reinforce anxiety about 'communication'. These same developments also have a significant impact on gender identities and relations since, on one hand, what is vanishing is the kind of work traditionally done by a male breadwinner, while, on the other hand, what is appearing is a kind of work traditionally done by women and requiring skills that are often considered 'feminine'. I regard the recent upsurge in verbal hygiene advice for women as partly a reflex of conflict engendered by these changes.

2. This 'mainstream' had its own biases; it was white and middle class (or perhaps more accurately, extensively educated). The fragmentation of this constituency (without, as far as I can see, any compensatory rise in feminist sympathy among working-class and minority ethnic women) is perhaps most

aptly illustrated by the demise of *Spare Rib* magazine, discussed e.g. by Wallsgrove (1993).

3. This remark was made by Meryl Altman, whom I thank.

4. Market research has found that self-help is a unisex market, and not as strictly divided as one might expect along the lines of men buying 'career' self-help literature and women buying 'relationship' literature (Wood, 1984). It is clear from my own small-scale research that relationship-oriented books, and specifically here *You Just Don't Understand*, may be read by both members of a heterosexual couple (typically, in my observation, at the woman's instigation). However, market research tells you little about how people read and from what positions. Those issues are better addressed by small-scale depth studies like Simonds's or my own. It is my view that women both read the relationship genre, and 'know how to read' it, more than/differently from men. The 'knowing how' is probably because of the ubiquity of the same generic conventions in girls' and women's magazine features. But in addition – and this is in fact Deborah Tannen's main thesis, though disingenuously played down in the unisex marketing of her work – the business of managing personal relationships is culturally gendered: it is women's work.

References

Cameron, D. (1993) 'Telling it like it wasn't: how radical feminism became history', *Trouble & Strife*, 27, Winter, 11–15.

Cameron, D. (1995) *Verbal Hygiene*. London: Routledge.

Dowling, C. (1981) *The Cinderella Complex: Women's Hidden Fear of Independence*. New York: Summit.

Fairclough, N. (ed.) (1992) *Critical Language Awareness*. Harlow: Longman.

Gray, J. (1992) *Men Are from Mars, Women Are from Venus*. New York: HarperCollins.

Jones, A. R. (1987) 'Nets and bridles: early modern conduct books and sixteenth century women's lyrics'. In N. Armstrong and L. Tennenhouse (eds), *The Ideology of Conduct: Essays on Literature and the History of Sexuality*. New York: Methuen.

Lichterman, P. (1992) 'Self-help reading as a thin culture', *Media, Culture and Society*, 14, 421–47.

Norwood, R. (1985) *Women Who Love Too Much*. London: Arrow.

Radway, J. (1987) *Reading the Romance*. London: Verso.

Rankine, J. (1996) 'Putting therapy on the couch', *Broadsheet*, Summer, pp. 11–14.

Simonds, W. (1992) *Women and Self-Help Culture: Reading Between the Lines*. New Brunswick, NJ: Rutgers University Press.

Talbot, M. M. (forthcoming) 'The acceptable face of feminism in contemporary advertising', *Journal of Sociolinguistics*.

Tannen, D. (1990) *You Just Don't Understand: Women and Men in Conversation*. New York: Morrow.

Wallsgrove, R. (1993) 'Sweet and sour: *Spare Rib* 1972–1993', *Trouble & Strife*, Summer, 26, 4–6.

Wood, L. (1988) 'Self-help buying trends', *Publishers Weekly*, 14 October, p. 33.

15. Fashioning the career woman: power dressing as a strategy of consumption

Joanne Entwistle

Introduction

In August 1997 the US edition of *Vogue*, along with its European counterparts, heralded the 'return of the suit'. The autumn/winter collections the same year had seen a return to the fashion phenomenon of the 1980s known as 'power dressing', with designers such as Alexandra McQueen and Dolce & Gabbana show-casing short skirts, shoulder pads and stiletto heels (see also Tredre in the *Observer*, 1997). In London in April the same year, the 24th Businesswoman of the Year award held at Claridges Hotel was attended by women in business and industry who, dressed in their best suits (Alexon, Escada, Planet, along with the more expensive Armani), spoke of the confidence that the tailored suit gave them at work (Sampson, 1997).

However, for these women the suit had not made a sudden return after nearly a decade's absence. The *New Yorker*'s editor Tina Brown summed it up when she noted that, while her magazine did its own feature on the return of the 1980s and power dressing, as far as she was concerned 'they never went away' (Posnick, 1997). What Brown's comments and the dress of the women attending the Businesswoman of the Year award point to is the fact that, whatever the fashion cycle, women in business and in many professions have worn and will continue to wear suits to work: it is a fact of life not a fashion statement. Indeed the suit has, in the words of the designer Billy Blass (himself a popular designer of female suits), become 'inevitable' for the woman who works (Blass, 1997, p. 210). This is not to say that the business suit is immune to fashion (on the contrary, suits adapt to fashion trends). However, what it does mean is that, whatever and wherever the fashion cycle goes next year (the 'return of the baby doll', for example), the women in business attending next year's Businesswoman of the Year award will be there in their skirt or trouser suit.

It may not have all started with power dressing in the 1980s (think of Joan Crawford or Marlene Dietrich earlier in the century and you have the prototype power dresser) but it is only during that decade that a distinct and self-conscious mode of dressing entered popular iconography and imagination, serving to establish a code of dress that is now widely recognized and adopted by women in a wide arena of professional and business settings. Power dressing emerged in the 1980s as a discourse on self-presentation ostensibly concerned with female empowerment in the workplace: it spoke to the emerging 'career women' about how to fashion themselves as competent and capable professionals. In doing so, it also laid out a strategy of consumption for career women which aimed to provide them with a set of principles for dressing that would enable them to purchase a trouble-free wardrobe for work. These principles have now been translated by numerous designers into a retail strategy. Since the 1980s, power dressing has opened up a new market within the retail trade, catering for the needs of professional women; a number of designers (Armani, Donna Karan, Jil Sander, for example) and high street shops (such as Jigsaw and Hobbs) are now recognized as providing tailored clothes for professional and business women. In addition, the phenomenon of power dressing has also stimulated the development of new patterns of consumption amongst women who can now purchase the services of image/dress consultants to help them put together their work wardrobe.

In this chapter I intend to explore the ways in which power dressing articulates a mode of dressing for the professional or business woman and consider what it has to say about the presence of a woman in what are typically male arenas of work. In particular, I want to explore how this discourse talks of 'empowering' women in the workplace. In order to do this, I will examine in the first part of the chapter the 'rules' of power dressing as laid out in the now classic dress manual of the 1980s, *Women: Dress for Success* (Molloy, 1980). In the second part of this chapter, I want to consider how the discourse of power dressing has informed the dress practices and consumption patterns of professional and business women in the 1990s. Drawing on interview extracts, I hope to illustrate the solutions power dressing has offered women, solutions which attempt to get around the problems of self-presentation at work, the problem of what dress to consume for work. However, as I will argue, while ostensibly about female empowerment, power dressing is inherently conservative and women's dress for the professional workplace is still fraught with more difficulties than men's.

Fashioning the career woman in the 1980s

The 1980s did not see women adopting suits for the first time. Women have worn the equivalent of the male suit to work for much of the twentieth century: for example, Edwardian ladies at the turn of the century moving into the expanding tertiary sector (in particular, clerical work and retail) wore tailored jackets and ties adapted from male riding dress (Steele, 1989). However, the 1980s saw the emergence of an explicit and popular discourse on female empowerment at work which addressed professional and business women in particular. More than simply rhetoric, power dressing set out a strategy for self-presentation which laid down particular 'rules' as to what clothes, hair and make-up to buy in order to increase one's chances of career success. It is no coincidence that this form of dress appeared at a time when women were beginning to reap some of the benefits of feminism and sex discrimination legislation and enter into positions at work which had hitherto been the preserve of men. It is also around this time that the metaphor of the 'glass ceiling' was used to describe the invisible barrier that is said to lie between women and the upper echelons of work. As a self-conscious 'uniform' for business and professional women, power dressing set out to increase a woman's 'authority' and her ability to do her job, thereby enhancing her prospects of breaking through the glass ceiling. John T. Molloy's influential 'self-help' manual on dress, *Women: Dress for Success*, provides a clear illustration of this concern with 'authority' and his manual lays out the 'rules' for its acquisition (Molloy, 1980). Molloy argues that in order for a woman to have 'authority' as a professional or executive, she must first be visible and recognizable as the 'boss' or the 'manager', in other words she must *look the part*. Molloy illustrates this need for visibility by recounting the story of how, sometime in the early 1970s, he was asked to meet three executives in a bar. After looking around unable to spot them, he finally paged them and discovered to his surprise that they were sitting less than ten feet away. The three executives were the three 'conservatively dressed' women sitting near the bar, 'yet I never considered the possibility that they might be my executives. I had been looking for three men' (1980, p. 35). The tale not only illustrates the implicit gendered assumption that 'executive' equals 'male', but demonstrates, according to Molloy, the degree to which, without a recognizable 'uniform' equivalent to the male business suit, professional and business women were 'invisible' within the public arena and therefore not being recognized and taken seriously in their professional roles. Molloy says that this made him come to the 'conclusion that here was a real need to develop a sign for business*women* to wear that is as effective as the sign worn by business*men*' (*ibid.*, p. 35). He went on to conduct a survey which, he claims, showed that there was no outfit that was widely recognized as a uniform for business and professional woman. Moreover, executive women entering into the careered occupations were finding themselves confused with the secretary and were therefore not getting the respect and recognition to which they were entitled. In his attempt to define a 'uniform' for professional and business women, Molloy set about 'testing' (in laboratory-like conditions) different garments and different colours and cuts. The end result of this 'wardrobe engineering', as he calls it, is a 'uniform' which aims to solve the problem of visibility at work for the career woman by providing her with a set of clear principles for the consumption of clothing. Molloy found that two things enhance a woman's visibility and authority at work: the first relates to status distinction, the second to sexuality. To take the first point, Molloy's manual stresses the need for career women to be marked out in terms of status from other female white-collar workers, in particular, the secretary. Indeed, his manual explicitly addresses the aspiring lower-middle-class woman (who might, in fact, be a secretary) and who is likely, in his words, to 'dress for failure' rather than success. The world of business and professional work, according to Molloy, is upper-middle-class and the upwardly mobile woman must dress for this context and not signal her lower-class status if she wants to succeed: in his words, she must 'learn the manners of the inner circle. And the inner circle is most emphatically upper middle class' (1980, p. 22). Therefore, the rule according to Molloy is 'dress for the job you want, not the job you have' (*ibid.*, p. 120). Furthermore, since women all too frequently occupy the lower echelons of work (as secretaries, clerical staff, cleaners, etc.), it becomes all the more important that the aspiring career woman adopts a style of dress which distinguishes her from low-status and low-power workers and enables her to assert her authority. The issue of status and the acquisition of 'authority' at work for the aspiring career woman is thus linked to the degree to which she can separate herself, sartorially, from clerical work. Thus, the dress considered to bestow 'authority' on the wearer is 'tailored' since this is the attire that men have traditionally adopted at work. For executive woman this means a tailored blazer or jacket and a knee-length fitted skirt in a neutral colour while items of clothing to be avoided are those associated with secretaries, especially sweaters and cardigans. Molloy argues that

> sweaters in the office spell secretary. Any woman at any level who wants to move up should not wear a sweater to work. In the office sweaters give out nothing but negative impulses. They say lower middle class and loser. (1980, p. 77)

In sweaters and jumpers, female executives are likely to be lost in the office (or a bar for that matter) while in a tailored suit they are more likely to be noticed as business or executive women.

The second issue in the acquisition of visibility and authority at work involves the smothering of sexual signals. The visibility Molloy suggests that business women need is not the visibility normally ascribed to women, namely visibility as an erotic object (Mulvey, 1989). Being seen in a sexual capacity is potentially undermining for professional women since one cannot be seen as 'authoritative', 'professional', or indeed even 'productive' if one looks too sexual. The fact that sexuality is a problem within the world of work is not only applicable to women: the sphere of work generally seeks to constrain sexuality (Bataille, 1986; Mills, 1993; Burrell and Hearn, 1993) as potentially subversive and undermining of productivity. However, women are more likely to experience problems with sexuality in the workplace than their male counterparts. A number of theorists (de Beauvoir, 1972; Gatens, 1991) have argued that women are more likely to be read as sexual than men because of their close cultural association with the body and reproduction. Furthermore, as feminist theorists such as Mulvey (1989) have argued, women within patriarchal society are subject to an eroticizing 'male gaze'. Given the fact that the workplace deems sexuality inappropriate, the erotic identification of women with the body and sexuality and the eroticizing 'male gaze' which underpins and reinforces this are potentially undermining to women seeking power and authority at work. In order to 'get on' within the business of professional spheres of work, the aspiring career woman must diminish these associations with sexuality since 'sexual attraction detracts from authority' (Molloy, 1980, p. 65). This second issue is, however, related to the first one since, as Pringle (1988, 1993) notes, the secretary not only has a history of low status (and low pay) in the office, but of sexual identification. Pringle points to the ways in which cultural associations pertaining to the secretary and the secretary–boss relationship are often sexual, with secretaries seen as the lovers or mistresses of the boss, or the 'wife' of the office. Making the coffee is therefore frequently seen as part of the duties of the office 'wife', and this identification is to be avoided if a woman is to be seen as a professional.

In view of this, the clothing recommended by Molloy is clothing that diminishes the potential sexuality of the female body. He advises women not to wear waistcoats for business because they draw 'attention' to the bust and his advice extends to the sort of jacket women should wear: it 'should be cut fully enough to cover the contours of the bust. It should not be pinched in at the waist to exaggerate the bust' (1980, p. 50). This is in contrast to the sweater which, as well as being associated with secretaries, is also, according to Molloy, a garment which is good for attracting men: 'a cashmere sweater on a woman with even moderate build is one of the greatest seduction garments in existence' (*ibid.*, p. 77). Unlike the tailored jacket which can obscure the bust, the cashmere sweater with its soft texture draws attention to the round contours of the female body.

However, while the body of the career woman must not be deemed too sexual, this requirement does not mean that women ought to dress like men: on the contrary, women must maintain their 'femininity' at the same time as resisting the potential problem of eroticization and objectification. In this way, power dressing attempts to negotiate what is a tightrope for women at work, balancing the need to diminish sexuality with the need to maintain femininity in a man's world of work. The aspiring career woman must therefore avoid being too 'masculine' if she is to succeed. The tailored jacket, as a throwback to the male suit, has the ability to connote 'business' and 'authority' but it should not, he argues, be pin-striped. While the pin-stripe signals power in a man's suit, it does not in a woman's suit and all such attempts to 'ape men', Molloy argues, 'destroy a woman's authority with men' (1980, pp. 51–2). This is one reason he offers as to why trousers are generally to be avoided in the boardroom and the office: according to Molloy the trouser suit 'is a failure suit' in most business environments (*ibid.*, p. 73). Although it can be acceptable in female-dominated companies, 'you are taking a chance if you have to deal with men' (*ibid.*, p. 73) because apparently men do not like doing business with women in trousers. However, as well as warning career women not to look too sexual or too masculine, Molloy also advises against being too 'feminine' at work: according to him, 'feminine' patterns such as floral print or 'feminine' colours such as salmon pink are undermining to a woman's 'authority'. However, women should be careful not to look too 'drab' either and can dress up their outfit with discreet jewellery and scarves. Indeed, Molloy suggests that scarves are good 'attention-seeking devices' at work as they draw attention to the face and away from the (problematic) breasts. While some of Molloy's rules seem rather dated today (power dressing in the 1990s comprised not only pin-stripes but trouser suits as well), his insistence on not looking too sexual and his concern to balance 'feminine' and 'masculine' styles of dress ring true today and testify to the thin line women have to walk between conventional notions of 'femininity' and 'masculinity' within the professional and corporate world. The dress advocated as the most appropriate for the female professional worker is a compromise between the demand to contain the potential eroticism of the female body and the demand to look like a woman at the same time. The female business suit sees the body of the woman divided in two: her torso is covered by a fitted jacket which de-emphasizes her breasts, but her 'femininity' is signalled by the wearing of a skirt. Unlike trousers which are worn now by both sexes, the skirt is the most obviously 'feminine' garment since in most circumstances men are forbidden to wear skirts. By wearing a skirt to the office, the business or professional woman signals her commitment to 'femininity' even though she might be operating in very male-dominated arenas of work. Indeed, despite the fashion for trouser suits, most business or professional women say that they are still frowned on in the workplace and even where they are acceptable, most consider skirts the most appropriate and professional thing a woman can wear to work. This need for 'femininity' within a man's world was put more plainly by an image consultant I interviewed who firmly advocates skirted suits for business encounters: 'Men,' she says, 'like to see a woman's legs.'

As a discourse ostensibly about female empowerment that seeks to improve the performance of women at work, power dressing is, however, inherently conservative. It does not set out to rock any boats or challenge the conventions and practices within the world of work which serve to undermine women in often subtle ways. On the one hand, its view of the female body takes for granted the idea that it is a sexual and 'sexy' body which is potentially disruptive at work rather than recognizing that this is only so because it is constructed as such by culture. On the other hand, its view of power, located as it is at the individual level of the body, fails to recognize the structural inequalities which are faced by women. Newman (1991) demonstrates this in her analysis of what she calls the 'enterprising' texts of the 1980s, that is, books written by successful business women about their experience of success. She maintains that these books speak of success as a question of individual motivation and effort in all aspects of work life, including overall self-presentation: as she puts it, 'image is depicted as the vital ingredient of success for women' (1991, pp. 245–6). Such focus on individuals is not surprising given the political landscape of the 1980s when such texts, including dress manuals, proliferated. I have argued elsewhere (Entwistle, 1997) that there is an ideological fit between power dressing, with its emphasis upon the individual and her body management, and the individualism of the 1980s which saw the extension of neo-liberalism into culture and everyday life with the rise of the New Right. In its various forms, liberalism and neo-liberalism emphasize the individual and encourage a view of the individual as an autonomous and rational subject. Within the terms of neo-liberalism, individual freedom is only secured once the State has been 'rolled back'. In Britain in the 1980s, Mrs Thatcher's government proclaimed the birth of 'enterprise culture' and this rhetoric argued for the necessity of individuals to take responsibility for their own future and use their own initiative in the pursuit of personal gain. The discourse of power dressing similarly places responsibility for success at work firmly on the shoulders of the individual woman who must signal her commitment to her work in every way possible. As a discourse on female advancement, power dressing is therefore limited: in translating career success into a matter of dress and appearance, texts such as Molloy's make light of the problems women encounter at work over which they have no control, problems such as sexual discrimination and sexual harassment as well as more subtle obstacles such as attitudes and practices within organizations which, while ostensibly gender-neutral, actually favour men and disadvantage women (see for example Mills and Tancred, 1992, and Hearn *et al.*, 1993). Instead of proposing real change in cultural attitudes and work practices, power dressing offers women a change of clothes: an option that leaves the status quo in place.

Power dressing and the professional woman in the 1990s

In this part of the chapter, I want to examine the ways in which power dressing has been taken up by women in a range of occupations. Between October 1994 and February 1995 I interviewed 24 women in a number of occupations about their dress and consumption practices for the workplace. The concerns they express about their self-presentation within the world of work, and the practices of dress they adopt to 'manage' their bodies, are remarkably similar to the points articulated by Molloy and a number of them cited his book unprompted. Even where they may not have read any such dress manuals, the 'rules' recounted were very similar to the extent that I would argue that the power-dressing phenomenon of the 1980s (of which Molloy's manual is only one albeit an influential example) has become 'common sense' to many professional and business women. I want to examine how power dressing has been adopted by women as a practice of dress which aims to solve the problem of how to present oneself as a career woman. I then want to consider how power dressing as a strategy for the consumption of work dress aims to solve the problem of consumer 'choice' for many career women. In summing up, I want to consider whether or not power dressing, a practice of dress and a strategy of consumption, can actually be said to empower career women.

Fashioning oneself as a career woman

The women I spoke to worked in a range of occupations: information management; consultancy; law; media. Most were in positions of some influence within their workplace, as managers or senior partners. The youngest woman interviewed was 33 but the majority of the women, as one might expect from their positions, were in their forties or fifties. All the women expressed concern to assert their authority as professionals or business women and in this respect, they echoed Molloy. Their concern was expressed in two main respects: on the one hand, they wanted to be recognized (as 'the manager' or a 'consultant' or a 'professional'). Except for those women in the media, all the women spoke of the need to be visibly recognizable as professionals and characterized this visibility in terms of looking 'professional' or 'businesslike' as opposed to 'clerical' or 'secretarial'. In this respect, they articulate a concern with status and distinction that is one of the cardinal 'rules' of Molloy's power-dressing code. The women all spoke of how a tailored jacket bestows the appropriate 'authority' on them and talked of avoiding clothes that might mean they are mistaken for the secretary. Jan Arnold, a diocesan manager within the Church of England, talked of avoiding 'jumpers and skirts' because 'they say secretary and I am not a secretary'. Amy Halden, an image consultant who advises business women on their self-presentation, also illustrates the importance of looking the part when describing how one senior woman's position in an international company was being undermined by the fact that she did not look like a professional woman. As Halden puts it, she 'looked like her own secretary – she had no status. This is no disrespect to secretaries whatsoever, but she didn't look like the senior woman that she was.' The problem with this woman was clearly one of status: she wore clothes which were cheap and did not suggest to others that she was a senior woman, in an important position, earning a high salary.

As well as articulating concerns to look professional and therefore gain the appropriate recognition and status at work, the women interviewed also articulated their concern to manage sexuality and femininity so as to not lose authority at work. Sexuality was deemed 'inappropriate' by the women and most of them said that women, more than men, are potentially read as 'sexual'. In her study of business women's dress, Sheppard (1993) argued that women feel responsible for the responses of men and this is echoed in the comments made by some of my respondents such as Judith Bush, a management consultant who argues that:

> with all these sexual harassment cases, I think women have to be sensible and sensitive to men and the response that [they] might produce . . . it is about not sending out the wrong signals, be they sexual . . . most men would be appreciative of women who don't dress provocatively. [Interview extract]

Women's dress therefore is not only about managing the potential eroticism of the female body, it is also about managing male sexuality and the potential 'threat' of unwanted gazes and comments from men. Hence the clothes many said they avoided are 'very short skirts', 'low-cut blouses', 'anything see-through'. The jacket was seen by most of the women as a prop to enable them to signal the 'appropriate' message and enable them to be 'taken seriously'. When asked why she insisted on always wearing a jacket to work, Janice Greaves, a senior manager with a Lloyds insurance firm, said that for her the jacket was 'a bit of a security blanket':

> because you know if you have got your top on there is no sex show, they can't look at your nipples or they are not looking down the front of your blouse, you know it is a kind of cover up . . . I just think it gives you a certain air . . . it makes you sexless really. [Interview extract]

Although 'they' are ungendered in this quote, it would seem that Greaves is invoking an anonymous but potentially eroticizing 'male gaze'. However, while sexuality is generally to be avoided in the workplace, most of the women were concerned to look attractive and 'feminine'. Negotiating sexuality in the workplace, then, for many professional and business women, is not a matter of dressing like a man. Bush notes that in the 1980s she learned how to 'soften' the lines of the suit with accessories: 'It was around this time that we learnt about accessories. You have to have pearl earrings, I remember reading', which, it would seem, was an attempt to 'feminize' the hard lines of the suit. The need to temper the suit with 'token female garb' (Armstrong, 1993, p. 278), such as bows, earrings and the like, demonstrates the degree to which femininity must be expressed in some way. The suit was meant to diminish feminine sexuality but not eradicate it.

Consumption and empowerment

Another issue that emerged in the interviews related to differences between male and female dress at work. One woman, when asked what is the main difference between men's and women's dress, replied 'men don't have to make choices'. The issue of choice was echoed by a significant number of other women who claimed that women have more choice of clothes open to them than men: women can choose to wear skirts or trousers (although some offices still frown on trousers); women also have more choice in terms of the colour and cut of suits and a greater latitude in terms of accessories, with earrings, rings, necklaces and scarves all permissible for women. However, this 'freedom' in dress comes at a cost: with more choices to make, deciding what to wear is more difficult since there is a greater possibility of making a mistake. One image consultant I interviewed summed up what she found when she did a session with a large bank:

> women were having like five million more problems because all the way from the tops of our head to our feet we have got decisions to make . . . men have simply got far fewer problems: they have got fewer clothes and women have got probably fifty garments they can choose. [Interview extract]

The anxiety produced by choice is described by Ulrich Beck (1992) and summarized by Don Slater (1997). Choice creates problems for individuals since consumer culture

> increases the individual's risk and anxiety by offering ever more choice and images of different identities and by increasing the sense of social risk involved in making the 'wrong choice'. (Slater, 1997, p. 86)

In consumer culture, every choice seems to implicate the self and yet, as Giddens (1991) notes, modernity is non-foundational and offers us little help as to what options to select. If, as I argued above, the burden of career success is increasingly placed upon the shoulders of the individual and she is called upon to think about all aspects of herself, including her appearance, as important to her career, then the stakes are very high for women and the problem of choice felt very acutely. Another aspect of choice which presents itself to working women is economic: a number of women noted that women need more clothes than men and this has implications for their consumer spending. According to one woman, men 'spend less on clothes than we do': 'women can't get away with one or two suits, they have got to have more flexibility'. Furthermore, as she pointed out, women have to spend on a plethora of other items like 'stockings and tights' which are easily damaged and need constant replacement, and also make-up, which most felt they have to wear to work each day. The reason offered as to why women experience these constraints and continue to put up with them is that, as one woman noted, 'women's dress is more noticed and commented upon than men's'. Women are simply looked at and scrutinized more closely and have to therefore monitor their appearance more closely (Wolf, 1991).

It is in the context of these pressures that power dressing could be said to empower women. At the heart of power dressing there is a concern with the reduction of choice of clothes to a set of basic principles for achieving 'authority'. In providing women with a 'uniform' for work similar in principle to the one that men wear to work, Molloy's rules of power dressing seek to reduce the choices one has to make about dress and therefore the risks that go with making the 'wrong choice', which would otherwise be a source of constant anxiety. His philosophy is essentially anti-fashion, to use Polhemus and Proctor's term (1978) to define an attitude of dress which emphasizes continuity and stability rather than fashion which emphasizes constant stylistic change. Molloy's attack on fashion stems from what he sees as its 'irrationality': fashion offers women a tyranny of constant change which makes no economic sense since clothes are not bought for the use-value and discarded when they are worn out, but worn for a short time until they are no longer the fashion. Furthermore, fashions for women are very often 'ugly' and silly and in this respect Molloy echoes the concerns of nineteenth-century sociologist and advocate of 'rational' dress, Thorstein Veblen (1953). In calling upon women to 'take this book with you when you go shopping' Molloy advocates a strategy of dress which circumvents fashion in the name of rational, sensible and economic consumption. His book aims to lay down such rational principles which, if followed, will never result in expensive 'mistakes' and 'impulsive' purchases. Given that the majority of women interviewed employed a number of limited 'techniques' or strategies for fashioning themselves as career women such as wearing a jacket, keeping their hair short, avoiding short skirts and low-cut blouses, etc., one could argue that they draw on a limited repertoire of dress which bears close resemblance to the power-dressing 'rules'. Moreover, the majority of the women said they felt better about themselves and gained more confidence once they acquired such 'rules' and learned how to dress professionally for work. In this respect, Molloy and the power-dressing phenomenon he helped to promote could be said to empower women by providing them with a strategy for consumption which disavows the endless cycle of fashion and the relentless call of consumer choice. However, while power dressing attempts to circumvent fashion by giving women a 'rational' strategy for consumption (as opposed to the irrationality of the fashion system as Molloy would argue), it has patently not avoided being consumed *by* fashion. As the Collections of 1997 demonstrate, power dressing has become another fashion style. Indeed, the idea that power dressing could stand outside the fashion system was a fallacy itself. The suits worn by business and professional women are subtly altered with each season as new colours and new cuts are promoted by designers. Men's dress is not immune from the influence of fashion either, but as the male business 'uniform' is more firmly established, the fluctuations are less noticeable. Furthermore, whatever the season, the colour range of men's suits remains very narrow with grey, black, sometimes brown, the predominant colours, while women's suits span the full spectrum and are more susceptible to swings in fashion (in 1996 brown was the key colour, but in previous years it has been red and sometimes pink). In this respect, power dressing will never provide women with a fixed formula for consumption. Moreover, make-up, hosiery, and accessories also change and require 'updating' (as fashion and beauty editors like to put it) and women's expenditure in these areas constitute an additional economic burden not experienced by men.

This strategy for consumption is one that depends upon knowledge and expertise: women moving into 'high-powered' careers do not automatically 'dress for success' nor have the skill to consume wisely the right suits and accessories for their work. Some women interviewed spoke of learning how to dress gradually through their career but others learned about image from an 'expert' or 'image consultant'. One significant development since the 1980s that runs in tandem with the rise of power dressing has been the growth of image consultancy which enables a woman to buy in the help of an 'expert' to help her with her image. Image consultancy refers to a range of services from 'dress for success' books such as Molloy's, to individual consultations such as those offered by Colour Me Beautiful, 'wardrobe audits' (where an image consultant reviews one's clothes) and corporate training schemes often offered as part of 'staff development'. Image consultancy could be said to be related to the rise of a therapeutic culture of the self which Nikolas Rose (1991, 1992) sees emerging at around the same time and which can be linked also to the rhetoric of 'enterprise' which, as discussed above, similarly emphasizes the self and calls upon individuals to work upon themselves. Half the women interviewed spoke of encountering such an 'expert' on image, either through reading a dress manual (in some cases Molloy's) or through courses offered by image consultants at work. A number of the women I spoke to had seen a colour consultant (Colour Me Beautiful is perhaps the most popular) and some had encountered image consultants on management training courses at work. All spoke of the confidence they felt they had gained by learning how to combine colours and clothes to 'look their best' and 'look professional'.

Conclusion

In this chapter, I have outlined the rules of professional dress that were established and promoted in the 1980s by the discourse of power dressing. This discourse spoke of how important it was for professional and business women to acquire visibility within male arenas of work. In addition, it spoke of how the female body is a sexualized body that must be de-eroticized at work.

On the face of it, power dressing, with its 'rules' and 'experts', would seem to have empowered these individual career women, such as those I interviewed, by offering them strategies for consumption. However, it is not an unproblematic discourse nor has it solved all the problems women might encounter with their image at work. To take the first point, power dressing, as discussed above, is an individualistic discourse which does not address the structural inequalities women face at work. It makes no challenge to the status quo but reproduces ideas about women's position in the workplace, i.e. that women are responsible for managing their own sexuality (by covering up the 'naughty' bits such as breasts) so as to manage the sexual responses of men (who are not responsible for their actions should a woman reveal too much flesh in the office). To take the second point, women still encounter more choice and have more options available to them than men which, while a source of pleasure for many women who like the 'freedom', also brings with it greater risk and greater anxiety as the image consultants I spoke with testify in their accounts of helping women dress for work. Thus, power dressing might provide women with a set of basic principles, but it does not offer them solutions to the problem of men's determination to see them as 'sexy' at work, nor does it offer them a steadfast 'uniform' which makes shopping for work clothes simple and economical. The ultimate issue at stake is the fact that women's appearance is a matter of greater concern than men's and as long as this is the case career women will experience greater risk and anxiety when getting dressed for work, a fact which no strategy of dress can eradicate.

Note

All names of interviewees have been changed.

References

Armstrong, L. (1993) 'Working girls', *Vogue*, October.
Bataille, G. (1986) *Eroticism: Death and Sensuality*. San Francisco: City Lights Books.
Beck, U. (1992) *Risk Society: Towards a New Modernity*. London: Sage.
Berger, J. (1972) *Ways of Seeing*. Harmondsworth: Penguin.
Beauvoir, S. de (1972) *The Second Sex*. London: Penguin.
Blass, B. (1997) *Vogue* (US edition), August, p. 210.
Burrell, G. (1992) 'Sex and organizational analysis'. In A. Mills and P. Tancred-Sheriff (eds), *Gendering Organizational Analysis*. London: Sage.
Burrell, G. and Hearn, J. (1993) 'The sexuality of the organization'. In J. Hearn, D. Sheppard, P. Tancred-Sheriff and G. Burrell (eds), *The Sexuality of the Organization*. London: Sage.

Entwistle, J. (1997) 'Powerdressing and the fashioning of the career woman'. In M. Nava *et al.* (eds), *Buy This Book: Studies in Advertising and Consumption.* London: Routledge.

Gatens, M. (1991) *Feminism and Philosophy: Perspectives on Difference and Equality.* Cambridge: Polity.

Giddens, A. (1991) *Modernity and Self-Identity: Self and Society in the Late Modern Age.* Cambridge: Polity.

Hearn, J., Sheppard, D. L., Tancred-Sheriff, P. and Burrell, G. (eds) (1993) *The Sexuality of the Organization.* London: Sage.

Mills, A. J. (1993) 'Gender, sexuality and organizational theory'. In J. Hearn, D. L. Sheppard, P. Tancred-Sheriff and G. Burrell (eds), *The Sexuality of the Organization.* London: Sage.

Mills, A. J. and Tancred, P. (eds) (1992) *Gendering Organizational Analysis.* London: Sage.

Molloy, J. T. (1980) *Women: Dress for Success.* New York: Peter H. Wyden.

Mulvey, L. (1989 [1975]) 'Visual pleasure and narrative cinema', *Screen,* 16(3).

Newman, J. (1991) 'Enterprising women: images of success'. In S. Franklin, C. Lury and J. Stacey (eds), *Off-centre: Feminism and Cultural Studies.* London: HarperCollins, pp. 241–59.

Polhemus, T. and Proctor, L. (1978) *Fashion and Anti-fashion: An Anthology of Clothing and Adornment.* London: Cox & Wyman.

Posnick, P. (1997) 'Well suited', *Vogue* (US edition), August, pp. 200–5.

Pringle, R. (1988) *Secretaries Talk: Sexuality, Power and Work.* London: Verso.

Pringle, R. (1993) 'Bureaucracy, rationality, sexuality: the case of secretaries'. In J. Hearn, D. L. Sheppard, P. Tancred-Sheriff and G. Burrell (eds), *The Sexuality of the Organization.* London: Sage.

Rose, N. (1991) *Governing the Soul: The Shaping of the Private Self.* London: Routledge.

Rose, N. (1992) 'Governing the enterprising self'. In P. Heelas and P. Morris (eds), *The Values of the Enterprise Culture: The Moral Debate.* London: Routledge.

Sampson, K. (1997) 'She's the business', *Guardian,* 18 April, pp. 4–5.

Sheppard, D. L. (1992) 'Women managers' perceptions of gender and organizational life'. In A. Mills and P. Tancred (eds), *Gendering Organizational Analysis,* London: Sage.

Sheppard, D. L. (1993) 'Organisations, power and sexuality: the image and self-image of women managers'. In J. Hearn, D. Sheppard, P. Tancred-Sheriff and G. Burrell (eds), *The Sexuality of the Organization.* London: Sage.

Slater, D. (1997) *Consumer Culture and Modernity.* Cambridge: Polity.

Steele, V. (ed.) (1989) *Men and Women: Dressing the Part.* Washington, DC: Smithsonian Institution Press.

Tredre, R. (1997) 'From boom to busts: the return of power dressing', *Guardian,* 12 October, p. 11.

Veblen, T. (1953) *The Theory of the Leisure Class: An Economic Study of Institutions.* New York: Mentor.

Wolf, N. (1991) *The Beauty Myth.* London: Vintage.

16. Non-occasion greeting cards and the commodification of personal relationships

Jane Hobson

Non-occasion greeting cards both constitute and are constituted in romantic discourses. Sometimes categorized as 'fun and love' cards, they realize romantic discourses in more or less serious ways: *I can count on the beauty of autumn once a year . . . / yours I can count on every day*, contrasted with *How could I ever look at another? / You're always watching me* (in each case the text preceding the / appears on the front of the card; the text following is inside).

According to some cultural critics of consumption, the use of greeting cards destroys the relationships they commodify. This view is exemplified in Papson's (1986) claim that women are unwitting agents in the destruction of the very domain they hope to bolster through the use of alienated, spectacular cultural artefacts, greeting cards, in the everyday realm. This is a claim many card-using women would want to dispute, although the use of greeting cards to negotiate intimate relationships certainly rings a warning about ways emotion may be organized discursively and used for greater social control. Discourses are social practices and include ways of thinking, talking and 'doing' in a community. Intricately tied to power, they 'define, describe and delimit what it is possible to say and not possible to say' (Kress, 1985, p. 7). Modern, Western romantic discourses determine how it is possible to think and carry on a romantic, intimate relationship, with the effect that, in the constitution of 'family', individuals involved in a romance that 'naturally' leads to marriage 'must' be a male and a female who then add children to the unit. 'Heteronormative'[1] discourses which project modern romantic coupling as given, natural and ahistorical have negative legal and social consequences for individuals; for example, same-sex couples who, no matter how many children they may each have, are not able to 'properly' constitute a family.[2]

In response to the position just outlined I would argue that the obvious pleasure in the consumption of greeting cards (billions of dollars are spent worldwide[3]) is highly productive, not reductive and destructive. The current thread of re-reading production and consumption relations provides a space to recontextualize commodification itself as productive; consuming is after all a complex and dynamic social process not a single physical event of 'ingestion [and] incorporation' (Radway, 1986, p. 440). Women's use of greeting cards can be initially contextualized as the selection of a particular semiotic (meaning-making) resource in social relations, contrasted to other (available) semiotic resources such as writing a letter, making a phone call or speaking 'face to face'. The idea, however, that choosing a commercial printed card is the choice of a synthetic substitute (in print) over authentic 'expressions' of emotion (in 'talk') signals the operation of two discourses: a phonocentric discourse (Derrida, 1976) where conflating and privileging speech and language over other modes such as writing forecloses any useful exploration of the social and cultural practices of giving greeting cards. Second, feminist and post-structuralist work has 'unpacked'[4] emotions, seeing them as historically contextualized, situationally context-dependent phenomena in contrast to being interiorized 'things'.

The profit context of greeting card production and the social exchange context that cards are used in closely articulate public and private domains in ways that are characteristic of post-modernity. Such articulations are often troubling and troublesome. 'The order of things' (Foucault, 1970) is upset when women deploy a mass-produced commodity in social contexts that are thought of as part of the private domain. I want to think this articulation as a problem of meaning making: what kinds of meanings[5] are being made with greeting cards? In particular, I want to examine *who* controls the meaning of the card. The producer? The consumer? What kinds of social subjects make meaning with greeting cards? (By social subject I mean a historically constituted positioned subject as suggested by feminist and post-structural/post-modern critical theorists.) From the point of view of discourses, the world offers us positions to occupy, which we are interpellated into. From these positions, individuals see the world and it 'sees' us (as male or female, as feminine or masculine, as belonging to a generation, as 'raced' individuals, and so on). It is from these positions that individuals make and understand meaning, producing the process of 'communication' rather differently than that realized in the 'signal transmission' model of communication between 'senders and receivers'.[6] In relation to greeting cards, gendered subjects occupy historically specific positions in relation to a range of discursive statements formulating discourses of romantic love, feminism and sexuality. *Who* can mean *what* with the texts, then, is ultimately a question of which social subjects can take up and deploy particular semiotic resources.

Greetings for every occasion and any-day 'non-occasions'

Traditionally, greeting cards have projected two distinct orientations to experience: as part of a birth to death lifecycle (birthday, marriage, birth, sympathy), or as events on a religious or secular calendar (Hanukkah, Mother's Day). From the first engraved Christmas card in 1843, greeting cards have proliferated in type and kind to be available for every conceivable occasion (Chase, 1971). The category of 'non-occasion' card has emerged since the 1970s.[7] Non-occasion cards are available to 'essentially *create* [an] occasion' (my italics, Hallmark Cards Australia, n.d.). On the occasion that *I Am Missing You*, for example, a card is available to 'say' so.

Non-occasion cards have proliferated into a range of 'friendship', 'fun and love' and 'lifestyle' cards and are distinguished from 'inspirational' friendship cards that often draw on religious belief for their inspiration, or are highly sentimental for example:

> *If friendship*
> *means harmony, then we have*
> *a perfect friendship, because we're*
> *so in tune with each other. That's why*
> *I'll often call you just when you're*
> *thinking of me, or you'll happen to stop by*
> *when I need to share something important*
> *with you . . . /*
> *I'm glad I share*
> *that special closeness with you,*
> *for it makes my life feel*
> *richer and fuller*

This extreme sentimentality is a strong contrast to the playfulness of the non-occasion 'fun and love' card: *Ours is a love so sweet, / No wonder it's making all our friends sick.* The non-occasion card is also clearly orientated to something other than 'just friendship'. The category of non-occasion card is available to negotiate romantic love (in contrast to kinship love) but the card isn't selected in response to an occasion such as St Valentine's Day.[8] A non-occasion card is selected as a response to a range of contexts that are generated in the specificity of a social relationship. A card may be given to get someone's attention, as part of a sexual pursuit, for example, *Have you ever noticed that the things we desire most are usually right under our noses? . . . / Yoo Hoo.*

The non-occasion category has in part been generated out of existing 'occasions' such as anniversaries. The importance of an 'Anniversary' is taken up and reworked in a non-occasion card to apply to a relationship beyond the 'date' of the anniversary itself, *Every day is an anniversary . . . / of something beautiful we've shared.* Of course, relationships aren't always rapturous and a non-occasion card can be used by individuals in an established romantic relationship when some difficulty arises, *Even when it's not going smoothly . . . / I trust our love,* or less seriously, *Alright, alright! I'm sorry! Okay? Can we fool around now?*

The productiveness of commodification

Giving a card is a social practice, a semiotic activity that uses a mass-produced commodity; it has a production (profit-making) context. Within that context, women's use of greeting cards is sometimes talked about in ways reminiscent of the 1940s and 1950s advertising for electrical appliances.[9] The suggestion is that greeting cards are a product that will ease increasing burdens on women. This rightly acknowledges that women's domain of operation has expanded into the public sphere while their level of responsibility in their traditional 'domain of influence', the private/domestic realm, has not diminished. Accordingly, non-occasion cards are available that provide ways for individuals to manage day-to-day complexities in social interaction. This 'altruism' of the card manufacturers is of course immediately undermined by the 'self-expression' industry's self-interest. Manufacturers are not involved in a simple case of service provision to meet a need, although such a position resonates ironically with Marxist analyses of commodities as 'the concrete forms of particular needs not met otherwise' (Williamson, 1980, p. 231).

Second, there is an exchange context, a particular social relationship in which individuals use a card. The greeting card industry projects the product as providing a means of communication, for 'self-expression' as a function of contemporary social relations (Hallmark Cards Australia, n.d.). These views of social interaction and cultural artefacts, however problematic, recognize the demands made on women to do what Di Leonardo (1987) calls 'kinwork'. This is the work that women do in order to keep family and community units ticking over. This is the glue of social relationships. Kinwork specifies that social relations and 'emotional life' involve effort being expended: that sending cards to acknowledge significant occasions in people's lives involves keeping track of those occasions, noticing those moments, choosing an appropriate message and image, writing on the card, finding a stamp and finally, posting it. Women use greeting cards to do what they feel they have always and must continue to do: interactional work.

Whose meaning is this?

As a mass-produced 'alienable' commodity, the meanings realized textually are those selected and produced by the card manufacturer. The images and linguistic text, the paper stock and the construction of the card are all determined in the production context.[10] The central question is whether such text, produced remotely from the card consumer, can be claimed by, and 'belong' to, the card consumer. It seems to me that such a question is only ever directed at mass-produced 'popular' culture texts. Quoting poetry to impress or seduce someone is, for example, typically excluded from this accusation. This reproduces the old high vs. popular culture distinction. 'High' culture is still regularly and effectively dragged out as a silencing operation on popular culture. All communication, however, is 'always/already' mediated. Some communication is doubly mediated, by technologies outside the body, technologies other than language.

Selecting a greeting card to do interactional work also of course involves selecting a semiotic resource that realizes meaning in writing, or rather print, in contrast to speech (although the 'voice' card[11] combines both of these). Various inflections of phonocentrism, an alignment of 'real', authentic and natural communication with spoken language, are mobilized in injunctions to stop doing relationship work with mass-produced texts. Face-to-face speech, however, is no proof or guarantee of 'ownership' of meaning, of truth, sincerity or anything else. The idea of orality as a real form of communication with which more authentic expressions of meaning can be realized is a naïve way of understanding both communication and social interaction. The idea of a real form of communication in which more 'authentic' expressions of sentiment can be generated is itself a discursive effect and operation. It is the desire for truth, the drive and necessity for some 'real' outside of representation, the operation of 'sincerity' that are mobilized in such conceptions of interaction.

Personalize it!

Meaning making with a printed, mass-produced greeting card is a matter of having chosen an at-a-distance[12] realization in contrast to those not at a distance, that is face-to-face in the same physical space. The non-occasion card is also a 'standardized', mass-produced object. This standardization[13] raises the question of how it can ever be 'right' for the specific social subjects and context that it is selected to be deployed in. The approach to meaning making here assumes that meaning made through the greeting card as a text and through its exchange is meaning that is always already available in the culture. But available to whom? Can meanings belong to particular groups and therefore shouldn't be used by individuals who don't belong to the group? Card manufacturers and their products are not somehow outside the culture, nor do products and meanings necessarily enter the culture and circulate only from the activity of the manufacturers. Greeting cards are not part of a colonizing process in which the market simply appropriates an existing, authentic interpersonal domain.

A colonizing view certainly gives prominence to the stakes and interests that are involved, but greeting card use is, in this conception, generated in production and by producers. The relationship between the ordinary, consuming user and the greeting card is rendered as fixed, unidirectional, and driven by an economic base. As a consequence, there is no possibility of accounting for consumer demands being made or responded to. As a consequence, those of us consuming greeting cards are rendered invisible or as 'duped' by the power embodied in the commodity.[14] By implication there are those who are not duped. These are a cultural elite who by virtue of their objective, theoretical stance towards the object, observe and pronounce on the practice, and on the 'ordinary' users of the object.[15] I want to exemplify the dynamic relation between production and consumption of non-occasion greeting cards by focusing in turn, on some consumption practices and production practice.

When women choose to use a greeting card to do interactional work there is no need to search the world, or even the mall, for the perfect card. The card buyer is not dependent on the manufacturer having imagined the exact context and a 'matching' card. Mass-produced goods like greeting cards are not 'completed' objects that a consumer cannot interact with further. Consumers intervene with 'pre-packaged' cultural artefacts; a perfect card can be made.

Greeting cards are inscribed in ways which make them 'right', provide 'specificity' in Miller's (1991) terms. There are simple interventions such as inscriptions on an anniversary card from a child to parents, *Happy Anniversary, Mum and Dad*, where the actual anniversary year, the *'17th'*, is inserted. The gender of pronouns may be changed – *she* to *he* or vice versa. Deletions may be made or the image altered to make a figure resemble the receiver – adding glasses to a figure for example, or the typographic text itself may be called up to be part of some personal joke. Re-inscribed, a greeting card may 'do' things or make meanings which were never anticipated by its (first and second) producers; the designer and manufacturer. The card recipient recognizes, or at least typically attempts to recognize, the ways that a card being given engages the particularities of the relationship between the individuals as well as appreciating the personalizing efforts (which may involve private jokes, etc.). This reciprocal effort of recognition is a stark contrast to the lack of appreciation for their kinwork that women often cite.

A production 'paradox' provides a further view of the dynamism that pertains between production and consumption relations. Relatively few non-occasion cards are actually sold compared to the overall sales quantities of greeting cards; a small number that belies the frequency and effort that producers put into 'inventing' new cards. Consumer demands for new non-occasion greeting cards cannot be dismissed as a mere response to fashion, or as demands for variety. Consumer demands are specifically tied to the ways non-occasion greeting cards are used and situated in the culture, uses that are generated in the social process of an intimate relationship.

Unlike occasion cards which have developed in type and kind in an expanded secular calendar, non-occasion cards proliferate in kind. More of the same is demanded by the consumer but not new 'moments'. There is a demand for new cards which take up the meaning potential (Halliday, 1978) of the social process of the romantic relationship. Social processes such as 'having a relationship' are 'made up of forms which past discursive practice, condensed into conventions, has endowed with meaning potential' (Fairclough, 1992, p. 75). Some detail about the social process of a romantic relationship illuminates some of the specific meaning potential of the romantic relationship as taken up and deployed through non-occasion greeting cards.

Is there a romance on the cards?

The origins and emergence of the romantic relationship are tied to the 'discovery' and constitution of the self and a concomitant rise of romantic love as a cultural ideal, as traced in both Foucault (1990) and Giddens (1992). Romantic love currently occupies a unique and privileged place in both the culture's and the individual's emotional repertoire – for some individuals it is even worth dying for (Romeo and Juliet being archetypal here). Love, like any other emotion, is generally rendered as falling outside the operation of the mind. The centrality and the 'reach' of the mind in modern Western conceptions of the self do not extend with ease over 'emotion'; it requires the effort of rationality. As an emotion, love is a 'state' that annexes the anatomy and physiology – the heart and blood in particular – but is necessarily perceived as not being within the control of that body. Love and the interpersonal domain more generally are, however, still represented as 'natural'. Love is discursively organized as feminine, un-organized, unpredictable, natural and over-whelming. Romantic love and other emotions, constituted as an authentic non-conscious 'expression' of the self, articulate uncomfortably with the rational corporate production of non-occasion greeting card 'sentiment'.

Between you and me there's a great love story being written

The 'logic' of corporate production realizes 'love' in non-occasion greeting cards grammatically as a noun, a 'thing'. This enables it to participate as a 'character' in a love story. This is not surprising, given that particular relationships in the culture are instantiated as social processes within the discursive realm of all 'great love stories': *Even before your divorce, I always knew you had a Chuck and Di relationship . . . / You were a princess and he was a royal pain !!!* Love's agentive capacities are solidified in such representations: *Love, it comes walking softly in silver sandals and steals our hearts away.* This is in contrast to the absence of agency an individual is projected as having when *love comes walking by* and *envelopes* them. Non-occasion cards project romantic love as 'idealization', *You are all I ever need*; as involving a 'state of absorption in thoughts about the other', *When I close my eyes, I can picture anything that I want to . . . / I only wish that when I open them, I could see you here with me* (Averill, 1985, p. 93). Love is a state of bliss occupied by special and unique individuals, *There's no one quite like you . . . / There's no two quite like us.* Interactional work with non-occasion texts is shaped by the always present, if implicit and dynamic, structure of the love story. Card giving acts, in turn, to shape other social processes: such as 'having' an intimate, romantic relationship.

Consuming cards, constituting couple

In the context of 'having a relationship' becoming 'a couple' is neither instant, automatic, 'natural' nor simply 'caused' by the 'presence' of love. The personal pronouns that litter non-occasion greeting cards are demanded in the construction of 'A Couple', *There's you, There's me, There's us . . . / and that's all that matters.* These are not the corporate voices of an advertising text (Fairclough, 1995). The undifferentiated addressee of the production context is always specified in the contexts of purchasing and giving of a greeting card. When a greeting card is given to someone there is no difficulty tracking the pronoun choices for the 'speaker', 'I' or 'we', the addressee 'you' or the 'us'. Personal pronouns also litter the language of individuals in a relationship constituting them as in a relationship and speaking from the position of being 'a couple'. The couple is constituted both as 'us' in relation to 'them' (solidarity 'against' the world) and as an 'us' in relation to 'you' and 'me' (how 'you' and 'me' become one/'us'). The couple, the 'us', is built through ways of talking about shared experiences, references to events such as 'the first time I saw you', and on mutual expectancies, *I want to grow older with you*. Becoming 'a couple' is in part achieved through the acquisition of a 'language'[16] with which to 'do' intimacy. An acquired 'language' that contrasts to the 'presence' of a pre-existing and authentic 'intimate language' that individuals 'in love' somehow access.

One of the central practices associated with the 'language' of intimacy and the constitution of a contemporary Western intimate relationship is disclosure. A non-occasion greeting card is in some senses a semiotic resource available for the social practice of confession,[17] building mutuality, shared knowledge and interdependence in negotiating the social process of 'having a relationship' (Forgas, 1985, p. 223). Intimacy itself is a process of straining towards some imagined authentic, 'real' self via a series of self-disclosures ('life stories', secrets, desires, childhood misdemeanours, sexual health status). It can't be assumed, however, that all individuals, all potential romantic subjects, 'know' or can 'do' the things with language that are expected in the culture as part of the social processes of 'intimacy'.

A woman's work?

That 90 per cent of all greeting cards are purchased by women has to do with the way women take up a 'ready-made' position and role of 'emotional manager' in relationships; their 'doing' kinwork and relationship work congruent with the ways historically women as a cultural category have come to be defined in terms of 'sensitivity' and 'sensibilities' and the cultural and social possibilities for realizing that subjectivity (Jordanova, 1989). Such definitions, subject positions and roles, however, aren't necessarily occupied by individual women unproblematically. Even without applying any explicit feminist analysis to their situations, individual women may take up these responsibilities reluctantly or resentfully, or less successfully than is expected. There are many instances of exasperated women proclaiming 'Why do I always have to be the one to do the relationship work?' and others who claim to be no good at interpersonal work. These social practices are difficult to avoid, however, as any woman who has tried not to be the emotion 'worker' in an intimate relationship will know. Women's use of greeting cards is 'tactical' in De Certeau's terms (1988). It is a 'making-do' in the context of women trying to have an intimate relationship while experiencing the very considerable personal conflict of having to be all things to all people:

superwoman. The force of competing discourses over what it means to be a woman in the late twentieth century generates a space for such tactical responses as well as the concomitant space that is generated for capital/ commercial responses. At ground zero – in relationships – many women struggle to only have to do their 'fair share' of the interpersonal work in the modern 'partnership'. For example, stereotypically, men are seen as doing relationship work only to get what they want in contrast to women recognizing the necessity to constantly grease the wheels.

Greeting card manufacturers, in keeping with that stereotype, have targeted men in relation to basically four cards: *Mother's Day, To My Wife* birthday cards, *Valentine's Day*, and the big one: *The Anniversary Card*. The anniversary card is typically the most expensive card sold in Australia – around $10 more than other cards of either non-occasion or occasion type. Manufacturers are clearly exploiting the obligation to give an anniversary card that is in part generated out of the absence of other 'relationship work' being done. There is some evidence,[18] however, that non-occasion greeting cards are being taken up by men to do relationship work; to do interactional 'repairs', to demonstrate affection (unbidden) and desire and to show gratitude to their partner, and so forth. Men are doing certain kinds of 'emotional' or relationship work that they 'hadn't even thought of doing before' (see note 9). Significantly, these informants self-identify, and are unproblematically identified by other people, as 'blokes',[19] as masculine subjects. They are also 'working-class' (a problematic category in itself). These are the very subjects constituted as absent in the feminine domain of the interpersonal.

That 'blokes' may be doing interactional work with non-occasion greeting cards in intimate relationships is not just the case of picking up a new tool to do an old job; the greeting card doesn't simply replace the bunch of flowers bought out of obligation on a partner's birthday, or as an act of contrition. Through processes of commodification, the domains of the intimate relationship and greeting cards connect in ways that are 'new', and unpredicted historically. These connections bring the possibility of new meaning potential to the social practices of interactional work in intimate relationships and of consumption. Non-occasion greeting cards are available to interacting subjects in unanticipated ways and can make certain social practices available to culturally unanticipated subjects.

Conclusion

The use of non-occasion greeting cards for doing intimate interactional work is an example of the deployment of a semiotic resource in creative ways by subjects engaged in construing intimacy (as they may understand it) in the context of contemporary socio-sexual relationships. Commodification of intimate relations through non-occasion greeting cards opens up the terrain that the cards occupy, the interpersonal and the intimate, in two important ways. First, interactional work using non-occasion greeting cards by individuals in intimate relationships is a practice that by its presence unsettles heterosexual intimate relationships, because such relationships can no longer be imagined unproblematically as something individuals come to, and experience 'naturally', in the course of 'a lifecycle'. Second, the use of non-occasion cards to negotiate intimate relationships foregrounds the constructedness of the relationship subject, the 'couple'. 'The couple' is recognized as constructed through, for example, a language of solidarity and unity ('us') and through iterated 'coupling' practices such as disclosure/confession and shared experience.[20]

The contemporary 'relationship' has become a site where men can do interactional work. This possibility contests both dominant discourses of masculinity and of intimacy. As masculine subjects begin to take up the texts, inserting themselves into the constitution of intimate relations, then there will certainly be changes to those relations. The intimate relationship remains a site over which subjects must struggle and there are losses and gains, for example, for women in 'giving up' or sharing occupation with men their 'traditional', if not natural, emotional and intimate domains. One of the ways in which that struggle is currently being played out is in essentialist 'men's movement' discourses which claim the emotional domain for men in a very particular way. Legitimate claims to the emotional domain are made but via attacks on a monolithic 'feminism' accused of reducing men to the status of victims. These claims and attacks are authorized through, in part, a refusal to acknowledge any recognition that the possibilities for such enunciative positions were (and are) produced in feminist discourses. How the site of intimate heterosexual (and therefore also same-sex) relationships are 'carved up' and occupied is not then just a matter of theoretical interest; it will continue to impact on the everyday lives of individuals and constitute the power relations that they engage in.

Notes

1. I have no idea who coined this term but it usefully captures the tendencies and forces of 'compulsory heterosexuality' as discursive and social practices (as developed by Adrienne Rich, 1980).
2. The legal status and discursive location of same-sex relationships vary nationally. In Australia there is no provision for legal partnerships of any kind for same-sex couples.

3. Greeting cards are bought at the rate of 21 cards a head per year in Australia, a consumption that generates 1.4 billion retail dollars a year for the 'social expression' industry (Prices Surveillance Authority, 1990, p. 5).

4. The term often used at this point in cultural studies is 'deconstruct'; however, I prefer to leave that term for the specific technique that Derrida describes.

5. The close linguistic and visual analysis of greeting cards that this discussion is based on are not detailed here for lack of space. The approach here uses Halliday's (1985) systemic functional grammar for the linguistic analysis and a related approach for the visual analysis as developed by Kress and van Leeuwen (1996).

6. As Ferdinand de Saussure's classic model presents it (1915).

7. The cards are generally accepted to have their origins in cards produced by Colorado artisans and Blue Mountain Arts (USA) in the late 1970s (Wandyzc, 1991). This 'sourcing' was the focus of litigation between Hallmark and Blue Mountain in the 1980s. In Australia, where this research has been focused, these cards have emerged strongly since the early 1980s.

8. In Australia, St Valentine's Day is very different from in America. Valentine cards in Australia are given to romantic and sexual intimates (potential or desired lover, boy/girlfriend, spouse/partner) whereas my understanding is that even primary school children in America would exchange cards.

9. This finding comes from the research done as part of my preparation of a doctoral thesis. Interviews with all major greeting card manufacturers, importers, distributors, retailers and consumers were carried out.

10. 'Manufacturer' includes all of those involved in the production process.

11. A 'voice' card has a printed greeting but can also be interactive. Cards are linked to a 'voice mail' system where the card giver can record a message that can be accessed by the card receiver via a personal identification number.

12. The dispersal of at-a-distance forms of interaction has been a particular characteristic of industrialization and the rise of capitalism (McCluhan, 1962).

13. This problem of 'standardization' is typically seen as 'the American problem'; America signifies homogenization and the destruction of cultural diversity and individual creativity for the non-American world, contradictorily, given that 'creativity 'and 'individualism' are also signified by 'America'.

14. The usual suspect in bringing about this 'duping' is advertising. There is, however, no retail advertising in Australia of greeting cards. Brand loyalty wasn't seen as achievable by most of the manufacturers at the time of interview (1992–1995).

15. A stance that Raymond Williams (1989) explicitly warns against in 'Culture is ordinary' and a position that Bourdieu (1990) very usefully explicates in Chapter 1, 'Objectification objectified'.

16. By 'a language' I mean a 'register' or a functional variety of language. See Halliday and Hasan (1986).

17. See Foucault (1978) on the emergent importance of the confession as a practice.

18. Findings from interviews. This can only be considered an untested trend at present. The manufacturers have no sense of any change, partly because the numbers involved are so huge – 90 per cent as opposed to 10 per cent – and partly because they aren't really looking for it at all.
19. The 'bloke' in Australian vernacular is at the heart of Australian masculinity in many versions. The 'bloke' is a Man without necessarily being macho. This is combined with unproblematized egalitarianism and a larrikin attitude to authority. His male friendships, his 'mates', are as important to him as his wife, if not more so; he is, however, homophobic, even if he is a man who has sex with other men. The recent coming-out process of a high-profile rugby player was testament to this, and to an obverse process that McInnes (1996) identifies as the 'blokification of gay'.
20. This is using Judith Butler's (1990) conception of subjectivity as inaugurated through iterated practice.

References

Averill, J. (1985) 'The social construction of emotion: with special reference to love'. In K. J. Gergen and K. E. Davis (eds), *The Social Construction of the Person*. New York: Springer-Verlag, pp. 60–102.

Bourdieu, P. (1990) *The Logic of Practice* (trans. R. Nice). Cambridge: Polity.

Butler, J. (1990) *Gender Trouble: Feminism and the Subversion of Identity*. New York: Routledge.

Chase, E. D. ([1926] 1971) *The Romance of Greeting Cards: An Historical Account of the Origin, Evolution and Development of the Christmas Card, Valentine and Other Forms of Engraved or Printed Greetings from Earliest Days to the Present Time*. Detroit: Tower Books.

De Certeau, M. (1988) *The Practice of Everyday Life* (trans. S. Rendall). California: University of California Press.

Derrida, J. ([1967] 1976) *Of Grammatology* (trans. G. Spivak). Baltimore: Johns Hopkins University Press.

De Saussure, F. ([1915] 1974) *Course in General Linguistics* (trans. W. Baskin). London: Collins.

Di Leonardo, M. (1987) 'The female world of cards and holidays: women, families, and the work of kinship', *Signs: Journal of Women in Culture and Society*, 12(3), 440–53.

Fairclough, N. (1992) *Discourse and Social Change*. Cambridge: Polity.

Fairclough, N. (1995) 'Critical discourse analysis and the marketization of public discourse: the universities', *Discourse and Society*, 4(2), 133–68.

Forgas, J. P. (1985) *Interpersonal Behaviour: The Psychology of Social Interaction*. Sydney: Pergamon.

Foucault, M. ([1970] 1984) *The Order of Things: An Archaeology of the Human Sciences*. New York: Vintage.

Foucault, M. ([1978] 1990) *The History of Sexuality: An Introduction*, vol 1. Victoria: Penguin Books Australia.

Giddens, A. (1992) *The Transformation of Intimacy: Intimacy, Sexuality, Love and Eroticism in Modern Societies*. Cambridge: Polity.

Halliday, M. A. K. (1975) *Learning How to Mean: Explorations in the Development of Language*. London: Edward Arnold.

Halliday, M. A. K. (1978) *Language as Social Semiotic: The Social Interpretation of Language and Meaning*. London: Edward Arnold.

Halliday, M. A. K. (1985) *An Introduction to Functional Grammar*. London: Edward Arnold.

Halliday, M. A. K. and Hasan, R. (1986) *Language, Context and Text: Aspects of Language in a Social Semiotic Perspective*. Victoria: Deakin University Press.

Jordanova, L. (1989) *Sexual Visions: Images of Gender in Science between the Eighteenth and Twentieth Century*. Hemel Hempstead: Harvester Wheatsheaf.

Kress, G. (1985) *Linguistic Processes in Sociocultural Practice*. Victoria: Deakin University Press.

Kress, G. and van Leeuwen, T. (1996) *Reading Images: The Grammar of Visual Design*. London: Routledge.

McLuhan, M. (1962) *The Gutenberg Galaxy*. London: Routledge.

McInnes, D. (1996) 'The footballer in me: making discursive space for gay blokes in the Australian press'. *Worlds of Discourse*, 21st Conference of the Applied Linguistics Association of Australia, 3–6 October, University of Western Sydney, Nepean.

Miller, D. (1991) *Material Culture and Mass Consumption*. Oxford: Blackwell.

Papson, S. (1986) 'From symbolic exchange to bureaucratic discourse: the Hallmark greeting card', *Theory, Culture and Society*, 3(2) 99–111.

Prices Surveillance Authority Australia (September, 1990) *Investigation into the Greeting Card Industry*.

Radway, J. (1986) 'Reading is not eating: mass-produced literature and the theoretical, methodological, and political consequences of a metaphor', *Book Research Quarterly*, Fall, 7–29.

Rich, A. (1980) 'Compulsory heterosexuality and lesbian existence', *Signs: Journal of Women in Culture and Society*, 5(4), 631–60.

Wandyzc, K. (1991) 'Love means never having to say anything', *Forbes*, 1 April, 147, p. 88.

Williams, R. ([1958] 1989) *Resources of Hope: Culture, Democracy, Socialism* (ed. R. Gable). London: Verso.

Williamson, J. (1980) *Consuming Passions: The Dynamics of Popular Culture*. London: Marion Boyars.

17. Girl power and the post-modern fan: the 1996 Boyzone concert tour

Maggie Andrews and Rosie Whorlow

Introduction: 'girl power' and feminism

This chapter focuses on the reactions of two groups of young girls, and their mothers, to the 1996 Boyzone concert tour. It is a case study of the contradictory and tense relationship women, and young girls in particular, have with one area of consumer culture at the end of the twentieth century. In discussing the 1996 tour we are emphasizing the historical specificity of this moment, when young girls' consumer culture embraced not only boy bands but the rising popularity of the Spice Girls and the 'girl power' phenomenon which encouraged new meanings for young girls' consumer culture. We are arguing against a dismissive perception of young girls as cultural dupes, suggesting instead that they are rather: tongue-in-cheek, knowing, aware consumers in a post-modern sense, who use consumption to construct and reconstruct their own identities.

'Teenybop culture' is an area of consumption that is not only central to many young girls' lives but, we shall argue, provides a space for the 'making' of their identity. Although in a 'post-modern age' identity is seen as fluid, made up of samenesses and differences based on belonging and not belonging to 'imagined communities' (Anderson, 1991), in this case study there were communities of Boyzone fans and the community constructed by fans under the heading of girl power. What was significantly new at this historical moment was the community between mothers and daughters across age boundaries which involved girl power and a space for feminism. These communities, which were focused upon consumption, were not fluid and temporary.

We see consumption as a site where women, girls and indeed all consumers are, to a greater or lesser degree, buffeted between the forces of creativity and constraint. Feminists of the past defending fan culture from a variety of criticisms and abuse have tended to focus on the significance of the female space this culture provided within which girls could express their sexuality (see Lewis, 1984), and indeed we will begin by looking at the representation of fandom in the past and some defences of it.

We also want to explore young female consumer consumption of young males in boy bands. For this we will draw upon our own participant observation with groups of young girls and their mothers at the 1996 Boyzone concerts and in the months afterwards. Although such interview material has its problems, we want to suggest that it is an essential source in trying to understand the meaning of consumption for the consumer, outside academia. We argue that although there is nothing new in the concept of fandom, there is something new in its recent articulation with girl power, and this offers possibilities for identity construction and reconstruction across generational boundaries.

Nancy Chodorow has suggested, using a culturalist object-relations theory of psychoanalysis (1978), that adolescent girls need to signify their difference from their mothers who tend to over-identify with them. The activities of teenage girl fans – expressing overt sexuality, revelling in consumption and identifying with an imagined community of other young girls – has been seen as one route for them to signify 'difference' from the cultural construction of motherhood. However, in a post-modern world of fluidity and uncertainty, motherhood itself is under tension, often represented in contradictory and oppositional ways – think of recent television sit-coms such as *Ab Fab*, *Roseanne* or *Grace under Fire*, for example. Consequently, relationships between mother and daughter may be better understood in terms of changing samenesses and differences. We argue that a new space was briefly opened up for sameness in 1996 when Boyzone produced new cover versions of teenybop songs of the 1970s and 1980s, the Monkees went on tour again and the Spice Girls released their song for Mother's Day entitled 'Mama' with the chorus line of 'Mama we love you, mama my friend'. For the post-modern fan attending the 1996 Boyzone concert tour, enthusiastically singing the Spice Girls 'Wannabe' song as they waited for the concert to begin, in an audience peppered by mothers, the divide between the mother and daughter identities that Chodorow saw as needing to be signified became blurred. The teenybop culture offered mothers and daughters both moments of sameness and difference. Fan culture is fluid, but some of the rhetoric of girl power enabled feminism not to be consigned to the dustbin of a mother's generation, but to remain firmly within the sphere of popular culture where it has always been most effective.

In 1996, young girls' magazines, the Miss Selfridge shop and the Spice Girls simultaneously promoted 'girl power' in a reworking and pillaging of what they see as the best of feminism's legacy: assertiveness, self-confidence, a celebration of female independence and achievement. An optimism, and a rejection of the rhetoric of romance for blunter discussions of sex, was accompanied by a loud assertion of their right to want to get what they 'really want'. In the words of *Company* magazine (November 1996, p. 5):

> A new girl has arrived, who's gutsy, irreverent and fun. A girl who's glad to be a girl – and into all that girl baggage that goes with it. A girl who loves fashion, makeup and men (so long as they know their place) and has the balls to get exactly what she wants . . . Okay it's a twist on feminism, but this time round it has a sense of humour – who wants to waste time burning bras when you could be out having a laugh.

Their wanting involved enjoying consumerism and all the possible trappings of that version of femininity: make-up, clothes, and presenting themselves as sexual objects, in a somewhat in-your-face way which others might see as the antithesis of feminism. However, Mel C, one of the Spice Girls, was quoted as having said, 'Feminism has become something of a misused and abused word. Girl power is the 1990s version. If women band together and show a unified front, solidarity creates power' (Spice Girls, 1997, p. 34). Thus from the shopping trolley dash that is post-modernism, some young girls have constructed a bricolage of iconographies and styles simultaneously readable as parody or masquerade, but from within which girl power may allow for a more sympathetic reading of post-feminism than is frequently the case.

Fans and fandom: past, present but hopefully not in the future

The phenomenon of 'teenybop' fans has long been discussed in the media, the music industry and more recently in the academic disciplines of cultural and media studies and requires some initial attention. Adorno and Horkheimer's criticisms of the standardization of popular music and 'the idolisation of the cheap making the average the heroic' (1979, p. 51) have passed through academic thought and into 'common sense' when young girls' musical tastes are being discussed. Many discourses concerned with 'teenyboppers' (young girls aged 8–15) construct them in terms of their naïveté, as immature and undiscerning consumers or cultural dupes entering into fandom as a time filler between adolescence and adulthood (Grossberg and Frith, 1993).

Furthermore, young girls reach the age for 'fandom' at an age when they are considered to be at their most vulnerable, and hence corruptible. Media discourse, in particular, has tended to focus attention on what was constructed as the 'infectious nature' of the hysterical behaviour of pop star-obsessed young girls. Often lurid headlines employed a metaphor of contagion, with young female fans being at risk 'of catching' perceived irrational and insane behaviour. For example, in the 1960s and 1970s the fan phenomenon was labelled 'Beatlemania' or 'Osmonditis' or 'Trextasy'. Labels such as these serve to locate the female fan simultaneously as a social concern and in need or moral protection and understanding.

The word 'hysteria' frequently found in the language of the tabloid press is worth remarking upon. Indeed, Ussher has argued that the term hysteria in itself has become a metaphor for anything considered unmanageable in the female sex (1991). Girls' lack of control appears to be voyeuristically eroticized by one male reporter who reported on a Beatles concert in 1963:

> Screaming like an animal and wearing almost as much leather as one, the young girl writhed and shook in some private ecstasy . . . There were hundreds like her and so much oblivious of their partners' presence that they stood at right angles to the boy they were 'with', shaking, screaming, supremely happy. (*Daily Mail*, 2 October 1963)

The author expressed concern over the apparent rejection of 'boyfriends' who were accompanying the girls and suggests that the primarily female enjoyment of the performance and the presence of the Beatles threatens the masculinity of 'the boyfriends'. This review fails to engage with ways that males might enjoy and consume the performance, focusing upon a more paternalistic or critical attitude to consumption which was by no means limited to young girls in the 1960s.

In the never-had-it-so-good years of the 1950s and beyond, attitudes to consumption were contradictory and rife with tension. Capitalist industries, governments, media pundits and advertisers heralded the consumer revolution, but at the same time too much spending and a desire for instant gratification were frowned upon as weaknesses from which women and other marginalized groups needed protecting. Despite, or maybe because of, the concern expressed by such media pundits, consumption of young male pop idols by teenage girls was consolidated in the 1970s, with the rise in manufactured teenage stars such as Donny Osmond, David Cassidy (Frith and Grossberg, 1993, p. 213) followed by 'boy bands' such as the Bay

City Rollers in the mid-1970s. When not engaged in discourses of sexual and moral danger, concerns focused on the financial aspects of the duping of the young and undiscriminating female consumers.

In the 1950s and 1960s concerns about fandom were, arguably, packaged in a class-specific language which reflected wider social concerns. In particular, the failure of the education system to 'pass on any more than the very rudiments of education'. One area where education was seen as lacking was in inculcating youth in the discriminatory and active use of their 'leisure'. Concerns about the consumption of mass culture, in particular, popular songs and films, were expressed by politicians and social commentators of the left and right. These frequently focused on Americanization which iconographically represented mass consumer culture desired by working-class youth. In 1975 a rather more direct and scathing commentary was made on the dangers, both physical and emotional, of the hysteria caused by

the most expertly packaged group in pop history, gift wrapped for young girls to love. As musicians they are so limited that they only recently attained the dizzy heights of playing all the music on their own hit records . . . They were discovered, manufactured and sold to an uncritical audience by former palais-de-danse bandleader and frustrated pop star Tim Paton . . . [starting with Scottish fans] . . . the movement burned across the border like a fever. And with it came Rollermania. Fans went hysterical when the group appeared, and a toll of teenybopper injuries followed. Throughout their 36 town tour this month [they] left a trail of crushed and unconscious schoolgirl fans to be treated by ambulance men and doctors. (*Daily Mail*, 26 May 1975)

Arguably, the Thatcherite 1980s challenged the negative connotations of consumption – the consumer was now king, but not necessarily queen. Chapman has argued that as consumption became central in society and as it acquired status it lost the identification with women that it once had (1988). Indeed, Mort suggests that consumption is the key element in the construction of the 'new man' and paves the way for radical reworkings of masculinity (1988). But, perhaps not surprisingly, young girls and boys appear to operate within different discourses of consumption, which reflect their different status and access to power within society. Girls are still more likely to be represented as 'unthinking' dupes, while boys represent themselves as 'discerning' consumers, differentiating between products in terms of 'authenticity' and technical expertise, for example. In attitudes to young girls' consumption and fandom there appears to be rather more continuity than change. However, the meaning of fandom to girls themselves may be very different.

Consumption as an active process: how girls make music and goodies their own

Condescension and condemnation is but one narrative of many surrounding the phenomenon of fandom. Some academics, such as Frith, have been more sympathetic than the journalists quoted above, and of course the girls themselves tell very different narratives of the meaning of consumption. Frith has drawn upon the memories of Sherl Garratt, who attended one of the Bay City Roller tour dates. For her, the whole notion of the Bay City Rollers being a strategically marketed product in no way detracted from the meaning of fandom for the young girls who made up the 'uncritical audience'. She theorizes the whole event in terms of the consolidation and celebration of female identities and friendships: what we, with the benefit of hindsight, suggest could be seen in terms of emerging 'girl power'.

> Looking back now, I hardly remember the gigs themselves, the songs or even what the Rollers looked like. What I do remember are the bus rides, running home from school together to get to someone's house in time to watch Shang-a-lang on TV, dancing in lines at the school disco and sitting in each other's bedrooms discussing our fantasies and compiling our scrapbooks. Our obsession was with ourselves; in the end the actual men behind the posters had very little to do with it at all. (Grossberg and Frith, 1993, p. 402)

Fandom can be a way that girls create a shared identity by defining themselves against others, both in their peer groups, as well as against other adults and parents, and a group's unpopularity may consequently be irrelevant. Garratt's narrative suggests it resulted in a feeling that 'it was us against the world – and for a while, at least we were winning' (*ibid.*, p. 403). The stars served a number of functions, one of them being the sense of community in the shared 'adoration' which brought the girls into the public sphere at concerts or at the disco and in private where fans could swap memorabilia, and create an alternative cultural economy based on knowledge about the star (Grossberg and Frith, 1993). Such knowledge, when shared, could increase personal status within a group of fans.

As Miller (1997) argues, the point of purchase is only a small part of consumption in the creativity/constraint dichotomy. The point of purchase may be where constraint is strongest, but it is after this at the point of use where creativity has most scope. For example, all the girls we interviewed had decorated their bedrooms and school files with images of Boyzone and the Spice Girls, they sang along to their music, and exchanged star-related gossip and information gleaned from magazines. Furthermore, claims from girls that they are a star's 'number one fan' are frequent in teen magazines, emphasizing the active individual role of fans.

I consume, therefore I am: identity in the making – interviewing Boyzone fans

Many young girls consume multiple media and magazine images and narratives on their selected star, providing the industry with an eager consumer market. The use placed on these commodities can confer community and status and, while also being creative, it can also serve as a vehicle for the expression of fantasies. As McRobbie has suggested, the multiple articles and trivia provide a bare framework for fantasies to be constructed around the star allowing fans to weave in, both collectively and privately, personal fantasies from which they construct their own identities (1991, p. 168). 'Is the rumour that Ronan is a virgin true?' three girls were asked in one of our interviews. 'He won't be for long if he met me,' Zoe replied, to uproarious giggles from the other girls. Frith argues that 'identity is mobile, a process, not a thing' (1996, p. 109). The celebration of a particular band or star by young girls may be seen as a celebration of themselves which confers power through multiple possibilities – one of which may be a new sense of assertiveness or confidence, in this case around sexuality.

Furthermore, we would suggest that the girls do not see consumer and producer as differentiated individuals – 'That's my video,' says Annie, of the Boyzone video of the Wembley Concert she attended. 'I'm on that video, Lucy and Zoe have seen me.' The girls we spoke to were aware and knowledgeable about the commercial aspects and origins of their favoured bands; the term 'manufactured' was mentioned often in relation to both Boyzone and Take That (a band some of them had previously been enthusiastic about), although their usage and understanding of the concept varied. That the Boyzone concert was 'manufactured' was pleasing to the girls. The choreography of the performance emphasized the inter-relationship between producer and consumer: control, it was implied, was fluid and not in the hands of the group. At the beginning of the concert the lads emerge from within a cage, their movements implying that they are chained only to be released when the adulation of the audience has reached fever pitch as they sang the 'Together' song.

> *Together . . . is better by far.*
> *That's what we are you'll see.*
> *Now that we're together.*
> *It's better by far you'll see.*

Prior to the rise in popularity of Boyzone, the band Take That was one of the most popular 'boy bands' with the young female pop market. It is perhaps not insignificant that many of the 10- to 11-year-old girls interviewed had recently transferred their allegiances from Take That to Boyzone just before, or round about the time that, Take That split up. It is evident from their discussions that, at one level, they were fairly upset about the split, and that the 'fresher' Boyzone had been in place to benefit from their decline. However, the girls' discussions revealed a number of contradictions as they constantly re-negotiated with each other the meanings of the split and their responses to it. Perhaps this provides a useful insight into their own fluid identities as they regrouped themselves, from their sense of belonging to the imagined community of Take That fans.

In several of our group interviews the girls insisted that they had 'blanked' Take That before the split. The reasons that they gave were related to Robbie Williams (the most popular member of Take That) leaving, and second, the change of image that Take That had undertaken shortly before their break. They moved from a fairly clean-cut trendy boy-next-door image, to a more overtly sexual image.

SAMMI: Because when Robbie left they were sort of boring really (the other girls in her group all agreed with this). They don't make their own songs.

BECKY: Not just that but we knew they were going to split up anyway, and their music was going down hill and Boyzone were there.

HEIDI: So we suddenly changed to Boyzone.

SAMMI: Yes . . . Boyzone is much fresher. I know they don't make up their own stuff but they give it a bit more life than the original.

The first aspect of this conversation of particular significance is the girls' insistence that they had rejected Take That first, and so had chosen to move their allegiance to Boyzone before Take That rejected them. In a sense fandom and stardom function on the basis on an inferred contract. One of the attractions of a 'relationship with a band is that it avoids many of the traumas of teenage sexuality: should you have sex? If so where? Will you get pregnant or catch unmentionable diseases?' (Lewis, 1992). Then another of the attractions is that it is the girls who do the chucking. When they move on to other bands they disregard the no-longer-fashionable males, in a reversal of the more familiar representation of women as disposable consumer items, in, say, porn or early James Bond films.

Much of the dialogue of Boyzone, during their concert, confers power to the fans, with comments such as 'thank you for all your loyalty, without you we wouldn't be here'. Thus there is a constant reassurance to the fans that they have personally played a role in the success of the band, their control is emphasized, the objects of their admiration need them. For a band to end the contract by splitting up shifts the sense of power away from the fans, thus breaking the implied contact between fan and star. A discussion between Becky and Sammi about Take That is illuminating in this respect.

BECKY: We bought magazines and everything and they just split up.
SAMMI: We bought loads of stuff and they just split up!
SAMMI: They take your money, but they don't really care, we expect more and they should give us that more, or give us our money back!

By splitting up Take That had, in terms of the 'fans' cultural currency', devalued all their photo collections, videos and tapes. Becky was implying that Take That had broken the contract, and so the girls had removed their allegiances to a newer band who would serve the same function in terms of style, attractiveness and inferred accessibility. In order to get on with exploring and reworking their own subjective identities they had acquired a more 'appropriate' focus for their consumer activities.

Constant comparison between the bands was another key feature of any discussion of shifting allegiances. It was as if the girls needed to show their new choice was preferable in terms of attractiveness, quality of performance and, as they were discerning customers, value for money.

BECKY: Take That concert tickets were £25 whilst Boyzone tickets were only £12.50, so you get more for your money.
SAMMI: I bet the show goes on longer too.
BECKY: Yes and their memorabilia will be a lot cheaper as well because Boyzone are not manufactured!

The above conversation exemplifies the contradictions of consumerist pleasure and anti-consumption rhetoric negotiated by the girls, presenting their particular band as authentic. This strategy for holding together contradictory ideologies has a long history amongst male and female fans. It is a fascinating tension when applied to Boyzone whose very trademark, and arguably their success, relies on their re-inflection of the music of a previous generation. (Their break-through British hit was a cover version of the Osmonds' song 'Love me for a reason'.)

At other points, however, the girls indicate a knowing awareness that what they buy at concerts is a 'rip-off' and remark on the exorbitant prices charged, not to show off, nor with the embarrassment that the mention of money or prices would have involved thirty years ago. For them, the premium charged for a T-shirt with a concert logo is a 'fact of life'. However, with a knowing discernment, or perhaps a certain acceptance of the capitalist system at work, they evaluate whether the consumer goods at a premium price on sale at a concert will be worth it. For them referring to the good value of Boyzone in relation to other bands such as Take That is an indication that they have already acquired the consumer logic of an older generation who, Miller argues, are able to deal with the contradictory pull of pleasure and duty by purchasing bargains and special offers (1977, p. 45).

It has already been suggested the manufacturedness of the teenbop groups contributes to the pleasure they provide. Many of the girls see whether or not the band actually sings during a performance as irrelevant, but their overtly choreographed dances are not. The very stylized movements are part of the pleasure for the audience, and echo the black vocal groups of the 1960s such as The Four Tops and The Temptations. Thus Boyzone, along with other boy bands, are mediating black culture for a white audience. That effort has been made to facilitate girls' enjoyment is a point emphasized on the video of the Wembley Concert when the lads discuss with concern 'getting their dances right'. Theirs is a performance for female pleasure, for active discerning and critical consumers who, it is understood, are more than prepared to discard them when they no longer appear to serve their needs.

Certainly, when standing, looking around the audience at the Wembley concert, the impression is of the irrelevance of those on stage compared to the size of the audience, and their sense of themselves, their presence and momentarily fixed identities. The 'imagined community' of Boyzone fans gets a sense of 'reality' when the lights go down and they scream and shout and wave their loomy-gloomies. It was very much a female community of consumers, and the status of having been part of this 'real community' of concert attendees had the potential to last way beyond the evening. 'What would you do if you met Boyzone?' Annie was asked, as we wandered around outside Wembley Stadium prior to the concert: 'Grab something of theirs, something they had touched.' 'Why?' 'To show everybody that we had really been there,' she replied. At a certain level, the Boyzone band serves only to service the girl community and only so long as it is wanted, until the girls choose to ditch it. 'I'm a bit off Boyzone now,' Annie explained, a couple of months after the concert. 'Who do you prefer?' 'The Spice Girls, but you should talk to Lucy, she prefers Backstreet Boys.' But only three days earlier Annie and her friends had been castigating Lucy as a traitor for her preference for Backstreet Boys. With girl power control is vital, but identity is fluid as they constantly rework boundaries of samenesses and differences.

And Mum came too: the possibilities of new communities and identities

What of the many mothers peppering the audience as fathers sat rigid in their seats at the sight of so much unleashed female sexuality? For many mothers it seemed that taking the girls to the concert was a rite of passage into the adult world of female sexuality and the shared consumption of masculine performance, although one in which the mothers' expectations and the girls' enjoyment may well be in conflict. The deliberately constructed musical repertoire of Boyzone, particularly their cover versions of songs of a different generation, encouraged cross-generational concert attendance. Hence the deliberately constructed polysemic nature of the music ensures that girls' mothers obtain a nostalgic enjoyment through the familiarity of the music.

We are not here implying that there is something negative in this nostalgia. As Wendy Webster has pointed out, nostalgia may be seen as a radical rejection of the status quo (1994) combined in this case with a reliving for the mothers of a time when they were young and free, prior to motherhood, domesticity, housework and other responsibilities. It has resonances with Radway's research on housewives' enjoyment of popular romantic fiction which, with a similar quotient of nostalgia, narratively emphasizes a pre-responsibilities phase in women's lives (1987). Such nostalgia has real commercial possibilities. For the girls themselves, their mothers' stake in the music of Boyzone might be a double-edged sword. On the one hand, it may increase the likelihood of concert visits and music purchases, significant for purchasers with only pocket money resources, alternatively, it also detracts from their enjoyment. As Lucy explained, 'It sort of ruins it when they know the words and sing along.'

But for the post-modern, nostalgic, second-generation fan the meaning of the concert may operate at several levels; taking their daughters into a space where female sexuality is celebrated, expressed and positively revelled in without any dangers. For the mothers who had escorted their daughters to the concert, especially those waiting in the ladies loo (the traditional place for women to share their emotions), conversations could be overheard reminiscent of an encounter group. As they talked, there was indeed a sense of 'knowingness', of sympathy and of shared experience, both with each other and with their absent daughters. Judging from their conversation, it would appear that many seemed to feel that, as mothers, they were introducing their daughters, in an almost ritualized way, to a very female 'rite of passage'. After all, many of the 1990s mothers were themselves daughters of the 1970s Osmond and Bay City Rollers era. Waiting around in the foyer Sammi's mum made comments like:

> I bet they're buzzing. Oh, my little girl, I can't believe this. I wish I could see her face . . . What are you looking at me like that for? My baby's in there . . . I'm really excited . . . I bet they're having the most amazing time . . . just stood there, I mean, fucking Boyzone. I only saw one of them through the door and I got a buzz.

It was as if Sammi aged 11 was moving away from both her mother and her childhood, and that womanhood would close in on her as soon as she entered the concert hall, and we somehow expected the girls to re-emerge different and more grown up and were surprised when what did emerge were two rather over-wrought little girls, whose excited babble soon gave way to a grumpy resentment at the tirade of questions hurled at them. Furthermore, after the consumption of Boyzone had been successfully completed it was the consumption of chips and Coke which became their main concern.

The post-concert 'reunion', instead of being a shared experience, revealed instead a number of tensions. Sammi's mum had been excited about seeing Sammi come out of the concert, saying things like 'I can't wait to see them. I wish I had a camera to catch their faces', and when the girls emerged all pink and giggling, she said to the girls, 'Was that brilliant or was that brilliant?' Sammi and Becky replied, 'It was so cool we screamed and screamed but can we have some chips now?' This response was not what had been envisaged. They were asked, 'OK, but what was it like, tell us about it?' To which Sammi replied, 'Sean Mcguire he was crap, Boyzone were totally brilliant and totally gorgeous but can we have some chips now?' Sammi's mum persisted and asked, 'What I really want to know is, do you feel any different about them now?' 'No, not really, we love them, but we want some chips . . . we stood on the stairs and screamed and screamed but we are hungry and we are thirsty and we want some chips.' On our way to the chippy two stroppy girls lagged behind giggling and whispering, their sense of difference in relation to their mothers' identity positions emphasized by sulks and demands for yet more consumption.

Nevertheless, if there was a sense of imagined community amongst the young girls at the concert, so was there equally amongst the mothers who smiled knowingly at one another. Some who had ventured into the concert climbed enthusiastically onto their seats to scream and wave, and all seemed to enjoy humorously the sight of the few fathers who had accompanied their daughters, and who sat, clearly uncomfortable and marginalized, rigid in their seats. It may be that in a 1990s post-modern culture shared consumption – of food, on shopping trips, at theme parks, in this instance at a pop concert – provides a significant focus for cross-generational contact. Arguably, at the Boyzone concert, mothers and daughters revelled together in a shared female consumer space where they could behave in ways oppositional to the social constructions of ideal womanhood. 'What are you going to do when you see them?' Annie was asked. 'Scream,' she replied, 'louder than anyone else', and we can report that she did. With the animal passion and private ecstasy of the 1970s fans maybe – but with tongue-in-cheek irony also.

Conclusion: boy bands come and boy bands go but Girlie Power lives on?

In popular media and academic circles young girls' consumer culture continues to be an object of scorn. The meanings of their activities and lives are often seen as silly and irrelevant; as feminist mothers we want to challenge that. Boyzone will be forgotten in a few years' time, like so many other boy bands. That does not mean that we should accept the negativity with which fandom has often been regarded, or allow fans to be lumped together with a sameness that negates their differences, and the changes over time. Young girl fans consumed the 1996 Boyzone concert tour within the dichotomy of creativity and constraint and moved on to consume chips or to an enthusiasm for some other group.

However, young girls use this area of consumer culture and the very act of consumption itself in the production of their own identities. At the moment of the 1996 Boyzone tour there was scope for these identities to relate to imagined communities of belonging which were drawable in a particular set of ways. The samenesses of girl power and feminism offered exciting scope for the future, but construction of difference was also important. Identities are never completed, always in the process of making. It is interesting to note that boy bands may come and go, but the Spice Girls found their way into the

Guinness Book of Records. Perhaps girl power and new versions of feminism will last a little longer.

Our thanks go to the girls we interviewed and for whom this is written – true enthusiasts of consumer culture: Annie, Becky, Heidi, Lucy, Sammi and Zoe.

References

Adorno, T. W. and Horkheimer, M. (1979) *Dialectic of Enlightenment*. London: Verso.

Anderson, B. (1991) *Imagined Communities: Reflections on the Origins and Spread of Nationalism*. Revised and extended edition, London: Verso.

Chapman, R. and Rutherford, J. (eds) (1988) *Male Order: Unwrapping Masculinity*. London: Lawrence and Wishart.

Chodorow, N. J. (1978) *The Reproduction of Mothering:Psycho-analysis and the Sociology of Gender*. Berkeley and London: University of California Press.

Ehrenneich, B., Hess, E. and Jacobs, G. (1992) 'Beatlemania: girls just want to have fun'. In L. A. Lew (ed.), *Adoring Audiences*. London: Routledge.

Frith, S. (1996) *Performing Rites on the Value of Popular Music*. Oxford: Oxford University Press.

Frith, S. and Goodwin, A. (1990) *On Record: Rock, Pop and the Word*. London: Routledge.

Grossberg, A. and Frith, S. (1993) *Sound and Vision: The Music Video Reader*. London: Routledge.

Lewis, J. (1984) *Women in England 1870–19??*. Brighton: Wheatsheaf.

McRobbie, A. (1991) *Feminism and Youth Culture from Jackie to Just 17*. Basingstoke: Macmillan Education.

Miller, D. (1997) 'Consumption and its consequences'. In H. Mackay (ed.), *Consumption and Everyday Life*. London: Sage.

Mort, F. (1988) 'Boys Own? Masculinity, style and popular culture'. In J. Rutherford and R. Chapman (eds), *Male Order: Unwrapping Masculinity*. London: Lawrence and Wishart.

Paddison, M. Adorno (1996) *Modernism and Mass Culture: Essays on Critical Theory and Music*. London: Kahn and Averill.

Radway, J. (1987) *Reading the Romance: Women, Patriarchy and Popular Culture*. London: Verso.

Spice Girls (1997) *Official Spice Girls Girl Power*. London: Zone Chameleon Books.

Ussher, J. (1991) *Women and Madness: Misogyny or Mental Illness*. New York and London: Harvester Wheatsheaf.

Webster, W. (1994) 'Nostalgia isn't nasty: the postmodernity of parliamentary democracy'. In M. Perryman (ed.), *Altered States*. London: Lawrence and Wishart.

Index